Advance praise for Fowl's *Engaging Scripture*

'After several decades of comparative neglect, the question of a distinctively theological interpretation of scripture is now back on the agenda of many biblical scholars and theologians. Stephen Fowl's new book is a most welcome contribution to this trend. In the past, Christian scriptural interpretation has always reflected the interpreter's participation in the Christian community and its patterns of life; and, in a series of sophisticated engagements with contemporary biblical interpretation, hermeneutics and theology, Fowl shows how and why this should still be the case.'

Francis Watson, Reader in Biblical Theology, Department of Theology and Religious Studies, King's College, London

'This is the book we have been waiting for from Stephen Fowl. The lush fruit of some years of writings in biblical criticism and in theology, this one puts all things together . . . *Engaging Scripture* is at once theologically adventuresome, textually disciplined, and practically instructive.

The author's approach refuses the bifurcations of modernity between academic and popular, confessional and scholarly. He retains a critical edginess worthy of a premodern era: remembering that the imperative character of the Word pierces through even academic studies of the Word's textual life.

Fowl exhibits a post-critical confidence in the capacity of scholars to speak dispassionately, yet with respect to particular communities of interpretation; to respect the evidences of historical critical research, while also generating imaginative and community-building hypotheses about elements of the Bible's message that lie beyond the limits of clear evidence.'

Peter Ochs, Edgar Brofman Professor of Modern Judaic Studies, University of Virginia

'This is a timely and creative study of genuine significance both to theologians and biblical scholars. One always expects from Fowl clarity of thought and expression. What makes this book special is the way it exemplifies the virtues it espouses: rather than remain safely in the realm of theory, Fowl risks readings of specific texts and specific life situations that "engage scripture" with courage and clarity. By so doing, he helps summon a community of readers willing to shape their lives by such reading and shape their readings by lives committed to the practices of Christian life.'

Luke Timothy Johnson, Robert W. Woodruff Professor of New Testament and Christian Origins, Emory University

Challenges in Contemporary Theology

Series Editors: Gareth Jones and Lewis Ayres
University of Birmingham and Trinity College, Dublin

Challenges in Contemporary Theology is a major series from Blackwell Publishers aimed at producing clear orientations in, and research on, areas of "challenge" in contemporary theology. These carefully coordinated books engage traditional theological concerns with mainstreams in modern thought and culture that challenge those concerns. The "challenges" implied are to be understood in two senses: those presented by society to contemporary theology, and those posed by theology to society. Each volume is firmly issue-based to enable it to encompass both these approaches.

Already published

Forthcoming

ENGAGING SCRIPTURE

A Model for Theological Interpretation

Stephen E. Fowl

First published 1998

2 4 6 8 10 9 7 5 3 1

Blackwell Publishers Inc.
350 Main Street
Malden, Massachusetts 02148
USA

Blackwell Publishers Ltd
108 Cowley Road
Oxford OX4 1JF
UK

Library of Congress Cataloging-in-Publication Data
Fowl, Stephen E.
  Engaging scripture : a model for theological interpretation / by Stephen E. Fowl.
    p.   cm. — (Challenges in contemporary theology)
  Includes bibliographical references and index.
  ISBN 0-631-20863-1 (alk. paper). — ISBN 0-631-20864-X (alk. paper)
    1. Bible—Criticism, interpretation, etc.   2. Bible—Theology.
  I. Title.   II. Series.
  BS511.2.F675   1998
  220.6—dc21
                                                                98-6188
                                                                CIP

British Library Cataloguing in Publication Data

A CIP catalogue record for this book is available from the British Library.

Typeset in 10½ on 12½ pt Bembo by Ace Filmsetting Ltd, Frome
Printed in Great Britain by MPG Books, Bodmin, Cornwall

This book is printed on acid-free paper

CONTENTS

ACKNOWLEDGMENTS

I initially began thinking about the issues and ideas that led to this book during my tenure as the Sir Henry Stephenson Fellow in the Department of Biblical Studies at the University of Sheffield. I am grateful to the trustees of the fellowship for starting me on my way. During the subsequent years I was often supported by Loyola College's faculty development funds. I am particularly grateful to the two deans under whom I have had the pleasure of working, David Roswell and John Hollwitz, for their support. The bulk of the current volume was written during a sabbatical year at Trinity College, Dublin. I was warmly welcomed by Sean Freyne and the rest of the staff and students of the School of Hebrew, Biblical, and Theological Studies. They provided me with the space to get on with my work and helped to make my time in Dublin very productive. Without the material help of each of these people and institutions I would not have finished this book.

Most important, however, have been the friends and colleagues who have helped me and, indeed, thought with me as I have prepared this volume. They will see their influence on almost every page, and my debt to them is greater than I can ever acknowledge. A. K. M. Adam, Margaret Adam, David Cunningham, Melinda Fowl, and Phil Kenneson patiently worked through a very rough draft of this volume. Margaret Adam also read through a late draft of the book, subjecting it to her keen editorial eye. She also generously compiled the index for this book.

My Loyola colleagues, Jim Buckley and Greg Jones (erstwhile), have read through pieces of this project at many different stages of its development. I have always benefited from their wise and insightful suggestions. Moreover, they, along with my other colleagues, help to make our department the stimulating and collegial place it is.

In addition, Jim Fodor, Mark Gornik, Kathryn Greene-McCreight, Stanley Hauerwas, Luke Johnson, Peter Ochs, Ray Pickett, and Bernd

Wannenwetsch all read drafts of the manuscript and offered numerous comments and criticisms which have improved the book enormously.

Above all, however, I am grateful to Lewis Ayres. Long before this volume was contracted to be in a series he co-edits, Lewis took the time to read carefully every page I wrote out. He pressed me to think in new and more rigorous ways. During my year in Dublin, he and his wife, Tamsin Simmill, were gracious hosts and good friends to my family and me. Throughout my stay, Lewis was a willing and challenging conversation partner. He has taught me a great deal and his help with this project has been invaluable. Needless to say, although all of these people have pointed out numerous errors in my work, I take full responsibility for those that have made their way into print.

This book argues that Christians must read scripture in the light of their ends as Christians – ever deeper communion with the triune God and with each other. My wife, Melinda, and sons, Brendan and Liam, constantly remind me in word and deed that our aims and ends as a family are closely and inseparably linked to our ends as Christians. I am grateful to them for impressing this on me.

This book is dedicated to all those I have been privileged to know who struggle to interpret and embody scripture and, in particular, to Mark Gornik.

I am grateful to the following for permission to reproduce previously published material:

Parts of chapter 2 appeared in "The Ethics of Interpretation; or What's Left Over After the Elimination of Meaning," in *The Bible in Three Dimensions*, ed. D. J. A. Clines, S. E. Fowl, and S. E. Porter (Sheffield: Sheffield Academic Press, 1990), pp. 379–98. Parts of chapter 3 appeared in "Texts Don't Have Ideologies," *Biblical Interpretation* 3:1 (1995), pp. 1–34. Parts of chapter 4 appeared in "How To Read the Spirit and How the Spirit Reads," in *The Bible and Ethics*, ed. J. Rogerson et al. (Sheffield: Sheffield Academic Press, 1995), pp. 348–65. Parts of chapter 5 appeared in "Who Can Read Abraham's Story?" *Journal for the Study of the New Testament* 55 (1994), pp. 77–95. Parts of chapter 6 appeared in "Making Stealing Possible: Criminal Reflections on Building an Ecclesial Common Life," *Perspectives* (September 1993), pp. 14–17. Parts of chapter 7 appeared in "Christology and Ethics in Phil. 2: 5–11," in *Where Christology Began*, ed. B. Dodd and R. P. Martin (Louisville: Westminster/John Knox Press, 1998).

Chapter One

INTRODUCTION

As the subtitle of this book indicates, *Engaging Scripture* is primarily an essay in the theological interpretation of scripture. The aims, methods, and practices of theological interpretation of scripture are not, however, immediately self-evident. A great deal depends on a particular account of "theological interpretation" and a particular understanding of the term "scripture." In the first pages of this book, then, I will try to lay out some of the assumptions and presumptions operating behind my use of these terms throughout the book. While my views differ from others', I do not think my account is idiosyncratic. I have tried to tie my account of scripture to fairly straightforward notions of Christian identity. From this, I will develop, argue for, and display a type of theological interpretation.

In this chapter I will introduce my own arguments about theological interpretation. I will also argue that, given my account of theological interpretation, the discipline of biblical theology, in its most common form, is systematically unable to generate serious theological interpretation of scripture. This is due to biblical theology's persistent concern with its own disciplinary integrity. This concern leads biblical theologians to bracket out constructive theological convictions. I will also examine the work of two biblical scholars who are advocates of theological interpretation, Francis Watson and Brevard Childs. I also look at the work of a systematic theologian who is deeply concerned with biblical interpretation, Werner Jeanrond. A thorough accounting of the works of these three would take a great deal of space. My interests in this chapter will be to present enough of their work to allow me to situate my own arguments. To begin, then, I offer a brief discussion of the Bible as the scripture of Christians and the authority of that scripture for Christians as a way of introducing my account of theological interpretation.

Christians and Scripture

The Bible, for Christians, is their scripture. As scripture, the Bible provides a normative standard for the faith, practice, and worship of Christian communities.[1] Scriptural texts, like all other texts, however, are not self-interpreting.[2] Asserting that scripture is the standard for their faith, practice, and worship does not get Christians out of the hard tasks of scriptural interpretation. Moreover, Christians are called to interpret scripture in a variety of different settings and contexts. One expects Christians to make recourse to their scripture in worship, as they reflect upon God, the world and their relationship to it, and as they argue and debate with each other over how best to live in particular circumstances. It would seem odd if they tried to engage in these activities apart from an ongoing engagement with scripture. Despite this variety of contexts in which Christians interpret scripture, their primary aim

---

[1] One of the common queries L. Gregory Jones and I received about *Reading in Communion: Scripture and Ethics in Christian Life* (Grand Rapids: Eerdmans, 1991) concerned the imprecision of the term "Christian community." Just what counts as a Christian community? I admit there is a vagueness in this term, but it is intentional. "Christian community" certainly covers the church both universal and local. In fact, there will be times in this book where I use the terms "church" and "Christian community" interchangeably. The phrase also recognizes, however, that there may be examples of Christian communities which are not obviously churches. These may be groups of people (who may well cross denominational lines) who meet regularly for prayer, study, and worship as part of their larger involvements with specific congregations. (Alternatively, university departments of theology probably are not examples of Christian community.) There may be other examples that I should consider as well. I am not, however, willing to make global judgments about any particular type of group. Using the phrase "Christian community" both allows me to include the church and allows for the possibility of considering a wide range of groupings that might not be strictly churches, but still manifest the relevant communal characteristics to find my arguments of value. Whether or not any particular grouping counts as a Christian community can only be worked out in conversation and debate.

[2] In making this claim, I am not undermining the classic Reformation notion that scripture is its own interpreter. The Reformers were well aware that a problematic text cannot be used to interpret itself. Rather, they advocated an inter-scriptural dialogue which used clearer texts to interpret less clear texts. To the extent that I understand Luther on this issue, however, it is clear that this principle of scripture interpreting itself should not be abstracted from Luther's convictions about the working of the Spirit and our own struggles against sin, for example. Further, for scripture to interpret itself, Luther insists on Christians being formed to read in particular ways. These are all emphases of this book as well. I am grateful to David Yeago for helping me understand some of these issues in regard to Luther.

in all of these different settings and contexts is to interpret scripture as part of their ongoing struggles to live and worship faithfully before the triune God in ways that bring them into ever deeper communion with God and with others. This means that Christians are called not merely to generate various scriptural interpretations but to embody those interpretations as well.[3]

I take it that these claims are relatively straightforward. They are simply logical extensions of fairly basic, and widely recognized, notions of Christian identity and its integral connection to scripture. That is, to identify oneself as a Christian is, at the same time, to bring oneself into a particular sort of relationship to the Bible in which the Bible functions as a normative standard for faith and practice. For the professional biblical scholar, the Bible is simply one (among many) texts upon which scholars might bring their interpretive interests and practices to bear. Christians stand in a different relationship to the Bible. The Bible, for Christians, is their scripture. In saying this I am implying that for Christians, scripture is authoritative.

Rather than making an assertion about a property of the text, however, Christians should best understand claims about scripture's authority as establishing and governing certain networks of relationships. One set of relationships is concerned with the Bible's status relative to its pre-history. When Christians call the Bible authoritative scripture they are implicitly, at least, claiming that the final form of the biblical texts, rather than any of the reconstructed stages its textual transmission, is the canon – the normative standard for faith, practice, and worship.[4] For Christians, then, the Bible is authoritative rather than J, or E, or Q. This is not to deny that that there may be interesting things to learn about these textual reconstructions. Neither do I wish to deny the various types of ambiguity in the notion of the "final form" of the biblical text. These ambiguities, however, are of a different order from discussions about reconstructed traditions of textual transmission.[5] Consider, for example, the text-critical issues surrounding the final form of Mark's gospel. Does the gospel end at 16:8 or 16:20? Such questions are important and show that the notion of the final form of the biblical texts can be

---

[3] This is one of the central arguments that L. Gregory Jones and I made in *Reading in Communion.*

[4] There are, of course, other ways of using the term "canon." For example, one could use it to refer to a list of books that was largely in place by the end of the second century and finalized by the middle of the fourth century. This is not the way I am using the term here. See also the further discussion in *Reading in Communion,* pp. 37–9.

[5] See also the similar arguments of Francis Watson in *Text, Church and World* (Grand Rapids: Eerdmans, 1994), part 1.

contestable. They are, however, arguments about what the authoritative form of Mark ought to look like, not about the authority of Mark relative to some posited *Urtext*.

Moreover, Christians disagree with each other over the contours of the canon depending on whether one is Roman Catholic, Orthodox, or Protestant. It is not clear, however, that this is a significant problem. Without doubt there are large differences between these Christian groups. Some of these differences are due to interpretive disputes. Nevertheless, these differences generally, and with a few possible exceptions, do not seem to depend on the shape of any particular group's canon. They all take the final form of the biblical text as authoritative even though they disagree about its contours. When such differences do depend on issues of canonical shape, such as the reference to "purgatory" in 2 Macc. 12:39–45, they have to be resolved in conversation between the interested parties.

Claims about scriptural authority also set the Bible into a network of relationships with a variety of other texts. One set of such texts is comprised of those texts that were more or less contemporary with the New Testament. Many (but not all) of these texts offered interpretive remarks about the Bible. Further, this body of texts includes some which Christians have come to regard highly as expressions of accomplished Christian scriptural interpretation, as profound articulations of Christian convictions, and/or as witnesses to faithful Christian life and worship. In addition, there were texts, which while valued by some groups, were never accepted (and sometimes actively opposed) by significant numbers of Christians. All of these texts, while valued more or less highly over subsequent centuries, were not and are not authoritative for Christians in the same way scripture is.

On the one hand, this may seem to be (and may only need to be) merely a formal point. This would especially be the case when one or more of these texts of the Christian tradition becomes (at least for a time) the conventional means of interpreting a scriptural text. Take, for example, the phrase "The Lord created me at the beginning of his ways and of his works" in Prov. 8:22 (LXX). Both Arians and their opponents read this verse's characterization of divine wisdom christologically. By the late fourth or early fifth century, however, it became dominant convention to read it as a reference to the eternal presence of the Son. In such cases the line dividing a passage or book of authoritative scripture and the conventional interpretation of that text becomes blurred. There is no reason to be concerned about reestablishing this difference unless and until the dominant interpretation comes under criticism. In such cases, those concerned either with defending or attacking the dominant interpretation will need to separate that interpretation from its close connection with scripture. Of course, while conceptually clear, this process itself is hardly straightforward and will always be a matter of discussion and debate.

On the other hand, the difference between scripture and that more or less fluid body of texts which help to comprise, articulate, reform, and advance the Christian tradition means that Christians theoretically could ignore or diverge sharply from the views of texts from the tradition, without in principle undermining both their identity as Christians and their participation in the same tradition – Christianity – as these authors from the past.[6] Christians could not ignore or diverge sharply from scriptural texts in this way. Of course, whether there is much wisdom in willfully cutting oneself off from previous generations of Christians is a different matter.

Without question, the decisions that led to the separation of the scriptural texts from both their hypothetical precursors and their actual contemporaries (and near contemporaries) were made by humans (almost always men). These decisions were (and are) contestable and contested (sometimes hotly). Neither were these decisions one-time affairs, that immediately set up a definitive result. Issues of theology and ethics played roles in these decisions; so did issues of power and self-interest. In fact, it is very difficult in many cases to separate the workings of theology, for example, from the workings of the interests of a particular group of people. I have no stake in arguing that the establishment of the Christian canon was an ideologically pristine process in which theological acumen, cool logic, and common sense were the only relevant criteria. Nevertheless, there are at least three reasons for Christians to avoid trying to re-make those decisions otherwise today. First, sociologically speaking, there seems very little chance of actually getting a significant number of Christians to agree to this (let alone agree on how to do this). Further, there is no reason to think that decisions made by Christians today would be any less influenced by the concerns and interests of particular groups than decisions made 1,700 years ago. Secondly, in some cases, the historical data on which such decisions might be based are extraordinarily equivocal. There is a high, and often unacknowledged, level of speculation involved in such things as scholarly reconstructions of Pententeuchal or gospel traditions. As David Clines has remarked, "Our

---

[6] An example of this might be found in the contrast between Justin Martyr's judgments about the Jews' relationship to Abraham and Paul's judgments (see the discussion in chapter 3). In this case it is clear that Christians would fundamentally distort their identity by opting for a position at variance with Paul's. At the same time, they should distance themselves from this aspect of Justin's views.

ability to analyze sources is not a sufficient reason for concluding they existed."[7] This would be equally true for historical accounts about the fixing of the list of authoritative books. In addition, to the extent that there is a scholarly consensus on any of these issues, it is a shifting one. Christians would have to be prepared to re-make decisions about the content and contours of scripture on a regular basis in the light of changing scholarly views. Third, Christians' convictions about God's providence must include the view that God has providentially provided in their scriptures what Christians require in order to live and worship faithfully before God. Moreover, if someone were to claim that any particular text, The Gospel of Thomas, for example, ought to be included in the body of Christian scripture, it would also be essential that rules for reading that text in ways that would maintain the coherence of Christian faith and practice be given at the same time. There is not much point in including a text within scripture that at the same time is going to, thereby, saddle Christians with a set of incoherent beliefs and practices. Given that an ideologically pure scripture is impossible, Christians would be better advised to interpret their scriptures and their traditional texts in ways that help them combat and counter the distorting effects of such texts' composition and transmission by sinful humans.[8]

The authority of scripture, then, is not so much an invariant property of the biblical texts, as a way of ordering a set of textual relationships. To call scripture authoritative also establishes a particular relationship between that text and those people and communities who treat it as authoritative.[9] In the absence of a community or communities of people who are struggling to order their lives in accord with that scripture, claims about the authority of scripture begin to look rather abstract and vague. Further, the vast majority of purposes for which Christians engage scripture both presuppose and work to establish and maintain particular sorts of communities. Indeed, great portions of both the Old and New Testaments are addressed to communities and directed towards forming and reforming the people of God. When Christians baptize, they welcome new members into this people. The specific communities Christians form become the primary contexts in which the formation and transformation of individuals takes place. If Christians are successfully to engage scripture in

[7] See *The Esther Scroll* (Sheffield: Sheffield Academic Press, 1984), p. 7.
[8] See the arguments in chapter 3.
[9] See Wayne Meeks' comment, "A book or a formal list of documents is not a canon unless there is a community that makes it authoritative" in "A Hermeneutics of Social Embodiment," *Harvard Theological Review* 76 (1989), p. 182.

all of the ways they seek to, then that will generally happen in the context of their participation in particular Christian communities.

Christians' relationship with scripture is not only multi-faceted in that they are called to engage scripture in a variety of ways and contexts; it is also ongoing. This is so in two interrelated respects. First, the purposes and aims of the Christian life cannot be realized through brief encounters with scripture. Because the Christian life is an ongoing process of formation and transformation, a journey into ever deeper communion with the triune God and with others, Christians can expect to engage scripture in more or less proficient ways throughout their lives. In addition, the formations and transformations that constitute the lives of Christians entail that they will need to bring an ever-changing set of interests and concerns to bear on scripture. Secondly, Christians' engagement with scripture is ongoing in that such engagement is part of the prior and ongoing life of a particular tradition. In this light, contemporary Christians cannot presume that they are the first to engage scripture. Rather, they are participants in a tradition that is geographically and historically extended and culturally diverse. In countless, and often subtle, ways, Christians' engagements with scripture are (and should be) shaped by the successes, failures, debates, discussions, and prayers of previous generations of Christians. As Kenneth Surin has argued, "[T]he perfected *communio sanctorum* has a critical regulative role to play in the process of helping all Christians to acquire the requisite skills for understanding the textual world created by the biblical narrative. The saints are the true interpreters of scripture."[10]

The various ways in which Christians' engagement with scripture is ongoing entail that the manner in which Christians and Christian communities engage scripture in any aspect of their lives is never a straightforward process of directly mapping a scriptural text onto a conviction, practice, or disposition. Rather, Christians will find that interpretations of scripture have already shaped convictions, practices, and dispositions which have, in turn, shaped the ways in which scripture is interpreted. Not only is it impossible to undo this process, it is not clear how one would ever know that one had done so. Christians therefore, interpret scripture in ways that shape and are shaped by their convictions, practices, and dispositions. One can see this particularly clearly in discussions about the role of the so-called "Rule of Faith" in scriptural interpretation. The "Rule" both guides scriptural interpretation and

---

[10] Kenneth Surin, "The Weight of Weakness," in *The Turnings of Darkness and Light* (Cambridge: Cambridge University Press, 1989), p. 219.

"arises" out of scripture in complex ways. Perhaps the clearest example of this is found in Irenaeus' articulation of the "Rule" in *Against Heresies*. As Rowan Greer characterizes this:

> We could say that the quest which Irenaeus accomplishes is basically the discovery of a principle of interpretation in the apostolic "Rule of faith." At the same time . . . it is scripture itself that supplies the categories in which the principle of interpretation is expressed. Text and interpretation are like twin brothers; one can scarcely tell one from the other. What emerges is an unbroken dialogue or discourse between a book and a people, between Scripture and tradition, between the letter and the spirit, and between the word and the experience of those hearing it.[11]

In these early discussions about the "Rule of Faith" the rule works to set out boundaries within which interpretation must operate if Christians are to read scripture properly. This is due to the fact that these specific discussions of the relationships between Christian convictions and scriptural interpretation are clearly shaped by the struggles against heterodox views in which the authors were engaged.

The arguments of this book are not as much concerned with establishing boundaries as with making constructive use of the interaction of Christian convictions, practices, and scriptural interpretation. In this light, the central argument of this book is that, given the ends towards which Christians interpret their scripture, Christian interpretation of scripture needs to involve a complex interaction in which Christian convictions, practices, and concerns are brought to bear on scriptural interpretation in ways that both shape that interpretation and are shaped by it. Moreover, Christians need to manifest a certain form of common life if this interaction is to serve faithful life and worship. Further, because there is no theoretical way to determine how these interactions must work in any particular context, Christians will need to manifest a form of practical reasoning. This practical reasoning will enable Christians to bring appropriate convictions, practices, and concerns to bear on specific texts, in the light of particular circumstances, so that the prospects for faithful life and

---

[11] James Kugel and Rowan Greer, *Early Biblical Interpretation* (Philadelphia: Westminster Press, 1986), p. 157. The relevant discussions in *Against Heresies* can be found in the most constructive arguments of books 1, 3, and 4. See also Greer's discussion, pp. 158–76. See also Paul Blowers, "The *Regula Fidei* and the Narrative Character of Early Christian Faith," *Pro Ecclesia* 6 (1997), pp. 199–228. For a particularly concise example of the complex interconnectedness of the "Rule" and scripture see Augustine's 18th tractate on John.

worship are enhanced rather than frustrated. This situation, combined with the variations in the temporal, cultural, and political contexts in which Christians find themselves, ensures that the precise shape of faithful Christian life and worship in any specific context, as well as Christian interpretation of scripture, will always be both ongoing and a matter of discussion, debate, and disagreement. Although one cannot determine in advance the course of a conversation or a debate, at various points in the book, particularly in chapters 3 and 6, I offer comments about habits and practices, themselves arising out of particular relationships between doctrines, specific interpretations, and a particular form of common life, which will aid those discussions and debates.

Because of the nature of the interaction between scriptural interpretation, and the convictions, practices, and concerns of Christians and Christian communities, I could not possibly display all of the convictions and practices and concerns that might shape and be shaped by scriptural interpretation. In this book I examine some of the convictions, practices, and concerns that seem most important to the lives of Christian communities in the United States and Britain. These are important because they seem to play no role in current debates and discussions over scriptural interpretation. No doubt someone else could point to other convictions and practices as equally important. My aim in this regard is not to say all that might be said about these issues. Rather, I am seeking to open up a different way of approaching issues of scriptural interpretation, a way that is both new and old. To the extent that it is old, it depends on recovering interpretive habits and dispositions that were once more common in Christianity. That is, I am particularly concerned that Christians learn from the best interpretive habits and practices of those who both clearly understood the purposes for which Christians interpret scripture, and were relatively adept at keeping convictions, practices, and scriptural interpretation together as part of a single, complex practice called theology. For reasons I will note shortly, it will turn out that most of these examples will come from what it is commonly known as pre-modern interpretation. I am not necessarily arguing that Christians should simply repeat pre-modern interpretive results. Rather, my point is that to the extent that contemporary Christians (theologians, professional biblical scholars, and lay people) have lost the skills and habits that allowed previous Christians to allow scriptural interpretation to shape and be shaped by Christian convictions and practices, they now need to learn those habits and skills anew and for their own time.[12]

---

[12] I take it that this is, in part, what George Lindbeck means when he claims that a theologically oriented history of Christian scriptural interpretation is "the theologically most crucial of all historical fields, including biblical studies, for those who think . . . that

To the extent that *Engaging Scripture* is opening something new, it will be as it offers an alternative to the current situation which sees biblical scholars and theologians working in isolation from each other and from the concerns of Christian communities. What I am proposing here is, then, a pattern or model for the theological interpretation of scripture. In addition to arguments about the ways in which scriptural interpretation might shape and be shaped by specific Christian convictions, practices, and concerns, almost all of the chapters are focused around the interpretation of a specific New Testament text. These, then, serve as examples of the sort of interpretation I am advocating.[13]

Having briefly laid out the central arguments of the book, I will here introduce each chapter. Following that, I will try to situate the arguments of this book in relation to other works. Chapter 2, "Stories of Interpretation," offers three accounts of interpretation: determinate, anti-determinate, and underdetermined. The aim of determinate interpretation is to produce, uncover, or illuminate the meaning of the biblical text. It seeks clarity, and closure. Determinate interpretation views the biblical text as a problem to be mastered. Anti-determinate interpretation is directly parasitic upon determinate interpretation. Its aim is to upset, disrupt, and deconstruct interpretive certainties. In its most sophisticated forms it argues that interpreters have a certain moral responsibility to read in this deconstructive manner. Underdetermined interpretation is underdetermined only in the sense that it avoids using a theory of meaning to determine interpretation. Underdetermined interpretation recognizes a plurality of interpretive practices and results without necessarily granting epistemological priority to any one of these.

I will argue that, of these three accounts, only an underdetermined account of scriptural interpretation will address the legitimate concerns raised by determinate and anti-determinate accounts without reproducing their weaknesses. At the same time, an underdetermined account of interpretation will

---

the church's future depends on its postcritical reappropriation of precritical hermeneutical strategies" (from his review of *Biblical Hermeneutics in Historical Perspective: Studies in Honor of Karlfried Froehlich*, ed. Mark Burrows and Paul Rorem (Grand Rapids: Eerdmans, 1991), in *Modern Theology* 10 (1994), pp. 101–6).

[13] While I discuss both the relationships between the Old Testament and the New, and offer comments on some Old Testament passages, no Old Testament text receives the attention that I give to specific New Testament texts. This is not out of any deep convictions about the inferiority of the Old Testament. Rather, it is the result of a variety of contingent factors mostly related to space and my own limitations.

be best suited to the aims and purposes which Christians bring to scriptural interpretation.

In chapter 3, "Vigilant Communities and Virtuous Readers," I address the criticism that the underdetermined account of scriptural interpretation I advocate in chapter 2 is open to the charge that it provides no resources to counter the historically well-attested tendency of Christians to interpret scripture in ways that underwrite their most sinful practices. To address this objection I first argue that this objection must be separated from claims about textual ideologies if it is to be made most forcefully. Having done this, I admit that it is impossible to develop a method that, if followed, will guarantee that Christians will not interpret scripture to confirm and underwrite their sin. Instead, what must be addressed are ingrained habits of perceiving and living in the world. Based on a reading of Luke 11:34–5, I argue that Christians are called to exercise a particular sort of vigilance over themselves and their interpretation. This further demands that Christian communities maintain the practices of forgiveness, repentance, and reconciliation in good working order. In addition to countering sinful interpretive tendencies, the good working of these practices will aid in the formation of virtuous readers capable of exercising charity in the midst of interpretive disputes.

Chapter 4, "How the Spirit Reads and How to Read the Spirit," addresses the role of the Spirit in scriptural interpretation. All Christians give some place to the Spirit in interpretation. In fact, however, this often amounts only to lip service. This is quite striking in comparison with a passage like Acts 10–15. Here, in regard to issues surrounding Gentile inclusion in the church, the Spirit plays a decisive role in a particular set of disputes involving scriptural interpretation. The characters in this passage demonstrate a remarkable facility for recognizing, interpreting, and acting upon the work of the Spirit. I argue that this facility is underwritten by two interconnected elements. The first is the ability to bear witness to the work of the Spirit in the lives of others. The second is that this ability is sustained by the particular friendships Christians are able to form. This leads me to look at a contemporary dispute over the role of homosexuals in the church as an analogous extension of the disputes over the inclusion of the Gentiles into the church in Acts 10–15. I conclude that to be in a position to debate, and perhaps enact, this type of analogical extension, Christians will need to begin by forming the sorts of friendships with homosexuals that would enable them to testify to the work of the Spirit in the lives of their friends. Without this initial step, Christians will be able neither to read the Spirit nor read with the Spirit.

Chapter 5, "Who Can Read Abraham's Story?," shifts to Galatians. There Paul powerfully reads both the Galatians' experience of the Spirit and the story of Abraham to argue that Gentile Christians in Galatia need not be circumcised and take on the yoke of Torah. These arguments are made in Gal. 3–4. I want to argue, however, that Paul justifies his powerful interpretive moves in Gal. 3–4 by means of the account of his character which he renders in Gal. 1–2. On this basis I will discuss the importance of the character of the interpreter, an issue as vitally important for Christian interpretation of scripture as it is irrelevant for professional biblical scholars. The issue of the character of the interpreter is particularly important for any consideration of whether and how contemporary Christians might interpret scripture like Paul does.

Chapter 6, "Making Stealing Possible," begins by observing that throughout the book I have presented Christian interpretation of scripture as an activity that is both marked and sustained by discussion, debate, and argument. Rather than eliminate debate, I have tried to point out ways in which Christians' convictions and practices should shape and be shaped by interpretive debates about scripture. If this ongoing debate and discussion about how best to interpret scripture is to advance the aims and purposes which Christians bring to scriptural interpretation (i.e. faithful life and worship), then Christians must manifest a host of verbal and rhetorical practices such as truth telling, as well as habits of gracious and edifying speech. This much is not very surprising. Based on a reading of Eph. 4:25–5:2, however, I want to argue that success in manifesting these verbal skills is connected to very material issues about how, for example, Christians get and hold wealth.

Chapter 7, "Practical Wisdom, Christian Formation, and Ecclesial Authority," concludes the book. This chapter begins by situating the type of theological interpretation advocated in the rest of the book in relation to professional biblical scholarship. Throughout the book I make ready and constructive use of professional biblical scholarship, while at the same time distancing the interests and purposes of theological interpretation from those of professional scholars. In this chapter I lay out the argument for making *ad hoc* use of professional scholarship. That is, the views, results, and works of professional biblical scholars can be usefully employed in Christian interpretation of scripture on an *ad hoc* basis. There is no sense in which these things are necessary to Christian interpretation of scripture. I also argue, surprisingly, perhaps, that one place where the church can learn much from the academy is in regard to the importance of forming people to be certain types of interpreters. Just as being formed to be a biblical scholar involves learning how to exercise a type of practical reasoning, so Christian communities need to form Christians to exercise Christ-focused practical reasoning if they are to interpret scripture in ways that enable rather than frustrate their struggles to live and worship faithfully before God. I illustrate the nature of this practical reasoning by means of a reading of Philippians. Further, I discuss some of the practices that will work to form Christians to be practically wise readers of scripture. Finally, I briefly turn to address the issue of ecclesial authority. On the one hand, the arguments of this book do not presuppose any particular account of ecclesial authority. On the other hand, the issue lurks in the background and should at least be brought to the surface. I cannot hope to address that issue in this book, but I do make some general remarks as a basis for further thought, and which I hope to address more fully at another time.

Of course, I am neither the first nor the only contemporary scholar advocating a form of theological interpretation of scripture. There are several recent works addressing similar issues. In addition, one might note that the discipline of biblical theology has endeavored to produce theological interpretation. In the rest of this introduction I want to situate the sort of interpretation I am advocating here in relation to these alternatives. I will begin by contrasting theological interpretation with the dominant form of biblical theology.

Theological Interpretation rather than Biblical Theology

On the one hand, one could without much difficulty write several volumes surveying varieties of biblical theologies and theologians. On the other hand, there is what I would call a dominant tradition in the discipline of biblical theology.[14] My remarks are largely about that dominant tradition, which I will trace out here. This tradition is deeply at odds with the type of theological interpretation I am advocating. I recognize that this is not true of all biblical theologies and theologians. It does, however, characterize a dominant approach.[15] By examining the beginnings of this discipline I want to show that, based on its initial concerns, it is systematically unable to provide the sorts of

[14] This dominant form is recognized by those holding very diverse and opposing views such as A. K. M. Adam, *Making Sense of New Testament Theology* (Macon: Mercer University Press, 1995); Heikki Räisänen, *Beyond New Testament Theology* (London: SCM, 1990); Thomas Söding, "Inmitten der Theologie des neuen Testaments," *New Testament Studies* 42 (1996), pp. 161–84; and Robert Morgan, "Can Critical Study of Scripture Provide a Doctrinal Norm?," *Journal of Religion* 76 (1996), pp. 206–32.

[15] There are some, like Robert Morgan, who advocate a similar approach to mine, but wish to keep the phrase "New Testament theology." Morgan characterizes biblical theology as "all theologically motivated interpretation" of scripture ("Can Critical Study of Scripture Provide a Doctrinal Norm?," p. 212). I wonder, however, if retaining the phrase "biblical/New Testament theology" for such work does not invite confusion.

theological interpretation I advocate here. Nevertheless, most biblical theologians want to be theological. I will try to show that this situation results in a variety of unfortunate practices, none of which can systematically advance the theological interpretation of scripture. Moreover, I will argue that, given the larger intellectual climate within which the discipline of biblical theology emerged, it is not all that surprising that it developed in the ways it did.

It is common to claim that biblical theology as a mode of academic discourse was born with Gabler's *Antrittsrede* in 1787.[16] I think, however, that Ben Ollenburger is right to indicate that Gabler's position was very quickly abandoned in favor of positions more clearly influenced by Kantian concerns culminating in Wrede's essay, "The Tasks and Methods of 'New Testament Theology'."[17]

Gabler's "pure biblical theology" was a two-staged affair that would have allowed for a blurring of the disciplinary distinctions between philosophy and theology. He proposed this at just the time that Kant was arguing for more rigid disciplinary boundaries within the emerging modern university's division of academic labors. In this respect, one could say that Kant's view won the day. Alternatively, even though they disagreed about how this was to be done, both Kant and Gabler were struggling to demarcate a space for biblical theology as a discipline within the modern university, a discipline which would interact with other newly disciplined modes of inquiry, but which would have its own integrity.[18] This quest for disciplinary autonomy is most thoroughly carried out in Wrede's essay.

Wrede's argument is a *tour de force* whereby the disciplinary integrity of New Testament theology is retained at the expense of both terms. The most famous lines from the essay come from its conclusion: "Nevertheless, the name New Testament theology is wrong in both its terms. The New Testament is not concerned merely with theology, but is in fact far more concerned with religion. . . . The appropriate name for the subject-matter is early Christian history of religion, or rather: the history of early Christian religion and

---

[16] As Gerhard Ebeling argues, prior to the Enlightenment the term "biblical theology" was used to refer to a pietistic attempt to reform scholastic dogmatics. See "The Meaning of 'Biblical Theology'," in *Word and Faith* , trans. J. Leitch (Philadelphia: Fortress Press, 1960), pp. 79–97.

[17] Ben C. Ollenburger, "Biblical Theology: Situating the Discipline," in *Understanding the Word,* ed. J.T. Butler, E. Conrad, and B. Ollenburger (Sheffield: Sheffield Academic Press, 1985), pp. 37–62. I have followed Robert Morgan in inserting scare quotes around the phrase 'New Testament Theology' in Wrede's title as a way of translating the German *sogenannte,* "so-called." See Morgan *The Nature of New Testament Theology* (London: SCM, 1973).

[18] See Ollenburger, "Situating the Discipline," pp. 44–6.

theology."[19] Wrede's proposals amounted to a call for a historical report on the "religion" of the first Christians. This meant that the scope of the inquiry could not be confined to the New Testament. Further, his romantic distinction between "religion" and "theology," and his demand that New Testament theology be strictly historical, effectively excluded all constructive theological work from this discipline. "Biblical theology has to investigate something from given documents – if not an external thing, still something intellectual. It tries to grasp it as objectively, correctly, and sharply as possible. That is all. How the systematic theologian gets on with its results and deals with them – that is his own affair. Like every other science, New Testament theology has its goal simply in itself, and is totally indifferent to all dogma and systematic theology."[20]

Wrede's proposals fit quite well with his own liberal Protestant views about theology.[21] Perhaps it is because this form of theology was ascendant at the time that Wrede's views seemed to win the day. This is true even though Wrede's untimely death meant that he never fulfilled the agenda set out in this essay. What strikes me as peculiar, looking back 100 years later, is that no one proposed that if Wrede were right, then the phrase New Testament theology simply ought to be abandoned. There really seems to be no point in keeping a phrase that is "wrong in both its terms." Let Wrede's work be called the history of the religion of early Christianity. Let New Testament theology describe something else. This would seem to have fit well with Wrede's desire for disciplinary autonomy. The fact that this option never really was proposed, although it has been followed in practice, and the fact that Wrede's proposals profoundly shaped the discipline, have tied biblical theology, as an academic discipline, to a series of unfortunate practices.

In the light of the success of Wrede's proposals, the discipline of biblical theology found itself caught up in two separate but related processes of fragmentation which have their roots in modernity.[22] First, there is the

[19] W. Wrede, "The Tasks and Methods of 'New Testament Theology'," in Robert Morgan's *The Nature of New Testament Theology*, p. 116.

[20] See Wrede, "Tasks and Methods," p. 69. As A. K. M. Adam nicely points out, however, while Wrede saw New Testament theology as radically separate from dogmatics, he also argued that dogmatics was utterly dependent on the findings of New Testament theology. See *Making Sense of New Testament Theology* , pp. 72–3. See also Ebeling's comment, "The more 'biblical theology' as a historical discipline derives its vitality from its detachment from dogmatics, the less it can be indifferent to the utterances of dogmatics," "The Meaning of 'Biblical Theology'," p. 89.

[21] See Morgan's comments in *The Nature of New Testament Theology*, p. 22.

[22] Given modernity's persistent desire to police theology, it is not clear that things would have turned out differently had Wrede never made his specific proposals.

fragmentation of theology into a set of discrete activities: biblical studies, systematics, historical theology, practical theology, and so forth. I do not mean to say that prior to the rise of modernity people would not have recognized rough and ready distinctions between various theological tasks. For example, Thomas Aquinas, as well as his contemporaries, would have recognized that in writing his commentary on John's gospel he was engaged in a different sort of task than in writing his *Summa Theologiae*. Thomas, and his contemporaries, however, would have been puzzled by the notion that in writing one he was acting like a biblical scholar and in writing the other he was working as a systematic theologian. These tasks were all seen as parts of a more or less unified theological program of articulating, shaping, and embodying convictions about God, humanity, and the world.

The fragmentation of theology became institutionalized when its various parts became professional disciplines within the structure of the modern university.[23] This institutional fragmentation is accomplished as, in the division of academic labor, spheres of knowledge are more and more narrowly defined and disciplined. At its best, this economy was designed to produce knowledge more efficiently. Instead, in its most advanced North American forms, each discipline struggles to maintain its own integrity and the integrity of its own sphere of discourse. To be counted as a professional within each of these disciplines, one has to master such a diverse body of knowledge particular to each field that it is rare to find a scholar in one of these fields whose work is read and used by those in another. Professionalization institutionalized the separation between biblical studies and theology. Because there is a strong temptation in most universities (as least in the US) to treat the work of professional scholars as commodities that can be exchanged for various professional rewards (e.g. tenure, promotion, and the like), there is little incentive to take the time needed to engage seriously with the work of those outside one's field. In fact, the commodification of scholarship works to specialize and fragment disciplines rather than to encourage the breaking down of disciplinary boundaries.[24]

[23] For a stimulating discussion of the effects of professionalization in American higher education see Burton Bledstein, *The Culture of Professionalism* (New York: W.W. Norton, 1976). Largely due to the policies of the Conservative government in Britain during the 1980s one can see similar patterns emerging in British universities. For a somewhat similar account of the fragmentation of theology see Francis Watson, *Text and Truth* (Edinburgh: T. & T. Clark, 1997), pp. 2–9.

[24] As I noted above, this phenomenon is particularly clear in the US; it seems increasingly the case in Britain as well. In the German context, the relationships between state, church, and university mean that the situation is and has been quite different. In developing countries a whole different range of pressures shapes the interests of academics.

It is within this economy that biblical theology has had to establish itself as a discipline since Wrede. One can see this struggle for disciplinary integrity carried out particularly well in New Testament theologies after Wrede. Many of these works persistently attempt to distinguish themselves from a History of Religion report on the religion of the earliest Christians, on the one hand, and "dogmatics" on the other hand. One of the primary criticisms one often reads of New Testament theologies is that they step over the boundary into systematic theology. From Wrede's explicit disregard for constructive theology, through Krister Stendahl's distinction between what a text meant and what it means, to Heikki Räisänen's desire to move beyond New Testament theology, the discipline of biblical theology seems inordinately concerned with images of boundaries and separations designed to keep constructive theological concerns at bay until some more properly historical work can be done by the biblical theologian.[25] While biblical theology might be more captivated by this sharp division of intellectual labor than other realms of biblical studies, this phenomenon is not unique. In fact, such a severe disciplining of knowledge is characteristic of the modern university. Just 20 years after Wrede's essay on New Testament theology, Max Weber gave his influential lecture, "Wissenschaft als Beruf," which lays out an almost ascetic program for the hyper-specialization of all academic work which is strikingly similar to Wrede's.[26]

My point is not to argue about causal relationships between Wrede and Weber. Rather, I wish to note that given the time when biblical theology became a form of academic discourse whose tasks are initially articulated by Gabler and more firmly established by Wrede, it is not surprising that it reproduces many of the intellectual practices of the modern university – an interest in the sharp division of intellectual labor, which results in fragmented and fragmenting disciplines each concerned with its own integrity as a discipline. This situation reinforces the fragmentation of theology into discrete disciplinary spheres and works to frustrate seriously theological interpretation of scripture.

---

[25] Ben Ollenburger has raised this issue in regard to Stendahl's work in "What Krister Stendahl 'Meant' – A Normative Critique of Descriptive Biblical Theology," *Horizons in Biblical Theology* 8 (1986), pp. 80–5.

[26] The original lecture was given in 1918. For an English translation see "Science as Vocation," in *From Max Weber: Essays in Sociology*, trans. and ed. H. H. Gerth and C. Wright Mills (New York: Oxford University Press, 1977), pp. 129–56. For an interesting critique of the effects on American academic life of Weber's views see Mark Schwehn, *Exiles From Eden* (New York: Oxford University Press, 1993), pp. 3–21.

While Wrede's aim of systematically establishing biblical theology as a separate discipline came to be widely, if not universally, shared, in practice biblical theologians have never really been comfortable making biblical theology simply a historical report on the religion of the first Christians.[27] There seem to be two interrelated reasons for this. On the one hand, the formal development presumed by the History of Religion school never really measured up to the historical evidence. At the very least, one would have to admit that it could be challenged by other constructs of historical movement.[28] Hence, offering a historical report that depends upon the plot assumed by the History of Religion school has become problematic. On the other hand, those aspects of biblical theologies which are strictly a report on the convictions, practices, and lives of the Israelites or the first Christians are simply not very satisfying theologically. Put another way, even if one could make Krister Stendahl's meant/means distinction theoretically serviceable (which cannot be done), most biblical theologies are not really satisfied with merely providing raw material for the systematic theologians. Most biblical theologies want to be theological.

The most common way biblical theologians' desire actually to be theological can be seen is in their attempts to manage issues relating to the unity and diversity of theological perspectives that one can identify within scripture.[29] These issues have been played out in various ways over time. Nevertheless, there seems to have been a basic pattern that biblical theologies this century have followed. A biblical theologian will posit that one or another theological view or biblical text is the controlling one that shapes and holds together all the others. This is countered by another scholar who argues, instead, that a different concept provides the lenses which best unify the theological perspectives found in scripture. More recently, however, scholars will argue that to privilege one perspective over another establishes a canon within the canon. Without invoking the external theological considerations that biblical theology has worked so hard to exclude, there is, in effect, no real way to unify

---

[27] This is the same point Wrede made of biblical theologies from Gabler to his own time. Heikki Räisänen has recently made a similar claim about biblical theologies from Wrede to the present in *Beyond New Testament Theology*, pp. x–xxviii. Both Wrede and Räisänen make this point by way of complaint. I see it as a sign of hope.

[28] I am thinking in particular of Norman Gottwald's *The Tribes of Yahweh* (New York: Orbis, 1979) and Elizabeth Schüssler-Fiorenza's *In Memory of Her* (New York: Crossroad, 1983).

[29] Again, Räisänen and I agree on our diagnosis of how theological concerns are made manifest in biblical theologies. We disagree about how to evaluate this phenomenon. For a classic example of the scholarly management of issues of unity and diversity see J. D. G. Dunn, *Unity and Diversity in the New Testament* (London: SCM, 1977).

the differing theological perspectives in the New Testament, much less the entire Bible, without doing a disservice to some of these perspectives. In response, biblical theologians have moved more towards simply cataloging the diverse theologies in scripture.[30] Again, any particular work of biblical theology may well have useful things to say about the theology of particular biblical books. The type of theological interpretation I am arguing for here, however, wants to take issue with this entire practice of seeking answers regarding issues of unity and diversity within the text of scripture.

The central problem with attempts to manage the unity and diversity of scripture is that they tend to treat this as an abstract problem. That is, they assume that the "theologies" of the Bible are simply specific examples of properties contained in the texts of the Bible which can be extracted by means of a general method available to anybody regardless of their larger interpretive aims. This approach seems to presume that unity and diversity are self-identifying and self-interpreting properties of texts or groups of texts. As I will argue further in chapter 2, the notion of texts having properties that can be mined by anyone using the appropriate method is deeply problematic on philosophical grounds. Moreover, it fails to account for the very different contexts in which interpreters operate and the diverse interests they bring to interpretation. Once these problems are recognized it becomes clear that the question of unity and diversity within scripture is not a single question. Rather, the question can be asked in a variety of different ways and it must be connected to the ends and purposes for which one interprets scripture.

Given the purposes for which Christians are called to interpret and embody scripture, there are senses in which they want to affirm the unity of scripture and senses in which the obvious diversity of material in the Bible is important. There are several respects in which Christians want to affirm positions which might be tied to the unity of scripture. For example, Christians want to affirm that the action of God witnessed to in the entirety of scripture is unified. That is, Christians want to affirm that, contra Marcion, scripture identifies one God whose will is unified in the sense that God does not act at certain times in ways designed to frustrate or counter God's ultimate purposes. On the evidence of Romans and Galatians, Paul himself recognized the importance of such claims

---

[30] Perhaps the best variation on this model is G. B. Caird's use of the image of an apostolic conference. "[T]o write a New Testament theology is to preside at a conference of faith and order. Around the table sit the authors of the New Testament, and it is the presider's task to engage them in a colloquium about theological matters which they themselves have placed on the agenda." See *New Testament Theology*, completed and edited by L. D. Hurst (Oxford: Clarendon Press, 1994), p. 19.

about God's activity. Given that Christians also recognize that God's actions can be surprising and that the path leading to the ultimate consummation of God's will for the world may well be filled with twists and turns unanticipated by humans, and which may require unconventional interpretive strategies, it does not seem too difficult to give an account of God's activity related in scripture that will be consistent with notions of God's unified will.[31] Of course, this claim cannot simply be extracted from scripture. Rather it presumes a doctrine of God (which is itself shaped by scripture) and God's providence, and is confirmed by the presence of a contemporary community which both testifies to God's continuing action in its midst and presents itself as the continuation of God's actions beginning with Adam and Eve through Abraham and Sarah, Moses and Miriam, and the prophets, reaching its climax in Jesus, moving on through Paul and Priscilla, down to the present, and looking expectantly towards the new Jerusalem.[32] Indeed, it is odd for biblical theologians to presume, if not explicitly argue, that the text of scripture is providentially ordered, but in a way that the vast majority of Christians cannot fathom apart from the very recent work of biblical theologians.[33]

Another related sense in which Christians want to affirm the unity of the New Testament is in regard to its presentation of Jesus. Christians must affirm that the gospels, despite (and, perhaps, through) their variety, still enable Christians to render a single, though complex, unsubstitutable character.[34] Within these notions of unity, there is quite a lot of room for diversity; though, again, that diversity cannot be spoken of in the abstract. There are, no doubt, other senses in which Christians would want to affirm notions of the unity of scripture. My point is not to list them all. I simply want to show that the

[31] See Morgan's comments on the theological unity of the New Testament, "Can Criticial Study of Scripture Provide a Doctrinal Norm?," p. 213.

[32] C.F. Evans, in his famous essay "Is 'Holy Scripture' Christian?," in *Is 'Holy Scripture Christian?* (London: SCM, 1971) rightly questions whether the issue of the unity of the New Testament would even be an issue apart from concerns about the unity of God (p. 34). He misstates the issue, however, by claiming that scripture, as a holy book, must reflect the unity of God. The issues of the status of scripture and the unity of God's action are logically separable. Further, Evans seems to imply that the notion that the issue of unity is imposed on the New Testament by doctrines about God is a bad thing, rather than simply a reflection of the way Christians interpret scripture.

[33] Of course, one way of countering this anomaly is to return to Wrede's notion that New Testament theology could not be confined to the canonical texts, a move that subsequent New Testament theologians have generally not made.

[34] See Hans Frei's *The Identity of Jesus Christ* (Philadelphia: Fortress Press, 1975) for this argument.

question of the unity of scripture is not a single question; it is not a question about content that can be answered in the abstract. Rather, it is a question that will be articulated and answered differently depending on the purposes and aims one brings to scriptural interpretation. Moreover, the specific ways in which Christians want to posit, answer, and argue about this question depend on bringing theological concerns and convictions into the discussion in a way that most biblical theologies either truncate or explicitly exclude.[35]

In this fairly brief sketch I cannot hope to have done justice to the differences between particular biblical theologies. Moreover, there are numerous examples of those who have resisted the dominant trends in biblical theology. Further, it would be a mistake to assume that Christians should ignore the work of biblical theologians. My point, rather, has been to identify a particular and dominant form of approaching biblical and/or New Testament theology. Having identified it, I have tried to indicate how, despite its *ad hoc* usefulness, it is systematically unable to serve the purposes Christians bring to the interpretation of scripture. This mode of biblical theology cannot advance theological interpretation of scripture because its aims and purposes differ from those of theological interpretation. For a variety of reasons, including the disciplining disciplinary concerns which have shaped so much of modern academic life, biblical theology has worked diligently to exclude the theological convictions it needs to engage in order to advance substantive theological arguments.

The aims of biblical theology seem explicitly to exclude considerations which are essential elements to the project of theological interpretation which I am seeking to advance in this book. In addition to those in the discipline of biblical theology, there are several other scholars advocating forms of theological interpretation. I will turn now to a brief discussion of two important advocates of theological interpretation.

Theological Interpretation and Some of Its Advocates: Francis Watson and Brevard Childs

Recently, Francis Watson has argued for a specifically theological interpretation of scripture in his book, *Text, Church and World*. Watson's book is a detailed argument in favor of re-invigorating theological interpretation, and

---

[35] For a similar argument against abstract accounts of the unity and diversity of the New Testament see Luke T. Johnson, *Scripture and Discernment* (Nashville: Abingdon, 1996), pp. 45–58.

in many respects Watson and I are plowing the same field. To engage Watson's book in all of the detail it deserves would require more space than I have here. At various points in the rest of this book I will engage specific points he raises. Here I will try to situate more generally our two works in relation to each other. Both of us are quite dissatisfied with those interpretive practices commonly known as historical-criticism, though we each tend to engage such work when it is useful.[36] Both of us recognize that some of the most significant and challenging conversation partners for theological interpretation come not from historical-criticism, but from what might be called post-modern perspectives, including the work of philosophers such as Jacques Derrida, on the one hand, and those (both inside and outside the church), on the other hand, who are critical of the ways in which Christians have interpreted scripture to underwrite some of their most oppressive practices.[37] We both try to make our cases in the course of offering theological interpretations of scriptural texts. As might be expected, in all of these aspects of similarity there are points of agreement, near agreement, and outright disagreement between Watson and me. Nevertheless, I think that those who read both works will find that despite our similar interests, these are two fundamentally different books.

My arguments in this book are primarily driven by attention to the purposes for which Christians engage scripture. As a result, I treat scriptural interpretation as a practice which both shapes and is shaped by Christian convictions and practices and which both calls forth and relies upon the presence of a community manifesting a certain sort of common life. Watson, too, makes some comments about the ends towards which Christians read scripture. Further, as the middle term of his title, "church," indicates, he believes that, "the primary reading community within which the biblical text is located is the Christian church."[38] Nevertheless, recognition of and attention to the purposes for which Christians interpret scripture seem to play little role in the

---

[36] In response to Christopher Rowland's "Open Letter to Francis Watson on *Text, Church and World*" (*Scottish Journal of Theology* 48 (1995), pp. 507–17), Watson makes the very perceptive comment with which I agree, "So far as I can remember, my book contains no disparagement at all of 'the historical-critical method', largely because I do not believe that such an entity exists in the singular form that is normally envisaged. What does exist is a shifting set of conventions, never clearly defined and constantly under negotiation, about questions that it is proper to address to the biblical texts and the answers that it is proper to expect from them" ("A Response to Professor Rowland," *Scottish Journal of Theology* 45 (1995), p.518).

[37] I am, however, much more interested than Watson in exploring the resources found in pre-modern interpretive practices.

[38] Watson, *Text, Church and World*, p. 3.

body of the text. Neither do the particular shape and practices of Christian communities play a significant role. This results in a book that reads very much like a contemporary systematic theology. Indeed, Watson notes that his use of the terms "theology" and "theological" "relate to a distinct discipline – that of 'systematic theology'."[39] Further, he characterizes his work as "interdisciplinary." That is, it seeks to traverse two disciplines, biblical studies and systematic theology. To the extent that, as a professional biblical scholar, he has produced a work that reads much like a systematic theology, his work must be judged a success.

What Watson's whole program seems to presume is that systematic theology has not been subject to the same anti-theological disciplinary forces of the modern university as biblical studies has been.[40] Alternatively, if John Milbank's arguments about the disciplining of theology within modernity are generally on target, then the discipline of "systematic theology" will be no better suited to serve the ends for which Christians are called to engage scripture than the discipline of "biblical studies."[41] This is because systematic theology has been dominated by models dependent upon the social sciences and modernist philosophy.

> The pathos of modern theology is its false humility. For theology, this must be a fatal disease, because once theology surrenders its claim to be a meta-discourse, it cannot any longer articulate the word of the creator God, but is bound to turn into the oracular voice of some finite idol, such as historical scholarship, humanist psychology or transcendental philosophy.[42]

This is not the only respect in which Watson and I differ in our views on the state of contemporary theology. A significant portion of *Text, Church and World* is concerned with the work of Hans Frei and George Lindbeck.[43] Watson's concern is that the intratextual theology advocated by these two threatens to degenerate into a self-referential theology in which God becomes simply the

---

[39] Watson, *Text, Church and World*, p. 1. Compare Watson's approach also with Robert Morgan's claim that ". . . it is the scholars' aims rather than their methods or conceptual choices that give the discipline [biblical theology] its coherence and justify the label 'theology'" ("Can Critical Study of Scripture Provide a Doctrinal Norm?," p. 216).

[40] I take it that this is, in part, behind Christopher Rowland's concern that Watson's book "reflects too much the pressing concerns of the academic context . . . ." See "Open Letter," pp. 511–13.

[41] See *Theology and Social Theory* (Oxford: Blackwell, 1990), esp. chs 5, 8, and 12.

[42] *Theology and Social Theory*, p. 1.

[43] Chapters 1, 7, and 8 are the central places where Watson discusses Frei and Lindbeck.

production of human textual interpretation.[44] "The God who may be said, intrasystematically, to have created the world becomes without remainder, the product of human linguistic practices."[45] To counter this, Watson strongly asserts both that there is extra-textual reality and that it is textually mediated. That is, there is no immediate access to this extra-textual reality.

There are several points to make in this regard. First, I do not think that it is possible to find anywhere in the works of Frei or Lindbeck a denial of the existence of "extra-textual reality." Further, in the light of Bruce Marshall's essays on Lindbeck, it should be clear that one could not even claim that Lindbeck implicitly denies the existence of extra-textual reality or that he gives up strong claims to truth.[46] The point of Lindbeck's advocacy of intratextual theology is to contrast a theology which accounts for things theologically, using language and concepts that derive from scripture interpreted under the Rule of faith and the creeds, with a theology whose account is determined by general, non-theological accounts of "human experience." There are several criticisms one might want to make of this type of theology, but they are not the ones Watson raises. For Watson to claim that "Theology has always been intratextual in the sense that its knowledge of the objects of its investigation is mediated in large part through texts" is true but completely misses the point Lindbeck is advocating.[47] In the end, I would argue that Watson's criticisms of what he calls "postmodern theologies" fail because they are not really directed at the strongest and most charitable presentations one might give of such theologies.[48]

That current scholarly concerns about theological interpretation are not completely idiosyncratic owes a great deal to the ground-breaking work of

---

[44] I do not here want to address the extent to which Frei and Lindbeck could be said to be working on the same project. Watson links them and my comments are primarily about Watson.

[45] *Text, Church and World*, p. 152.

[46] The key essay in this regard is "Aquinas as Post-Liberal Theologian," *The Thomist* 53:3 (1989), pp. 353–406.

[47] *Text, Church and World*, p.152.

[48] In *Text and Truth* Watson continues his assault on what he calls post-modern theologies. In this case his criticisms are directed at interpretive pluralism (see ch. 3). Here Watson addresses methodologically flat-footed accounts of interpretive pluralism. By ignoring more sophisticated accounts Watson ends up with unconvincing arguments against straw figures. For two accounts of interpretive pluralism that do not make the sorts of claims that Watson finds so objectionable, see the essays by Mark Brett and by me in *The Bible in Three Dimensions*, ed. D. J. A. Clines, S. E. Fowl, and S. E. Porter (Sheffield: Sheffield Academic Press, 1990).

Brevard Childs. When many of us were finding the theoretical and theological limitations of various types of historical criticism extraordinarily frustrating, we found someone who gave voice to our frustration and helped to relieve it in the course of working through Childs' commentary on Exodus or his *Introduction to the Old Testament as Scripture* or any number of his essays. Childs' subsequent works continued to make a case for scholarly engagement with the biblical texts as the scripture of the church, culminating in his magisterial *Biblical Theology of the Old and New Testaments*. In the course of this book, however, it will become clear that I have particular disagreements with Childs over such things as the role of the Spirit in scriptural interpretation, and the nature of the "literal sense" of scripture. Perhaps the best way of situating my positions in relation to Childs' is by looking at one of his very recent essays on theological interpretation. In "Toward Recovering Theological Exegesis" Childs addresses an earlier essay by David Yeago, "The New Testament and Nicene Dogma." In this essay Yeago shows the logical continuities between specific New Testament texts and later trinitarian formulations. He seeks to argue that "The Nicene *homoousion* is neither imposed *on* the New Testament texts, nor distantly deduced *from* the texts, but, rather, describes a pattern of judgments present *in* the texts, in the texture of scriptural discourse concerning Jesus and the God of Israel."[49]

Childs is wholly sympathetic to Yeago's position, and seeks to advance further a notion of theological exegesis. Childs, in ways similar to, yet different from, the arguments of this book, also argues that theological interpretation involves a complex (Childs says dialectical) interaction between scriptural interpretation and Christian convictions and practices.[50] Because of the theoretically underdetermined nature of this interaction, Childs argues for a multi-layered interpretive approach that is both similar to and different from the medieval four-fold sense of scripture. Only such pluriform interpretation can address the variety of contextual concerns with which the text operates.[51] In this respect, Childs' position and my own arguments in chapter 2 overlap in significant ways. Our difference lies in Childs' commitment to what he calls a literal historical reading of the Old Testament. For Childs, literal historical interpretation is essential for theological interpretation because it allows the "discrete voice of the Old Testament" to be heard.[52] Indeed, Childs' essay is

---

[49] "The New Testament and Nicene Dogma," in *The Theological Interpretation of Scripture: Classic and Contemporary Readings*, ed. S. E. Fowl (Oxford: Blackwell, 1997), p. 87.
[50] "Toward Recovering Theological Exegesis," *Pro Ecclesia* 6 (1997), p. 19.
[51] "Toward Recovering Theological Exegesis," pp. 22, 24.
[52] "Toward Recovering Theological Exegesis," p. 20.

filled with claims about the "voice" of scripture and the discrete voice of the
Old Testament in particular.[53] As I will argue more fully in chapter 2, I am not
in principle opposed to using language of human agency in regard to texts
either in relaxed, informal conversation or as a verbal shorthand to refer to
well-established interpretive views. This language can do no conceptual
work, however, when it is invoked as part of an argument about contested
approaches or interpretations. That is, I can advance no argument by claiming
that my interpretation conforms to the "voice" of scripture and my oppo-
nent's does not allow the "voice" of scripture to be heard.

Childs' language about the "voice" of scripture seems to buttress arguments
addressing two legitimate concerns, but which can be addressed otherwise –
without recourse to textual voices. First, Childs is concerned to rule out
allegory, particularly "uncontrolled allegory."[54] While he notes a few examples of bad allegorical practices in Origen and Jerome, he does not give any
examples of "uncontrolled allegory" which were actually accepted by large
numbers of Christians. Simply citing examples of bad practice does not really
count as an argument against allegory in principle. As I will argue in regard
to Paul's reading of the Old Testament, whether one uses the term "allegory"
or not, some type of "counter-conventional interpretation" was both
practiced and recognized by the first Christians. Further, such interpretation
is theologically necessary to maintain Christian claims about the continuity of
God's activity. Nevertheless, the "controls" for such activity are not found so
much in a "literal historical" account of the voice of the Old Testament as in
communal judgments about whether such interpretations will issue forth in
faithful life and worship that both retain Christians' continuity with the faith
and practice of previous generations and extend that faith into the very specific
contexts in which contemporary Christians find themselves. Throughout his
essay Childs seems suspicious of any interpretive claims which finally rest on
the judgments of actual living Christians. No doubt, Childs could produce a
depressing list of recent ecclesial documents filled with self-affirming, lax, and
ultimately flawed interpretations to support his suspicions. Again, however,
these examples of bad practice do not speak in favor of using a notion like the
"voice" of the Old Testament to regulate them. As I will argue in chapters 2
and 7, failed interpretation, bad theology, and sinful practices do not need an
(ultimately question-begging) interpretive theory to regulate them. Instead,
Christians need to be more intentional about forming their members to be

---

[53] "Toward Recovering Theological Exegesis," pp. 20–4. In addition to having a "voice"
Childs also speaks of scripture as exerting a coercive pressure (p. 17).
[54] "Toward Recovering Theological Exegesis," pp. 20, 22.

certain types of readers, readers who, by virtue of their single-minded attention to God, are well versed in the practices of forgiveness, repentance, and reconciliation.

The second set of points that claims about the "voice" of the Old Testament seem designed to buttress is related to the place of critical Old Testament scholarship. Childs, more than any other Old Testament scholar, keenly recognizes that his call for theological interpretation of scripture (whether Christian or Jewish) renders the place of the Old Testament/Hebrew Bible scholar profoundly ambivalent. On the one hand, such a scholar distances herself from the profoundly atheological concerns of most professional biblical scholars, resisting the professionalizing tendencies I noted above. To introduce such theological concerns from a Christian perspective is to relativize the Old Testament.[55] That is, such theological concerns will always understand the Old Testament in relation to the New.[56] This is not to imply that the Old Testament is inferior to the New. Neither does it obviate the complexity of the relationships between the two testaments. On the other hand, there is little, if any, professional space for those who wish to read the Old Testament either through lenses ground by the New Testament and Christian theology or by the Talmud and midrashim. Asserting the fundamental importance of the "discrete voice of the Old Testament," as determined by literal historical exegesis, secures a professional place for such scholars. Having said this, I want to be very clear here. I am not accusing Childs of special pleading, of advocating a problematic notion of scriptural voices in order to secure his own job. Rather, I am simply noting that this is a residual effect of such notions. Moreover, as Childs' own work ably testifies, there is much work that is filled with rich theological potential that, in our current situation, could only have been produced by someone with the skills of a professional biblical scholar. Further, Childs is quite explicit that one of the theologically important reasons for advocating the "discrete voice of the Old Testament" is that it can remind Christians that they share at least part of their scriptures with Israel. The scriptures that give Christians life also animate Jews.[57] This is particularly important in a post-holocaust world. While I am sympathetic with this concern, I do not think that problematic notions of the "discrete voice of the Old Testament" will render Jews secure from Christian violence any more than a thoroughly christological reading of the Old Testament will open Jews

---

[55] Introducing Jewish theological concerns will also relativize the Old Testament, but in a different way.

[56] Morgan, "Can Critical Study of Scripture Provide a Doctrinal Norm?," p. 209.

[57] "Toward Recovering Theological Exegesis," p. 20.

to Christian violence. Jews will have nothing to fear from Christians only when Christians follow their Lord and forswear violence.

Thus far I have tried to situate my arguments for a theological interpretation of scripture in relation to the dominant form of biblical theology and in relation to two of the most significant advocates of theological interpretation. In regard to the dominant mode of biblical theology, I have argued that it is systematically unable to advance the type of theological interpretation I advocate here. This is largely due to the fact that as a discipline it is unable to account for the theological concerns that must generate and underwrite Christian interpretation of scripture. In regard to the work of Francis Watson and Brevard Childs, I have too briefly expressed my critical appreciation of their work, noting some significant points at which our works overlap and tend towards agreement. Rather, I have spent more time pointing out what I take to be some of the most significant points of difference between their work and mine. At this point I want to comment on the work of someone who seeks to advance a type of theological interpretation of scripture by grounding it in a general hermeneutical theory.

Theological Interpretation and Texts: Werner Jeanrond

Over the past 15 years Werner Jeanrond has demonstrated a keen concern to bridge the gaps between systematic theology and biblical studies. Moreover, he has rightly noted that the bases for the disjunction between theology and biblical studies are deeply embedded in the curricula of theology faculties. Hence, no large-scale progress will be made in bridging this gap in the academy without substantial revision to the disciplinary boundaries currently in operation.[58] In order to span the chasm between these two disciplines he has focused on the view that theology is a thoroughly hermeneutical discipline.[59] For Jeanrond, hermeneutics in general, and a developed theory of texts or textuality in particular, provide a common ground on which biblical scholars and theologians can meet. Again, there would be a variety of

---

[58] See the final section of "After Hermeneutics: The Relationship between Theology and Biblical Studies," in *The Open Text,* ed. Francis Watson (London: SCM, 1993), pp. 95–101.
[59] The most extensive account of Jeanrond's views here can be found in *Text und Interpretation als Kategorien theologischen Denkens* (Tübingen: Mohr, 1986). There is a very poor English translation of this work under the title *Text and Interpretation as Categories of Theological Thought* published by Gill and Macmillan, 1988.

points on which Jeanrond and I agree and many on which we would disagree. For the purposes of this introduction, I want briefly to lay out his notion of theological interpretation as a way of distinguishing it from the positions I take in this book.

The clearest and briefest statement of Jeanrond's views is from his essay "After Hermeneutics: The Relationship between Theology and Biblical Studies." Here he notes:

> While it is perfectly possible and legitimate to treat the Bible as an object for all kinds of specialized readings and investigations, some form of theological reading of the scriptures, though not necessarily according to the ecclesial lines suggested by Barth, is imperative for any critical reader of the biblical texts who wishes to respond to their semantic potential . . . I am arguing that the biblical texts themselves offer theological perspectives to the reader which a reader who claims to respond to the texts' own communicative perspectives cannot afford to ignore. By "theological perspective" I mean that these texts raise in their different ways the question of God.[60]

Two elements in particular support Jeanrond's claims in this quote. First, Jeanrond's claim that it is imperative that all critical readers read theologically depends on his overly formal notion of theological interpretation. That is, theological interpretation is that interpretation which attends to the "theological perspectives" of the text. These, we are told, are related to "*the* question of God" (emphasis mine). While it is not clear what "the question of God" is, it is clear that the Bible presents a variety of diverse claims and pictures of God. What sort of attention to these accounts really counts as theological interpretation? Does an interpretation that attends to the picture of God found in the Succession Narrative wholly in terms of the social and political forces that led to the production of that particular view of God count as theological?[61] If so, then the vast majority of professional biblical scholarship has been theological for quite some time. Moreover, it is not clear that systematic theology has anything to contribute to that discussion. At its most basic level, the difference between Jeanrond's notion of theological interpretation and my own is that Jeanrond desires to have theological interpretation exist in

---

[60] "After Hermeneutics," p. 88.

[61] In a subsequent essay Jeanrond is slightly clearer about what he takes the Bible's theological perspectives to be. See "Criteria for New Biblical Theologies," *Journal of Religion* 76 (1996), pp. 240–1, 246–7. Even here, however, I would claim that his account is overly formal, designed to keep biblical theology (in this case) separate from the incursions of Christian doctrine.

separation from the distinct purposes, convictions, and practices that Christians do, and must, bring to the interpretation and embodiment of their scripture.

Secondly, while I share with Jeanrond a commitment to interpretive pluralism, I do not think that it is "imperative" for all critical readers to read the Bible theologically in order to respond to the text's "semantic potential."[62] Anyone who recognizes the diversity current among biblical scholars cannot at the same time assume there is a "semantic potential" within these texts that somehow holds all of these interpretive approaches together. These approaches issue in too many diverse and contradictory interpretations. Yet, if there is an imperative to read theologically, it must rest on the fact that there is some sort of cumulative unity provided by the "semantic potential" of these texts that would be incomplete without a theological approach. This would require an extraordinarily problematic notion of "semantic potential," and it is hardly necessary for a commitment to interpretive pluralism. Some such notion of "semantic potential" is required, however, if one is to claim that there is some sort of demand to read these texts theologically that is incumbent on all readers.

My own claims in this regard are much more modest. Christians, by virtue of their identity, are required to read scripture theologically. Others may wish to do so, and Christians can certainly benefit from the insights of outsiders who engage scripture theologically. Most obviously, these readings would come from Jews who are reading their scripture theologically, but are not necessarily limited to them. My claims here neither limit the extent of the universal claims Christians want to make, nor seek to eliminate the interpretive practices of others. Christian biblical scholars can in principle engage in the whole panoply of diverse, and irreducibly distinct, interpretive practices characteristic of the profession of biblical scholarship. Neither the profession nor the "semantic potential" of the Bible requires all critical interpreters to read theologically.

In the course of this introduction I have laid out the various arguments I advance in this book regarding the theological interpretation of scripture. In addition, I have tried to situate my concerns in relation to the dominant strain of biblical theology from Wrede down to the present. In this regard, I have tried to lay out theological, philosophical, and historical reasons why this dominant strain of biblical theology cannot advance theological interpretation.

Further, I have briefly laid out some of the central differences between my

---

[62] Jeanrond's notions about textuality largely rely on work from text-linguistics and the work of Wolfgang Iser. Chapter 2, parts 3, 4, and 5 of *Text und Interpretation* make this clear.

version of theological interpretation and the work of Francis Watson, Brevard Childs, and Werner Jeanrond. These three are not the only scholars advocating forms of theological interpretation. These are, nonetheless, some of the most significant contemporary examples of such work. At this point, however, I will move to make my own position clearer by presenting a case for keeping theological interpretation of scripture "underdetermined" by theories of textual meaning.

Chapter Two

STORIES OF
INTERPRETATION

Introduction

In this chapter I want to lay out three different accounts of biblical interpretation. One account argues that biblical interpretation is determinate. The aim of this determinate interpretation is to produce, uncover, or illuminate the meaning of the biblical text. One might even say that the aim of this type of interpretation is to render interpretation redundant by making the meaning of the biblical text clear to all reasonable people of good will.[1] Determinate interpretation views the biblical text as a problem to be mastered. On this view the clarity and coherence of Christian believing depends on the determinacy of biblical interpretation.[2]

The second account argues that interpretation is marked by a sort of indeterminacy. The aim of indeterminate interpretation is to upset, disrupt, and deconstruct interpretive certainties. In this light, and for reasons I will explain more fully later, it might be better to call this view of interpretation "anti-determinate." Anti-determinate interpretation is always parasitic upon determinate interpretation. In its more sophisticated forms it argues that interpreters (including biblical interpreters) have a certain moral responsibility to read in this

---

[1] Even if such interpreters recognize that human fallenness being what it is means that interpretation will continue until the Kingdom comes in its fullness, the aim of interpretation is to end interpretation. See also the comment of Benjamin Jowett, one of the pioneers of determinate interpretation, "The true use of interpretation is to get rid of interpretation and leave us alone in company with the author." See "On the Interpretation of Scripture," *Essays and Reviews*, 7th edn (London: Longman and Green, 1861).

[2] "A Christian faith concerned to retain its own coherence cannot for a moment accept that the biblical texts (individually or as a whole) lack a single, determinate meaning, that their meanings are created by readers, or that theological interpretations must see themselves as non-privileged participants in an open-ended, pluralistic conversation." See Francis Watson in *Text and Truth* (Edinburgh: T. & T. Clark, 1997), p. 97.

deconstructive way. The aim of anti-determinate interpretation is to keep interpretation an ongoing event, avoiding the illusion of mastering the text.

The third account claims that biblical interpretation should be underdetermined.[3] While determinate and anti-determinate interpretation depend on accounts of textual meaning, underdetermined interpretation is underdetermined only in the sense that it avoids using a general theory of meaning to determine interpretation. This is based on the conviction that all interpretive quests to produce a general theory of meaning are bound to be question-begging and should be eliminated. Underdetermined interpretation recognizes a plurality of interpretive practices and results without necessarily granting epistemological priority to any one of these. An underdetermined biblical interpretation allows space for Christian theological convictions, practices, and concerns to shape and be shaped by biblical interpretation without being ruled by a determinate theory of meaning.

The argument of this chapter is that of these three stories, an underdetermined account of biblical interpretation will address the legitimate concerns raised by determinate and anti-determinate accounts of interpretation without reproducing their weaknesses. At the same time, an underdetermined account of interpretation will be best suited to the aims and purposes which Christians bring to biblical interpretation.

I will begin, then, by offering my three stories of interpretation. I make no pretense at offering an "objective" account of these three views. I do not consider each of these views equally viable as theories; neither are they equally suitable to the purposes for which Christians are called to interpret and embody scripture. My aim here is to offer accounts of determinate and anti-determinate views of interpretation that display what I take to be their strengths, to expose their weaknesses and, by means of an account of underdetermined interpretation, offer a better proposal.

Determinate Interpretation

A determinate view of biblical interpretation will stress that biblical texts have a meaning. This is not simply a claim about the basic intelligibility or even the meaningfulness of the biblical texts. Rather, meaning is conceived of (at least implicitly) as a sort of property with which the text has been endued. Further,

[3] I take this term from Eugene F. Rogers, Jr, "How the Virtues of the Interpreter Presuppose and Perfect Hermeneutics: The Case of Thomas Aquinas," *Journal of Religion* 76 (1996), pp. 64–5.

such meaning can be uncovered through the application of some set of interpretive procedures. On this view, the biblical text is seen as a relatively stable element in which an author inserts, hides, or dissolves (choose your metaphor) meaning. The task of the interpreter, whether lay, clerical, or professional, is to dig out, uncover, or distill the meaning of the text. Lest anyone think I am creating a straw person here, let me quote from a book published in 1995 by a mainstream biblical scholar, "Meaning resides in the text and is placed there by the author by means of his or her configuration of its words and phrases. Therefore, though the writer may be deceased, his or her words and meaning can still live on without our trying to impose a modern meaning on the text that violates the author's intended sense."[4] Even those biblical scholars who recognize the theoretical validity of a variety of interpretive methods and approaches tend in practice to be quite monistic, implicitly regarding their own approach as superior to alternatives.[5]

In terms of the purposes and interests Christians bring to scriptural interpretation, once the biblical text has yielded up its stable and determinate meaning, then issues of Christian doctrine and practice take on a concomitant stability and determinacy. Failure adequately to determine biblical interpretation will result in doctrinal and practical anarchy. The operating assumption here is that matters of doctrine and practice are straightforwardly determined by biblical interpretation and never the other way around. The complex interaction between doctrine, practice, and biblical interpretation for which I am arguing in this book is replaced by a one-directional movement from determinate meaning to stable doctrine and practice. Even here, however, one will find in both ecclesial and academic communities that those committed to a determinate account of biblical interpretation will still disagree sharply on the implications or applications of a biblical text on whose meaning they all agree. At this point, many of the theological convictions and ecclesial practices and concerns on which this book will focus come to play a decisive role in the way such disagreements are

---

[4] See Ben Witherington III, *Conflict and Community in Corinth* (Grand Rapids: Eerdmans, 1995), p. xiv n.13. I would also direct someone to the way the term "meaning" is used in John Barton's "Reading the Bible as Literature: Two Questions for Biblical Critics," *Literature and Theology* 1 (1987), pp. 135–63. See also the recent comments by Francis Watson in *Text and Truth*, ch. 3.

[5] Rowan Williams rightly characterizes this type of interpretation as viewing the text as a puzzle or problem to be solved. This is opposed to seeing interpretation as offering "social proposals for common reading and common, or at least continuous, activity (a gesture of performance that in some sense goes on with or takes up from mine)." See "The Suspicion of Suspicion: Wittgenstein and Bonhoeffer," in *The Grammar of the Heart*, ed. R. Bell (San Francisco: Harper and Row, 1988), p. 40.

articulated, argued, and resolved. These factors, however, can only be brought
into the discussion once the meaning of the text has been established. Indeed, one
of the ways those holding to this determinate view of interpretation can trump
others who also hold to this view is to show how one's interpretive opponents
have allowed theological concerns, prejudices, or preferences to determine their
interpretation, rather than rigorously mining the text for its meaning and then
letting that meaning shape their theology. By separating the establishment of
textual meaning from some other activity called theological application, the
clarity and stability of the meaning of the biblical text is preserved.[6]

Stendahl

Given that some of the same theological convictions and ecclesial practices
with which I, too, am concerned ultimately play a significant role in this way of
thinking about biblical interpretation, one might well ask why I do not opt for
some such view myself. In response I would like to point out both the conceptual
problems and the theological limitations of this view of biblical interpretation.

First, one must admit that this way of thinking/talking about texts works
pretty well as long as people agree on what it is they are looking for when they
mine a text for its meaning. Further, one can see that in periods when there
is a large degree of interpretive agreement, agreement both in terms of
methods for attaining meaning and in terms of interpretive results, there is an
illusory plausibility to the notion that interpretation is determinate. Problems,
however, arise when someone questions the very definition of meaning, thus
throwing the object of any textual mining expedition into question. As the
history of literary criticism over the past 50 years has shown, someone has only
to ask, for example, "Why should something like the author's intention count
as the meaning of a text?" to make both the contingency and the fragility of
those interpretive agreements clear.

At such points several things may happen. On the one hand, there will
probably be an outpouring of lengthy, but ultimately question-begging,
philosophical polemic designed to show that the author's intention (to stick
with the original example) really *is* the meaning of a text. These responses will
all be question-begging, because they will presuppose some notion of textual
meaning which is the very point at issue.[7] The problem does not lie so much

---

[6] One of the most well known articulations of this type of separation is found in Krister
Stendahl's distinction between what a biblical text meant and what it means. See his article
"Biblical Theology, Contemporary," in *The Interpreter's Dictionary of the Bible*, ed. G.
Buttrick (Nashville: Abingdon, 1962), vol. 1, pp. 418–32.

[7] Let me state categorically that I am not opposed to people using the word "meaning" in
either general conversation or scholarly debate as long as it is used in its everyday underdetermined sense. What this sense of "meaning" cannot do, however, is resolve an interpretive
dispute where the parties involved disagree about the nature of their interpretive tasks.

with the interpretive methods as with a fundamental lack of clarity about the ends towards which those methods are directed. This means that refinements in methodology will not resolve the problem.[8]

Of course, when people start arguing about what counts as textual meaning, some authoritative interpreters may exercise their institutional power and decree arbitrarily that meaning equals authorial intention. Those coming under the institutional control of such interpreters must either assent, leave, or be driven out. This phenomenon is as well known in modern academic settings as it is in churches. Displacing one's interpretive opponents may provide a limited of amount of institutional stability but it does not make arguments about the determinate meaning of biblical texts any more coherent.

In addition, there are several theological limitations to a determinate account of interpretation which should make it more unattractive to Christians than it often is. First, this view must force Christians to view the overwhelming majority of the history of Christian biblical interpretation as a series of errors, of failed attempts to display the meaning of the text.[9] No doubt, there is much in the history of Christian biblical interpretation for which Christians ought to repent. The use of biblical texts to underwrite the kidnapping of Africans and their enslavement in the United States and the Dutch Reformed Church's use of the Bible to support apartheid come immediately to mind. Nevertheless, there is much in the history of Christian biblical interpretation which speaks truthfully about God, enables faithful living, and inspires Spirit-directed worship, all of which was either done in the absence of a determinate theory of interpretation or under the direction of competing theories of meaning. In either case, such interpretation would be excluded from consideration by a determinate theory of interpretation.

A second related problem is that if the biblical texts have a single, stable, determinate meaning, then Christians are put in an awkward relationship to the Old Testament. The Christian church has always regarded itself in relationship to Israel. While not continuous in every respect, the church has claimed to be in continuity with Israel. This claim of continuity is crucial for Christian affirmations regarding the integrity or righteousness of God. As Paul understood so well, a God that abandons promises made to Israel, may not be able to keep promises made to Christians. For my purposes, the important element here is that Christians have always maintained the importance of

---

[8] I discuss this issue further in my account of underdetermined interpretation, below.
[9] Of course, there are Christian groups who tell the story of the church from the post-apostolic age down to themselves as a long history of decline. These groups will be quite content to view the history of biblical interpretation as a series of failures.

interpreting the Torah, the Prophets, and the Writings as their scripture. A determinate view of interpretation, however, results in a variety of problems in this regard. As David Steinmetz has nicely put it:

> How was a French parish priest in 1150 to understand Psalm 137, which bemoans captivity in Babylon, makes rude remarks about Edomites, expresses an ineradicable longing for a glimpse of Jerusalem, and pronounces a blessing on anyone who avenges the destruction of Temple by dashing Babylonian children against a rock? The priest lives in Concale, not Babylon, has no personal quarrel with Edomites, cherishes no ambitions to visit Jerusalem (though he might fancy a holiday in Paris), and is expressly forbidden by Jesus to avenge himself on his enemies. Unless Psalm 137 has more than one possible meaning, it cannot be used as a prayer of the Church and must be rejected as a lament belonging exclusively to the piety of ancient Israel.[10]

Whether or not this situation leads one to adopt the medieval four-fold sense of scripture, it clearly points out a key theological limitation for those who hold that biblical interpretation must be determinate. Indeed, a similar version of the problem arises when one attempts to read the prophets christologically (as many of the New Testament writers themselves did). To illustrate this problem further, imagine a French monk living in Paris in 1200 – no relation to the priest of Concale mentioned above. As part of his daily prayer, both communal and personal, he reads (and interprets!) the Psalms. In the course of his daily work he lectures on Psalms at the university of Paris. Being a gifted artist, he is also illuminating a manuscript of the Psalms. On Sundays he preaches from Psalms. All of these activities involve interpretation, but they cannot all fit under a single determinate theory of interpretation. If one privileges the interpretation done in the university, for example, claiming that it provides "the meaning" of the text, what is one to say about these other interpretive activities? Such a view of determinate interpretation risks subordinating or abandoning scripture's liturgical and ascetical roles in favor of a determinate theory of meaning.

Someone wishing still to hold to the determinate view of biblical interpretation might respond by noting that even within the medieval four-fold sense of scripture, the literal sense (*sensus literalis*) of scripture served as a determinate meaning of the biblical text which disciplined and limited all other types of

---

[10] See "The Superiority of Pre-Critical Exegesis," in *The Theological Interpretation of Scripture: Classic and Contemporary Readings*, ed. S. E. Fowl (Oxford: Blackwell, 1997), p. 28. Strangely enough, this is very close to the strategy Francis Watson adopts in regard to this very Psalm. See *Text and Truth*, pp. 119–21.

reading. Further, that literal sense was often equated with the intention of the author.

In response one must note several things. First, there is no single determinate account of the literal sense of scripture. Lyra, for example, seems to hold to a double literal sense, which would not really serve the ends of determinate interpretation.[11] More contemporary advocates of the literal sense of scripture such as George Lindbeck, Hans Frei, and Kathryn Tanner treat the literal sense as that meaning established within the community of those who take the Bible to be their scripture.[12]

The most obvious person to turn to if one wants to corrolate a notion of the literal sense of scripture with a determinate theory of interpretation is Thomas Aquinas. As Eugene Rogers has recently shown, however, while someone like Aquinas argued that the literal sense is that which the author intends,[13] "It turns out that Thomas' reflection on the literal sense leaves matters surprisingly underdetermined and that the author's intention functions in his hands more to promote diversity than to contain it."[14] This is largely because, for Aquinas, God is the author of scripture. "Now because the literal sense is that which the author intends, and the author of Holy Scripture is God who comprehends everything all at once in God's understanding, it comes not amiss, as St. Augustine says in *Confessions* XII, if many meanings

---

[11] See, for example, the Second Prologue to Lyra's *Postilla litteralis super totam Bibliam,* para. 14. Translated and introduced by Denys Turner in *Eros and Allegory* (Kalamazoo: Cistercian Publications, 1995), p. 385.

[12] George Lindbeck, "The Story Shaped Church: Critical Exegesis and Theological Interpretation," in *The Theological Interpretation of Scripture,* ed. S. E. Fowl, pp. 39–52. Frei's most concise presentation of his views can be found in "The 'Literal Reading' of Biblical Narrative in the Christian Tradition: Does it Stretch or Will it Break?," in *The Bible and the Narrative Tradition,* ed. F. McConnell (New York: Oxford University Press, 1986), pp. 36–77. See also Kathryn Tanner, "Theology and the Plain Sense," in *Scriptural Authority and Narrative Interpretation,* ed. Garrett Green (Philadelphia: Fortress Press, 1987), pp. 59–78. Brevard Childs seeks to distance himself from his erstwhile colleagues in "Toward Recovering Theological Exegesis," *Pro Ecclesia* 6 (1997), p. 20 n.8. He claims that their position implicates them in a form of theological liberalism. He contrasts their views with his own position laid out in "The Sensus Literalis of Scripture: An Ancient and Modern Problem," in *Beiträge zur alttestamentlichen Theologie: Festschrift für Walter Zimmerli,* ed. H. Donner et al. (Göttingen: Vandenhoeck and Ruprecht, 1977), pp. 80–94. It is not clear from this essay why Childs should contrast his position so sharply with Frei's and Tanner's except that theirs operates with a clearly thomistic notion of the literal sense and Childs, while misstating Aquinas' views, shows a clear preference for the Reformers'.

[13] See *Summa Theologiae,* I.1.10.

[14] Rogers, "Virtues," p. 65.

[*plures sensus*] are present even in the literal sense of one passage of Scripture."[15] Rogers argues that Thomas' account of the literal sense is determined not by a theory of meaning or a method, but by common consent. The literal sense of scripture is that which commands communal assent.[16] In this respect, Thomas' view is much more compatible with the views of Frei and Tanner than with a determinate theory of interpretation.

Rogers argues that rather than seeing the literal sense as a form of determinate interpretation, the literal sense, for Thomas, becomes a "whole category into which many readings may fall . . . . As a whole category the appeal to author's intention promotes diversity rather than a restriction of readings, particularly since we can point so rarely to relatively independent indications of what it is."[17]

Further, as Thomas argues in *De potentia*, there is a theological importance to maintaining a plurality of readings within the literal sense. Maintaining a plurality within the literal sense avoids such a situation,

> That anyone confine scripture so to one sense, that other senses be entirely excluded, that in themselves contain truth and are able to be adapted to scripture, preserving the way the words run; for this pertains to the dignity of divine scripture, that it contain many senses under one letter, in order that it may both in that way befit diverse intellects of human beings – that all may marvel that they are able to find in divine scripture the truth that they conceived by their minds – and by this also defend more easily against the infidels, since if anything which someone wants to understand out of sacred scripture appears to be false, recourse is possible to another of its senses . . . . Whence all truth which, preserving the way the words run, can be adapted to divine scripture, is its sense.[18]

For Thomas, a determinate literal sense would limit edifying scriptural interpretation to the well trained, possibly leaving the untrained at the mercy of the "infidels." Moreover, it would inevitably bring scripture into disrepute since the literal sense might be forced to teach something obviously false.

Rather than eliminating interpretation, a thomistic account of the literal sense fosters ongoing interpretation within the community of believers. Disputes about the literal sense can only be hashed out by means of *ad hoc*

[15] *Summa*, I.1.10; see also Rogers "Virtues," pp. 65–6.
[16] See Rogers, "Virtues," p. 67. As Rogers goes on to show, the community Thomas appeals to in regard to the Old Testament extends to the Jews as well (see p. 68).
[17] Rogers, "Virtues," p. 72.
[18] *De potentia* q.4, a.1,c, *post init.*, quoted in Rogers "Virtues," p. 74.

argumentation by interpreters guided by the virtue of prudence and by God's providence working through the Spirit rather than by appeals to a determinate theory of interpretation. It appears then that appeals to thomistic notions of the literal sense of scripture will not help those holding to a determinate account of interpretation to overcome the theological limitations of such a view. To argue that the intention of the human authors of scripture should count as the literal sense of scripture might secure the sort of determinacy of the literal sense that this view requires. It would only do so, however, by shifting all of the problems associated with the term "meaning" onto the term "literal sense."[19]

In the end, this view of determinate biblical interpretation seeks to secure stability and coherence for Christian faith, worship, and practice, by ascribing a particular, stable and coherent property to the Bible (i.e. meaning). Following the proper interpretive procedures for extracting meaning will be a necessary first step. This view, however, is theoretically mistaken in thinking of meanings as properties of texts, and theologically mistaken in locating the bases of coherent and faithful Christian faith and practice in the text of the Bible interpreted in isolation from Christian doctrines and ecclesial practices.[20]

Anti-determinate Interpretation

I want now to move on to discuss anti-determinate interpretation.[21] Almost anyone who has been involved in some form of church-based Bible study, particularly within mainline Protestant denominations, will be familiar with the following claims: Nobody's interpretation is better than anyone else's; everyone has a right to his/her own interpretation; it is rude and not inclusive to fail to accept someone's interpretation as true for that person. These are all

[19] This seems to be one of the results of Watson's arguments in *Text and Truth*, pp. 107–24.

[20] For a further critique of this notion of meaning as a textual property see Ben Ollenburger, "What Krister Stendahl 'Meant' – A Normative Critique of Descriptive Biblical Theology," *Horizons in Biblical Theology* 8 (1986), pp. 85–8.

[21] I am acutely aware here of lapsing into neologism. There are several reasons for this; hence, this long note. The obvious phrase to use here would be "Indeterminate Interpretation." Derrida, who is the focus of this section, has explicitly distanced himself from this term (though he uses the term "relative indeterminacy" in one case). This is because of its connotations of randomness, laxness, and absolute relativity – charges often leveled at Derrida. These charges are, as I will argue, misguided. As an alternative, Derrida describes his own concerns as focused around the notion of "undecidability," which he defines as "a determinate oscillation between possibilities." (See *Limited Inc.* (Evanston: Northwestern University Press, 1988 [Fr. 1977]) pp. 143–50 and Gary Phillips' discussion

forms of anti-determinate interpretation. They are not, however, the result of a theory of interpretation. Rather they reflect many American Christians' deep and unshakable commitments to the doctrines of liberal democracy in a market economy. A different theory of interpretation will not address the type of anti-determinacy represented in these views. For the purposes of this chapter I want to give an account of anti-determinate interpretation that relies on a serious theoretical account.

The view of anti-determinate interpretation I want to discuss begins from a particular vision of determinate interpretation. That is, a particular account of determinate interpretation provides the foil against which to offer the view that interpretation is not determinate. On this view, the notion that biblical (or any other) texts have a single, stable, determinate meaning is simply one aspect of a larger set of assumptions and practices that are seen as characteristic of the whole history of western philosophy. This so-called metaphysics of presence seeks mastery over all external things, including texts. The meta-physics of presence, of which determinate interpretation is simply one manifestation, favors speech over writing, reduces the other to the same through processes of exclusion and reduction, and seeks ultimately to stop interpretation by rendering texts absolutely clear. It seeks wholeness, clarity, and closure.

I shall have reason later on to raise questions about the all-encompassing nature of this metaphysics of presence. For now it is enough for these notions to provide a backdrop against which to set an account of anti-determinate interpretation. The version of anti-determinate interpretation I will focus on here often goes by the name deconstruction. The figure most closely associated with deconstruction is Jacques Derrida. It is important to under-stand, however, that rather than a method of reading, deconstruction is more like an attitude. It sets out to undermine systems of wholeness, clarity, and

---

" 'You are Either Here, Here, Here or Here': Deconstruction's Troublesome Interplay," *Semeia* 71 (1995) esp. pp. 204–6.) While "undecidability" dodges the charges associated with silly notions of indeterminacy, it has problems of its own. For example, while Derrida's account does allow for specific determinations of possibilities of meaning and action, it refuses to specify in advance what those determinants might be and how they might work in regard to particular interpretations. Moreover, it never really addresses the nature of decision-making – i.e. who it is that might actually be making decisions and for what purpose. In recognition that no term is going to be problem free, I have coined the term "anti-determinate." At least one virtue of this term is that it keeps deconstruction's parasitic nature always in view. It would be a mistake, however, if one assumed that anti-determinate interpretation is not interested in offering its own concrete interpretations.

closure with the aim of manifesting what is excluded or reduced or obscured within those systems. This subversion is not offered in order to make the system better, but to undermine the very practice of system-making.

Given this attitude, it becomes very difficult to offer an adequate account of deconstruction that does not risk making deconstruction into the sort of system that it is designed to oppose. Further, Derrida's work is breathtaking in its scope, complexity, and its volume. There is great opportunity for misrepresentation and caricature which I wish to avoid. Hence, in rendering my account of this type of anti-determinate interpretation I will rely on Simon Critchley's work, *The Ethics of Deconstruction*, as a guide, and on Gary Phillips' deconstructive reading of John 4 as an example. While there are many ways of getting at the issues raised by deconstruction, these two works are important for my account for two specific reasons. First, they both show the serious intellectual rigor involved in reading deconstructively. Many have, perhaps over-hastily, dismissed Derrida and deconstruction because they thought Derridian deconstruction lacked intellectual and moral seriousness. What makes Critchley's and Phillips' work particularly important is that they demonstrate the intellectual rigors of deconstructive reading. Secondly, these works also take steps towards addressing the charge that deconstruction lacks moral seriousness. Critchley, followed by Phillips, goes so far as to make a claim that there is a sort of moral duty or responsibility to read deconstructively.[22] I will now lay out the various elements of deconstructive reading as a way of displaying the ethical demands it seeks to register.

Anti-determinate interpretation in this vein will always be a two-staged affair, a double reading. The first stage involves a close, scholarly, rigorous, and necessarily historical interpretation of a text's "dominant interpretation."[23] Derrida calls this "a respectful doubling of commentary which acts as a guardrail on interpretation."[24] Later, however, he qualifies this use of the term commentary to indicate that he realizes that commentary is not simply the repetition of a text, that commentary always involves interpretation. Rather,

---

[22] In doing this Critchley takes insights from the work of Emanuel Levinas to push Derrida's work in a direction that Derrida himself has not yet fully explored. Even if Derrida would not make the same moves Critchley does, it is not damaging to his argument; Critchley's account stands or falls on its own and is a more important account of deconstruction because of the moral claims it seeks to lodge. See Critchley, *The Ethics of Deconstruction* (Oxford: Blackwell, 1992).

[23] Derrida, *Limited Inc.*, p. 143.

[24] Jacques Derrida, *Of Grammatology*, trans. Gayatri Chakravorty Spivak (Baltimore: Johns Hopkins University Press, 1976 [Fr.1967]), p. 158.

Derrida sees the act of commentary as representing the "relative stability of the dominant interpretation (including auto-interpretation) of the text being commented upon."[25] Such commentary represents the various points of (at least) minimal scholarly consensus on a text. As Critchley notes,

> Thus, although "commentary" alone does not open genuine reading, the latter is not possible without a scholarly competence in reading, understanding and writing, without knowledge of texts in their original languages, without knowing the corpus of an author as a whole, without knowing the multiple contexts – political, literary, philosophical, historical and so forth – which determine a given text or are determined by that text.[26]

For biblical scholars, this practice would most closely conform to what is done in modern commentaries and monographs. In fact, thus far, there is little with which a modern biblical scholar would wish to quarrel. In the course of this first stage, however, the deconstructive reader will come across some element in the text (usually a word or phrase) that, it is claimed, is "other" to and resists the dominant interpretation. This textual element becomes the lever used to open the dominant interpretation and thus expose what is obscured, reduced, or neglected. One can see how this second stage of interpretation is deconstructive as one remembers that the primary texts which Derrida seeks to deconstruct are (with some exceptions) modern texts of western metaphysical philosophy, whose goal, Derrida has argued, has been to present Truth in all of its clarity; to master texts through interpretation; to construct an epistemological system marked by wholeness, completeness, and finality. As Derrida notes in an illuminating passage regarding the goals of deconstruction,

> I wished to reach the point of a certain exteriority with respect to the totality of the age of logocentrism. Starting from this point of exteriority a certain deconstruction of this totality which is also a traced path, of that orb (*orbis*) which is also orbitary (*orbita*) could be broached.[27]

"The goal of deconstruction, therefore, is to locate a point of otherness within the philosophical or logocentric conceptuality and then to deconstruct this

[25] Derrida, *Limited Inc.*, p. 143.
[26] Critchley, *The Ethics of Deconstruction*, p. 24. He goes on to say, "This is what one might call the deconstructive duty of scholarship." This "duty," however, should not be confused with the moral responsibility to read deconstructively, which I noted above.
[27] *Of Grammatology*, pp. 161–2.

conceptuality from that position of alterity."[28] It is in the course of the first respectful reading of a text that one discovers this position of alterity within the text itself. Hence, deconstruction must always be a two-staged or double-handed engagement with a text.[29]

Critchley goes on to supplement Derrida's position with resources from Emanuel Levinas, to argue that there is a moral demand to read deconstructively.[30] The moral call of deconstruction stems from a responsibility to the "other" that is submerged in the texts of the western metaphysical tradition, and which can only confront us if we read deconstructively. "The ethical moment that motivates deconstruction is this Yes-saying to the unnamable, a moment of unconditional affirmation that is addressed to an alterity that can neither be excluded from nor included within logocentric conceptuality."[31] Critchley goes on to claim that this moment of Yes-saying is an unconditional categorical imperative. "There is a duty in deconstruction which both prompts the reader to the rigorous and ascetic labour of reading and produces a reading that commands respect in so far as it opens an irreducible dimension of alterity."[32] Much of the rest of Critchley's book seeks to show how one can take Levinas' claim about the ethical, pre-reflective call that the other person exerts on us and argue that it can be inscribed in a book without betraying it.[33]

Despite some very good books that have recently sought to introduce deconstruction to biblical scholars,[34] this account of anti-determinate inter-

---

[28] Critchley, *The Ethics of Deconstruction*, p. 26.

[29] "What takes place in deconstruction is double reading – that is, a form of reading that obeys the double injunction for both repetition and the alterity that arises within that repetition. Deconstruction opens a reading by locating a moment of alterity within a text" (Critchley, *The Ethics of Deconstruction*, p. 28).

[30] To be fair to Critchley, he does not claim that this call extends to all acts of reading. His focus implies that this claim extends to the texts of the western metaphysical tradition.

[31] Critchley, *The Ethics of Deconstruction*, p. 41.

[32] Critchley, *The Ethics of Deconstruction*, p. 41.

[33] Critchley, *The Ethics of Deconstruction*, p. 48. For Critchley, all of this work is preparatory for showing that derridian deconstruction supplemented by levinasian ethics can be developed into an adequate politics. In this last effort I think he is ultimately unsuccessful, reproducing a typically modern result. That is, he desires the moral force of Levinas' ethics without the convictions about God which underwrote Levinas' views. This claim, however, takes me far beyond the confines of this book and I will have to leave it here, underdeveloped.

[34] See Stephen Moore's various works; in particular, *Mark and Luke in Poststructuralist Perspective* (New Haven: Yale University Press, 1992) and *Poststructuralism and the New Testament* (Minneapolis: Fortress Press, 1994). Also see The Bible and Culture Collective, *The Postmodern Bible* (New Haven: Yale University Press, 1995); and A. K. M. Adam, *What is Postmodern Biblical Criticism?* (Minneapolis: Fortress Press, 1995).

pretation will seem unfamiliar in a way that my account of determinate interpretation did not. This is in part why I want to invoke the exemplary work of Gary Phillips. In a recent essay Phillips has vigorously and clearly presented this case that there is a moral duty or responsibility to read the Bible deconstructively.[35] Moreover, in the course of this essay, Phillips offers a deconstructive double-reading of John 4. Phillips, too, largely follows Critchley's account as he argues against the view that deconstruction lacks intellectual rigor and moral seriousness. He then goes on to offer a respectful reading of the dominant modern interpretation of John 4. While this reading will act as a "solid guardrail" for Phillips' reading of John 4, he finds that both historical and literary readings of this passage "can not do justice to the *textuality* and *otherness* of John's narrative."[36] One might expect that a text with as many narrative fissures as John 4 clearly has would not be able to generate a dominant interpretation substantial enough to be deconstructed. Phillips focuses his attention on the fact that modern critics are so uncomfortable with the numerous interpretive problems posed by John 4. What dominates modern interpretation of John 4 is a critical discomfort with the text's interpretive wrinkles. This discomfort is manifested in the numerous methods for reading this text which have been proposed, methods designed to iron out all textual wrinkles. These methods, Phillips argues, always tend to domesticate the figure of the Samaritan woman to some methodological or theological agenda.[37] He asks, "Does the Johannine text deliberately call its readers to a textual awareness designed to make us 'uncomfortable' not only with the Samaritan woman but with the Gospel text as Other?"[38]

From this point Phillips offers the second stage of his deconstructive reading, a reading designed to attend to "Johannine textuality." Phillips focuses on the woman's refusal to give Jesus the drink he has asked for. This,

---

[35] Gary Phillips, "The Ethics of Reading Deconstructively, or Speaking Face to Face: The Samaritan Woman meets Derrida at the Well," in *The New Literary Criticism and the New Testament,* ed. Elizabeth Struthers Malbon and Edgar McKnight (Sheffield: Sheffield Academic Press, 1994), pp. 283–325.

[36] Phillips, "The Ethics of Reading Deconstructively," p. 291. The metaphor of using the dominant interpretation as a guardrail comes from Derrida, *Of Grammatology,* p. 158.

[37] See Phillips, "The Ethics of Reading Deconstructively," pp. 297, 299.

[38] Phillips, "The Ethics of Reading Deconstructively," p. 293. Also, "The alterity of the Johannine text reserves to itself the potential to keep readers reading and signing on in new and different ways by intervening in the text in an unpredictable manner" (p. 301). (The image of signing on to a text comes from Derrida's "Signature, Event, Context" in *Limited Inc.*) "Does the Johannine text resist giving itself up completely to any reader for critical consumption and digestion?" (p. 303).

he notes, stands in sharp contrast with other "woman at the well stories" (e.g. Gen. 21:18; 24:18). In v. 28 the woman departs never having complied with Jesus' request, but leaving behind her water jar; "She leaves behind something else, namely a lasting impression about who she is. More than any other man or woman in the Johannine narrative, the Samaritan woman makes a mark with her 'attitude'."[39] The dominant interpretation has tried to erase (through allegorizing?) the traces of this woman from our consideration. A deconstructive reading recovers these traces. The water jar she left behind becomes for Phillips an allegory of the aims of "Johannine textuality." "The jar continues to sit in the well text as a reminder to the reader of a woman who is *other* to Jesus – and as a textual figure who is *other* to the male disciples and to the text's readers, too – a face that cannot be completely effaced from the text."[40]

The call of deconstructive reading practices is to remind us of these overlooked signs of "otherness." "The deconstructive reader seats herself by the narrative well and makes use of that jar to dip into the text, to draw new meaning and to challenge masculinist reading practices and institutional structures."[41] This is what it means to be responsible to the "other" which confronts readers in the face of the woman at the well.

Phillips concludes his essay by noting some of the larger implications that would follow for professional biblical scholars should they attend to their duties to read deconstructively. First, biblical scholars would recognize the failure of all determinate critical strategies that aim to exhaust a text's meaning and to restrain ways of reading the text. It is important to note here that for deconstructive interpretation it is the otherness of the text itself that guarantees that interpretation can always continue.[42] Phillips claims that widespread adoption of this attitude would significantly alter the reading practices and institutional structures which support professional biblical criticism. "What sets deconstruction apart is its response to what is other about the text by orienting a way of thinking, of writing and reading in relation to this Other that demands we face up to institutional configurations of power, gender and ideology. In short, deconstruction calls for a way of living with the Bible in a postmodern world today that reinscribes biblical studies in a certain responsible way within the culture of criticism and the criticism of culture."[43] This claim, however, is

---

[39] Phillips, "The Ethics of Reading Deconstructively," p. 304.
[40] Phillips, "The Ethics of Reading Deconstructively," p. 306.
[41] Phillips, "The Ethics of Reading Deconstructively," p. 308.
[42] See Phillips, "The Ethics of Reading Deconstructively, " pp. 315, 317 and elsewhere.
[43] Phillips, "The Ethics of Reading Deconstructively," p. 316.

left underdeveloped. The most significant institutional and disciplinary implication that Phillips leaves us with is that deconstruction will lead us to "resist any personal and disciplinary effort to complete the text and to sign off with that Final Sign and signature, to engage in a summative semiotic effect that even the Johannine narrator concedes not even the world could contain (cf. 20:30; 21:25)."[44] Almost as an afterthought, Phillips notes that this sort of reading would require scholars to be formed and transformed in particular ways. Note again, however, that it is " the work," – that is, the text in question – that does this work of formation, not other people or institutions.

I have tried here to give a respectful reading of this view of deconstructive interpretation. I think all scholars would recognize that this is not the dominant interpretation in the sense that there are very few deconstructive biblical scholars.[45] On the other hand, I would argue that Phillips is a, if not the, dominant deconstructive voice in biblical studies. Given my respectful reading, one might now expect a deconstructive, double-handed, opening up of that reading. How one characterizes what follows is out of my hands. I hope to display some of the assumptions that underwrite this view and to take issue with them. I would like to show the limits of the moral demand to be deconstructive. In addition, I think the political implications of deconstruction need further developing. In doing this I ultimately want to make the case that this deconstructive account of anti-determinate interpretation will not serve the aims and purposes Christians bring to their interpretation of scripture.

First, it must be noted that the moral demand to read deconstructively that both Critchley and Phillips present is a professional ethic in the most limited sense of that phrase. Only professionals can participate in deconstructive double-reading because only they have the requisite background knowledge to engage the dominant interpretation, which is the necessary first stage of a deconstructive reading. In fact, on Critchley's account, it is only philosophers interested in metaphysics that come under the call to deconstruct. I suspect, however, that he would want to apply this call more broadly. In any case, only those who could possibly fulfill the rigorous intellectual demands of deconstructive reading can be held responsible for doing so. This disparity is less obvious in philosophy, where basically only professionals study and teach the texts to be deconstructed. The Bible, of course, is read more widely and for more diverse

---

[44] Phillips, "The Ethics of Reading Deconstructively," p. 318. Of course, the commodification of scholarship has achieved the same result.

[45] While there are many more derridian philosophers like Critchley, they, too, could not be considered the dominant interpretive voice in contemporary philosophy.

purposes.[46] Limiting the ethical call of deconstruction to professionals does not undermine the moral demand to deconstruct in principle, but it does significantly circumscribe its importance. What this circumscription particularly leaves out is the overwhelming majority of biblical interpreters, those who seek to order their lives in accordance with their biblical interpretation.

As Critchley and Phillips present and develop Derrida's views, the moral demand to read deconstructively is supported by two separable but interrelated claims. One is historical; the other, I will argue, entails a metaphysics. First, the moral demand to deconstruct is supported by a particular historical account of what is generally referred to as the western metaphysical tradition. This tradition is the source of all things in need of deconstruction. It privileges speech over writing; it desires mastery over the world by bringing all things under its systematic domain and methodically rendering them present to us. It seeks methods for making all things clear and in doing so it reduces difference to sameness.[47] On Derrida's account, this tradition is so dominant and pervasive that one cannot really escape it. One can (and must) only use this tradition's own tools, its key texts, against it. In short, deconstruction both requires and is parasitic upon the presence of this metaphysics of presence. If, therefore, one can show that this, surprisingly monolithic, account of the history of philosophy and theology is problematic, if not badly inaccurate, at certain crucial points, then the demand to deconstruct will be altered significantly.

Just such an account has been offered by Catherine Pickstock in *After Writing: On The Liturgical Consummation of Philosophy*. For Derrida, a key text in the rise and formation of the metaphysics of presence is Plato's *Phaedrus*. His most systematic treatment of this dialogue comes in his essay, "Plato's Pharmacy."[48] A central component of Pickstock's argument is the claim that Derrida badly misreads the *Phaedrus*, using Socrates' expressed preference for speech over writing to argue for Plato's complicity in a metaphysics of presence. On Derrida's account, the Socratic preference for speech links speech, capital,

---

[46] In this respect it is inaccurate for Phillips to try to class Gerald West's work as "contextualized deconstruction" since it is primarily interested in the reading practices of ordinary, non-professional readers (see Phillips, "The Ethics of Reading Deconstructively," p. 316 n.43). Further, while West's work, and the work of others operating with a liberationist hermeneutic, does seek to deconstruct very specific types of interpretive and practical habits, it also has a clear sense of offering something constructive in their place.

[47] Part 1 of *Of Grammatology* gives an account of this metaphysics of presence in terms of its effects on theories of language.

[48] See "Plato's Pharmacy" in *Dissemination*, trans. Barbara Johnson (Chicago: University of Chicago Press, 1981 [Fr.1972]) pp. 66–172. The basic structure of Derrida's reading of the Phaedrus can be found five years earlier in *Of Grammatology*.

logos, the father, and the good in opposition to writing, which is false, orphaned, and absent.[49] Derrida then deconstructs this opposition. His aim is to show that the priority of writing allows for the flourishing of supplementarity and difference. Such flourishing will counteract the suffocating tendency of a metaphysics of presence to move towards completeness and sameness.

By attending to the dialogue in a more detailed way, Pickstock is able to invert Derrida's deconstruction of it. The crux of her disagreement with Derrida hinges on the fact that Derrida treats Socrates' attack on the Sophists as part of his larger argument in favor of speech over writing in particular, and a metaphysics of presence more generally. Pickstock's account sets the preference for speech within the context of a more systematic attack on Sophists. Socrates' preference for speech must, therefore, be seen in the context of his hostility to the Sophists' commodification and ultimate humiliation of language in pursuit of a corrupt way of life.[50] "His [Socrates'] critique of writing and rhetoric does not presuppose a desire for a supralinguistic philosophical logos, independent of time and place, but to the contrary, it is precisely such a preference which Socrates associates with a *sophistic* vision of purely commercial reality"[51] By removing his critique of the Socratic preference for speech over writing from the larger context of Plato's attack on Sophistry, Derrida, ironically, ascribes to Socrates the very views Socrates attacks in the Sophists.

Pickstock systematically addresses Derrida's claims and turns them on their head. Rather than advocating a mercantilist metaphysics of presence, Socrates becomes the champion of difference. Alternatively, it is the Sophistic commodification of language and of subjectivity itself which suppresses real difference.[52]

---

[49] See "Plato's Pharmacy," pp. 76–7 and 168; also *Of Grammatology*, pp. 3–8.

[50] "Instead of the notion that orality is a mask for 'presence', it will be shown that orality is primarily linked to an account of the subject as doxological. For in the *Phaedrus* and other Platonic dialogues there are clear indications that the measure of good ethical practice is as much, or more, determined by its orientation toward liturgical praise of the divine as by the ideal of rational contemplation" (Pickstock, *After Writing: The Liturgical Consummation of Philosophy* (Oxford: Blackwell, 1998) p. 4).

[51] Pickstock, *After Writing*, p. 4

[52] See "Plato's Pharmacy," pp. 82–4 for the connection of speech and the good with capital. Derrida here relies primarily on the *Republic*. Pickstock, pp. 5ff., however, focuses both on Phaedrus' persistent determination to place Socrates and his fascination with the quantity of points in a speech (234e–236). She shows that while this may seem to show that Phaedrus favors differentiation, "his act of differentiation is coterminous with manipulation or violence, for by using sophistic categorization to hold in fixity the components of his taxonomies, Phaedrus does not allow for the contingency of their boundaries. Thus, this 'differentiation' is, in fact the reduction of difference to identity, and like sophistic rhetoric is 'the same when concerned with small things as with great' (261b)" (Pickstock, *After Writing*, p. 6).

In "Plato's Pharmacy," Derrida connects speech and the good with capital. This allows him to characterize the good as at once radical absence and original presence. Having argued that it is only the Sophists who are linked to capital, Pickstock goes on to identify the Platonic good as

> [A]n inaccessible, inexhaustible, and incircumscribible plentitude. This conception explains Socrates' demur at speaking directly of the good, preferring instead an economy of figures and traces. His withdrawal from direct speaking of the good is neither a matter of capital's fear of itself nor a metaphysical construal of the good as an unapproachable and therefore fetishized ideal. It is rather that the good cannot be *circumscribed* in the manner of ordinary, empirical data, and is not accessible to technical knowing, but instead must be allowed to rise in and through the excess of supplementary figures.[53]

That the superabundant good can be apprehended only in the physical world means that Socrates does not and cannot disparage the physical, exterior world at the expense of interiority.[54] This is seen, for example, in Socrates' attention to the beauty of his surroundings at the beginning of the dialogue (230). This attention leads Phaedrus to characterize him as "atopic" (230c). This is

> because according to his [Phaedrus'] commercial sensibilities, the environment is mere background extension, so that Socrates' treatment of each tiny detail as significant seems strange, out of place, foreign, and insane. However, for Socrates as also for the philosopher-lover, spontaneous adoration is inspired, via *eros*, by the memory of the beautiful itself which now infiltrates every aspect of life, great and small, in such a way that the 'ordinary' becomes 'extraordinary'. Whilst Phaedrus has relied upon physical particulars remaining secondary, as a backdrop, Socrates' holistic, harmonious understanding of interconnectedness disallows any such hierarchical demarcation of phenomena.[55]

---

[53] Pickstock, *After Writing*, p. 11. See *Phaedrus* 249c–d, where memory aids the philosopher in ordering the plenitude of physical manifestations of the good into a coherent order which can rightly direct the philosopher/lover's life.

[54] "So contrary to Derrida's claim that Platonic metaphysics is to be found in a privileging of truth-as-presence, and of subjectivity as interiority, from the enumeration of the myriad of stimuli in which the philosopher-lover is immersed there seems instead to be derived an account of the self as constituted by its opening to receive its environment, both physical and divine" (Pickstock, *After Writing*, p. 32).

[55] Pickstock, *After Writing*, p. 16.

The importance of this is that rather than simple oppositions between interior and exterior, Plato is primarily concerned with the economy within which the interior and the exterior are ordered. It is the economy in which the philosopher-lover participates, rather than the mercantilist economy of the Sophists, that allows true difference to flourish.[56]

On Pickstock's account, Platonic knowledge of the good comes through the apprehension of traces. Yet, "despite this implicit epistemology of supplementary traces, Derrida argues that 'what Plato dreams of is a memory with no sign. That is, with no supplement', whereas this is to overlook Socrates' erotic and hermeneutic understanding of the philosopher-lover's striving towards the good as commensurate with the act of knowledge. Whilst signs, both natural and conventional, are the essential and only route, via the trace of memory, to the good, it is the *sophists* for whom the supplementation effected by language is regarded as a secondary form, a mere vehicle for exchange and transaction."[57]

Pickstock's reading of the *Phaedrus* decisively undermines arguments about Plato's complicity in this construct called the western metaphysics of presence.[58] Such a claim is limited, but important. It is limited in that it only addresses Plato; one, albeit a central, figure in the history of philosophy. It is important, however, for several reasons. First, it suggests that the only way to get beyond a monolithic account of the metaphysics of presence is to take it apart piecemeal. One can, thereby, show in specific cases where and how it operates. Further, one can begin to counteract the habits and practices underwritten by a metaphysics of presence by showing historically embodied alternatives to it. I am not claiming that the intellectual habits and practices characteristic of the metaphysics of presence are not apparent in philosophy,

---

[56] See *Phaedrus* 266b where Socrates says, "Now I myself, Phaedrus, am a lover of these processes of division and bringing together, as aids to speech and thought; and if I think any other man is able to see things that can naturally be collected into one and divided into many, him I follow after and 'walk in his footsteps as if he were a god'. And whether the name I give to those who can do this is right or wrong, God knows, but I have called them hitherto dialecticians." On this Pickstock comments, "Dialectical differentiation is quite other from sophistic classification because it is thus combined with *synopsis*, which sees things together as one and only thereby as different and exhibiting novelty through time" (*After Writing*, p. 17).

[57] Pickstock, *After Writing*, p. 21. The quote from Derrida is from "Plato's Pharmacy," p. 109.

[58] For a similar attempt to show Plato's ambiguous relationship to platonism see S. Rosen, "Antiplatonism," in *The Ancients and the Moderns: Rethinking Modernity* (New Haven: Yale University Press, 1989), pp. 37–64.

theology, and elsewhere. Rather, my claim is that they are not characteristic of the entire history of western thought.[59]

Secondly, and more importantly for my purposes, dismantling this monolith also begins to reframe one element of the moral call of deconstruction. Remember that deconstruction is Derrida's response to the pervasive intellectual habits and practices of the metaphysics of presence. The moral call to deconstruct is in part based on the need to open up fissures in the smooth surface of this metaphysics. If the surface is not, and has never really been, smooth, then the most one can say is that where this particular form of metaphysics is present, one must try to undermine it.[60] If, as Pickstock's study of Plato indicates, however, there are lots of spaces within the history of philosophy and theology which cannot be situated within the metaphysics of presence, then one may also expect, to find within those spaces alternative resources for undermining the metaphysics of presence which are not deconstructive. If, as appears to be the case, all of philosophy and theology is not complicit in this metaphysics of presence, there may be alternative resources for addressing the intellectual habits and practices of a metaphysics of presence when one does confront them.[61] The upshot of this is that failure to be deconstructive may not signal a moral deafness which consigns one to participation in the metaphysics of presence. One need not be oppressed by the metaphysics of presence if one can find spaces where it does not (and maybe never did) operate.

The second element which underwrites the claim that interpreters have a moral duty to read deconstructively has to do with what I wish to call a

[59] Interestingly, when Phillips presents his respectful reading of the dominant interpretation of John 4, it is only modern interpreters who comprise this interpretive tradition. One might argue that this is because pre-modern interpretations simply are not part of the purview of modern biblical studies. This, however, reinforces my claims about the limited historical scope of the metaphysics of presence.

[60] In this respect Critchley's ethics of deconstruction starts to look like a professional ethic designed to rescue the practice of metaphysical speculation from modernity. I am not unsympathetic to this. My point, however, is that this is a very limited sort of ethical demand, and it in no way commits one to relying on the practices of deconstructive interpretation to do this.

[61] John Milbank in *Theology and Social Theory* (Oxford: Blackwell, 1990) indicates several other points where alternatives to a metaphysics of presence are particularly striking. For example, he contrasts Scotus' "fundamental ontology" with Aquinas' account of analogical difference (pp. 302–6). In addition, he contrasts the Christian doctrine of the Trinity ("The Son who is always given with the Father is a supplement at the origin; the Spirit who is always given with the Father and the Son is the infinite necessity of deferral") with Derrida's reliance on the myth of Theuth, god of writing (pp. 306–11).

metaphysics of textuality. One can see this metaphysics at work in a fairly benign way in Phillips' discussion of John 4. Throughout his discussion textual features and/or textuality as such take on an almost human agency. Here are a few examples: "Johannine irony *demands* an otherness that exceeds gender . . . "; "By gathering up the ironic force or power of the *text itself* and attributing it to the Evangelist, she subordinates text to reader"; the text has a "generative power" which can be shut down long before the text is ready; "The Johannine text reserves to itself the potential to keep readers reading . . . "; ". . . it is the textuality of John's narrative that invites us as readers to read otherwise."[62] In some interpreters one might let such language slide by, arguing that it reflects a sloppy way of speaking rather than a particular course of reasoning. This is not the case for Phillips. This language is quite intentional and signifies the view that textuality as such calls interpreters to read deconstructively. Textuality is "the other" to which interpreters must be responsible. Indeed, having gone to some effort to criticize those who allegorize the woman at the well in order to make a theological point, Phillips effectively sees the woman as an allegory for Johannine textuality.[63] Textuality (as opposed to, for example, the purposes, interests, and aims that readers bring to texts) calls us to keep interpretation always ongoing. It is part of one's moral responsibility to textuality to rescue it by reading deconstructively whenever the dominant interpretation threatens to close interpretation down.

Although Phillips presents this metaphysics of textuality in an understated form, it conforms to the fuller account of originary writing offered by Derrida in *Of Grammatology*. Several points need to be made about this metaphysics of textuality. First, to the extent that it depends on Derrida's claims about the ontological priority of writing over speech, it reflects an arbitrary claim about language founded on a misunderstanding of Platonic views about speech and writing.[64] As was noted above, Socrates' preference for speech over writing was not a preference for a metaphysics of oral presence over of a metaphysics of written absence. Rather, his preference

---

[62] "The Ethics of Reading Deconstructively," pp. 297–305.

[63] See Phillips, "The Ethics of Reading Deconstructively," pp. 303–5.

[64] This is different from Critchley's claim that "All deconstructive discourse is strategic and adventurous; which is to say that it cannot be justified absolutely" (Critchley, *The Ethics of Deconstruction*, p. 35). While deconstructive discourse is provisional and contingent, my claim is that the metaphysics which drives the discourse is arbitrary. To the extent that Derrida's claim is simply a radicalizing of Saussure, it appears to be an radicalizing based on his arbitrary claims about writing.

reflected the contingent and specific nature of the moral and political threat posed by sophistry.[65]

Further, this metaphysics of writing is a metaphysics without people. Unlike that of Levinas, whose ethic of responsibility to the other argues that alterity is recognized in the human face of the other,[66] Derrida's ethic of responsibility to the other locates alterity in writing or textuality as such. ". . . Derrida's written model suggests no people at all, only a word which comes from nowhere, or an autonomous word, which conceals or violently eradicates its origins and dictates to its 'author', rendering him entirely passive before a disembodied and (spiritual?) power."[67] A metaphysics of textuality or writing effectively truncates real difference. It allows only the differences conceivable within a radicalized account of Saussure's linguistics. It "disallows the play of real traces permitted by a series of embodied speakers."[68]

When posed against the claims of determinate interpretation, there may be something to be said on behalf of this sort of anti-determinate interpretation. For example, it avoids the quest for mastery over the text in the name of a determinate theory of meaning. It warns against the temptation to see established interpretations as the "natural" ones. It renders interpretation provisional and urges a sort of humility in interpretation.

As a moral claim it might even suffice for professional interpreters as a sort of rule of thumb against closing down interpretation prematurely. It is pretentious, however, in suggesting that the history of biblical interpretation must be seen within the pervasive scope of the metaphysics of presence and that, thereby, there is a moral demand to resist this by reading deconstructively. In addition, a strong moral claim to deconstruct must come along with a metaphysics of writing or textuality that is, at best, questionable.

Further, accounting for biblical interpretation as systematically anti-determinate will make it difficult for Christians to interpret and embody their scriptures over time in ways that are essential to living faithfully before God.

---

[65] Further, one can make the sorts of criticisms that Derrida makes in chapter 2 of *Of Grammatology* against Saussure's preference for the priority of speech over writing (a very different preference than Socrates') without necessitating Derrida's counterproposal regarding the ontological priority of writing to speech.

[66] See, for example, *Totality and Infinity*, trans. A. Lingis (Pittsburgh: Duquesne University Press, 1969), pp. 50–2. Levinas' claim, as Critchley seems both to note and try to avoid, cannot ultimately be sundered from his theological commitments. It is Critchley's attempts to do so in the final chapter of his book which ultimately render his project typically modern. See, for example, *The Ethics of Deconstruction*, pp. 219–36.

[67] Pickstock, *After Writing*, p. 22.

[68] Pickstock, *After Writing*, p. 34.

For example, Christians who resisted and deconstructed attempts to interpret the Bible in ways that underwrote the practices of apartheid would not want to continue the deconstructive process in ways that re-opened the door to apartheid. Systematic interpretive anti–determinacy (as opposed to humility and charity) will paralyze actual attempts to order one's life in accordance with one's interpretation. To avoid this problem, any alternative to deconstruction will have to recognize both the provisionality and plurality of biblical interpretation, and be self-reflexively critical of Christian practice, without practicing deconstruction.

Thus far I have told a story of determinate biblical interpretation and one of anti–determinate biblical interpretation. While determinate interpretation appears to secure a sort of stability and coherence for Christian faith, worship, and practice, it is achieved by means of question-begging theories of meaning. Moreover, a determinate account of meaning could not adequately account for the diverse and particular ways Christians will need to be able to interpret scripture if they are to live faithfully before God. Further, I argued that attempts to retain interpretive determinacy and a limited diversity by means of establishing a determinate "literal sense," from which other subsidiary spiritual senses could be derived, misunderstood the most common notions of the literal sense.

Anti–determinate interpretation is dedicated to continuously opening texts to further interpretation. In its deconstructive form, this involves constructing a text's dominant interpretation and then using the fissures and cracks in that dominant interpretation to open the text to further interpretation. In some of its most sophisticated forms, one can even argue that the pervasive drive of the metaphysics of presence for textual mastery and interpretive closure combines with the very nature of writing or textuality to issue a moral call to interpreters to read deconstructively. In reflecting on the nature of this moral call I offered several considerations. First, the ethical demand to read deconstructively can only apply to professional readers. This in itself would make it irrelevant to virtually all those who read the Bible. Secondly, the metaphysics of presence which is the pervasive construct against which deconstructive readings struggle is probably not really all that pervasive. It certainly was not universally characteristic of Plato, the supposed source of this metaphysics. At the very least, it exists contemporaneously with alternative possibilities. Hence, where one finds the metaphysics of presence threatening to close down interpretive options prematurely, there will be more than one way to resist. Finally, the metaphysics of originary writing or textuality which stands behind the call to derridian deconstruction needs further examination. In its most benign form, it simply and arbitrarily ascribes an agency to textuality that could be located less arbitrarily in readers and the social, political, and material contexts in which interpretation takes place.[69] In its less benign forms, it transfers an alterity from the human face of the other, where Jews, like Levinas, and Christians would want to locate it, to textuality. Rather than preserving difference, this has the effect of severely truncating it.

In terms of how Christians read and embody scripture, anti-determinate accounts of interpretation offer a version of interpretive plurality. This plurality is crucial in the light of the diverse and particular aims Christians bring to biblical interpretation. In this light, a version of anti-determinate interpretation might seem preferable to accounts of determinate interpretation. Christians, however, will need to make decisions about how they are to live in the light of their biblical interpretation. Systematic anti-determinacy in interpretation will result in paralysis and instability in practice.[70]

Underdetermined Interpretation

This brings me to my account of underdetermined interpretation. The central interpretive claim here is that our discussions, debates, and arguments about texts will be better served by eliminating claims about textual meaning in favor of more precise accounts of our interpretive aims, interests, and practices. The theoretical argument for underdetermined interpretation is most succinctly laid out in Jeffrey Stout's essay, "What is the Meaning of a Text?"[71] Stout

---

[69] Phillips, "The Ethics of Reading Deconstructively," p. 299, is quite clear about which option he prefers. His claim is that readers and institutions work to domesticate the text. Textuality presumably cannot be so easily domesticated. I agree with the implicit warning in Phillips' remarks about the tendency of readers to read in ways that confirm rather than challenge their prejudices and practices. I disagree that ascribing agency to textuality can insure occasions where texts challenge and transform us. I will say more about this in the next chapter, on vigilant communities and resistant readers.

[70] Gillian Rose attributes just this sort of paralysis to Derrida in "Of Derrida's Spirit," in *Judaism and Modernity* (Oxford: Blackwell, 1993), pp. 65–88, where she discusses Derrida's apologia for Heidegger's complicity in National Socialism.

[71] In *New Literary History* 14 (1982), pp. 1–12. I first discussed this position in "The Ethics of Interpretation, or What's Left Over After the Elimination of Meaning," in *The Bible in Three Dimensions*, ed. D. J. A. Clines, S. E. Fowl, and S. E. Porter (Sheffield: Sheffield Academic Press, 1990), pp. 379–98. Eugene Rogers' essay cited above also links his view to Stout's essay. In addition, Peter Ochs offers an account that runs parallel to mine, relying on many of the same philosophical resources, as he argues for an interpretive pragmatics. In particular, Ochs' position retrieves and revives the work of Peirce and brings it into conversation with both the post-liberal reading strategies of Hans Frei and George

begins by noting the variety of competing notions of textual meaning, and notes that there does not appear to be any way of adjudicating between them.

> If interpretation is a matter of discovering meaning, and is therefore bound to run amuck when informed by mistaken assumptions about what meaning is, then literary criticism, religious studies, classics, history – in short, all disciplines involving the interpretation of texts – will consist largely in failure to deliver the goods.[72]

This would not be so bothersome if, as in the natural sciences, we could say that we were moving forward by systematically reducing error. Failure would be tolerable if it were leading to increased probability of success. But in the case of developing a theory of textual meaning without a clear conception of what meaning is, we do not even know what "success" would look like.

The reason we cannot agree on what the meaning(s) of a text is, Stout proposes, is that our concerns with textual meaning are confused. The source of this confusion is the term "meaning" itself.[73] Obviously, most of us can use the term in informal conversations with relative ease and clarity. This is because in these informal conversations the contexts in which the term is used are so clearly circumscribed (or open to circumscription in the course of conversation) that it poses no serious impediment to discussion. The problem arises when we move to formal discussions of meaning as such. Here the term meaning is not so clearly circumscribed. Take for, for example, discussions about a theory of meaning:

> What is a theory of meaning a theory of? Evidently, it may be a theory of any number of things. A question of the form, "What is the meaning of x?", retains all of the ambiguity of its central term but none of the grammatical features that . . . would diminish its tendency to confuse.[74]

Stout's remedy for this confusion is to eliminate it at its source. That is, we should eliminate talk of meanings in favor of other terms that will both suit our interpretive interests and be precise enough to put a stop to futile

---

Lindbeck and rabbinic reading practices. For a concise account of this form of "scriptural reasoning" see Ochs' introduction in *The Return to Scripture in Judaism and Christianity* (New York: Paulist, 1993) pp. 3–51.

[72] Stout, "What is the Meaning," p. 1.

[73] See John Lyons' description of the various meanings of "meaning" in *Semantics* (Cambridge: Cambridge University Press, 1977), vol. 1, pp. 2ff.

[74] Stout, "What is the Meaning," p. 3.

discussions. To do this, Stout suggests that we employ a form of explication in regard to the term 'meaning'. Stout here is following W. V. O. Quine's view of explication, in which "We fix on the particular functions of the unclear expression that make it worth troubling about, and then devise a substitute, clear and couched in terms to our liking, that fills those functions."[75] "Good explication . . . tells us how to translate theories from familiar but confusing idioms into idioms better suited to our purposes."[76] When explication is applied to a term like meaning, the result is that instead of answering our questions about meaning, we replace our present question – What is the meaning of this text? – with different questions.

Instead of talk about meaning we would, for example, claim that we are interested in an author's communicative intentions – what an author's words would have communicated to someone in the context in which the author wrote them.[77] One can perform the tasks necessary to display this more or less well. Further, it is a task that can be evaluated both in terms of the clarity of its definition and in terms of the way it is carried out. Most importantly, both this interpretive activity and its evaluation can be performed without recourse to the term meaning. Alternatively, we may want to display a text's contextual connections to the material or gender-based means of its production. Having defined this concern closely enough, we can perform the necessary analysis and come up with some sort of account. There is no need to cloud the issue further by calling the result of this interpretive activity "meaning" at the expense of other interpretive interests one might pursue.[78]

Explicating textual meaning in terms of varied and diverse interpretive aims, interests, and practices will provide us with a much more manageable way of addressing interpretive disputes. One set of disputes we will confront is disputes that are internal to a specific interpretive practice. These are disputes

---

[75] See W. V. O. Quine, *Word and Object* (Cambridge, MA: Harvard University Press, 1960), p. 260.

[76] Stout, "What is the Meaning," p. 2.

[77] See Mark Brett's useful distinction between motives and communicative intentions in "Motives and Intentions in Gen. 1," *Journal of Theological Studies* 42 (1991), pp. 1–16.

[78] A good example of such interpretive gerrymandering is E. D. Hirsch's position in *Validity in Interpretation* (New Haven: Yale University Press, 1967). Hirsch revised his position somewhat in subsequent works (cf. "Meaning and Significance Reinterpreted," *Critical Inquiry* 11 (1984), pp. 202–25. For powerful criticisms of these revised views see Richard Rorty, "Texts and Lumps," *New Literary History* 17 (1985), pp. 1–16, and Lutz Dannenburg and Hans-Harald Müller, "On Justifying the Choice of Interpretive Theories," *Journal of Aesthetics and Art Criticism* 43 (1984), pp. 7–16, with a reply by Hirsch on pp. 89–91.

where interpreters are agreed that they are pursuing the same set of interests in regard to a particular text. Their disagreements lie in how to adjudicate a relatively common set of interpretive problems and issues. While they may disagree over such things as how to apply particular methods, what counts as evidence, and how to interpret that evidence, there would still be reason to expect enough commonality in their interests that they have some bases for resolving disputes.

Alternatively, interpreters will be able to see that some of our most intractable interpretive disputes were not really disputes about the same thing. Rather, they are the result of pursuing very different, and perhaps incompatible, interpretive aims. Only a common reliance on the term "meaning" clouded those fundamental differences. Eliminating meaning through explication, then, results in an underdetermined account of interpretation as such. What we are left with is a series of much clearer, more circumscribed issues and practices related to the interpretation of specific texts.

Given the diverse and particular ways Christians need to interpret and perform specific scriptural texts, an underdetermined account of scriptural interpretation will allow Christians to articulate this diversity without having to fit it all under a single determinate theory of interpretation. The imaginary French monk I presented in my account of determinate interpretation can give an account of each of his interpretive activities with the Psalms in ways that are both rigorous and clear, and in each case capable of evaluation without having to provide an overall account of interpretation that would set them in some sort of theoretical order.

Nevertheless, in the interpretive activities of this monk there clearly was an order, even a discipline. This order, however, was not provided by a theory of interpretation. This order received its intelligibility within a set of doctrinal, moral, ecclesial and communal concerns. It came from the very specific contexts in which that monk carried on his scriptural interpretation. It was an order that was contingent upon a specific time and place. Nevertheless, when called upon to do so, one could argue that this order was continuous with the practice of faithful Christians from past generations. Hence, the results of scriptural interpretation within this scheme could not easily be evaluated apart from some account of how those larger contextual concerns shape and were shaped by scriptural interpretation.

An underdetermined account of interpretation may well dissolve some serious interpretive issues. It is more likely, however, that this account will relocate and reframe those issues in ways that will be more likely to generate fruitful results. I can, however, imagine two interrelated sets of objections to this relocation and reframing. The first objection would note that I criticized determinate accounts of interpretation for proceeding as if meaning were a property of a text. Further, I also criticized anti-determinate interpretation for treating textuality as if it were an agent. In reaction to these moves have I not gone to the other extreme and simply reduced biblical interpretation to its theological, ecclesiological, social, and institutional determinants? Have I not really eradicated the possibility that interpreting the biblical text might transform individuals and communities in ways that the social contexts of those interpreters could not have anticipated?[79]

By advocating an underdetermined account of biblical interpretation I do not wish to reduce interpretation to its various other determinants. Rather, I wish to argue that theological convictions, ecclesial practices, and communal and social concerns should *shape and be shaped by* biblical interpretation. The options are not either to make conceptually questionable claims about certain properties of the biblical text or simply to reduce the text to its contexts. Rather, for Christians, at least, biblical interpretation will be the occasion of a complex interaction between the biblical text and the varieties of theological, moral, material, political, and ecclesial concerns that are part of the day-to-day lives of Christians struggling to live faithfully before God in the contexts in which they find themselves. What I cannot do is provide a method for specifying in advance how these interactions will work. In the rest of this book, however, I will try to display how some of these interactions are displayed in the New Testament. Moreover, in the course of offering interpretations of specific biblical texts, I will try to display how some specific theological, moral, ecclesial, and social interests shape and are shaped by an engagement with the Bible. For example, in chapter 6 I will show why issues of how Christians acquire and hold wealth are related to truthful scriptural interpretation. In chapter 5 I will try to show how issues of character become important for evaluating and adjudicating interpretive disputes. Further, I will try to show how Christians' convictions about the importance of the role of the Spirit in scriptural interpretation cannot be rightly understood or, more importantly, given practical force, apart from the workings of other ecclesial practices (see chapter 4).

More immediately, however, I will need to address the second related objection to the sort of underdetermined account of biblical interpretation I

---

[79] This is the force of the criticisms that A. C. Thiselton makes of interpreters he calls "social pragmatists," of whom Stanley Fish is the most prominent example. See *New Horizons in Hermeneutics* (Grand Rapids: Zondervan, 1992) pp. 535–50. For a criticism of Thiselton's views on these matters see A. K. M. Adam's review in *Modern Theology* 10 (1994), pp. 433–4.

have advocated here. This objection concerns whether my underdetermined account of interpretation provides sufficient resources for Christians to resist simply using the Bible to underwrite sinful practices that have become embedded in the theological, social, and institutional contexts which play such a large role in my account. In Gary Phillips' account of reading the Bible deconstructively there is a strong sense of using deconstruction to resist interpretive practices and habits that have become so solidified and petrified that the Bible in a sense becomes a closed, quiet, and domesticated book. Reading deconstructively opens the text so that it can breathe again. Moreover, feminists would also share a similar aim even if many of them would not see deconstructive reading practices as a way to achieve this. How does my account help Christians avoid becoming complicit in, for example, the patriarchal ideologies in the Bible?

Without question, it is important for Christians to be aware of the ease with which they have in the past (and continue in the present to) become complicit in sinful practices and have interpreted the Bible to underwrite and justify their sin. On Phillips' account it is a metaphysics of writing or textuality and a readerly respect for the alterity of the text that keeps biblical interpretation from closing down prematurely. The inherent instability of such biblical interpretation would keep the Bible from underwriting sinful practices. Of course, it also inhibits scripture's role in ordering faithful Christian living. In a similar vein, for feminists or liberationists, a vigilant eye which exposes the ideology(ies) of the Bible is the best way to avoid becoming complicit in those ideologies in the present.

I have already argued against adopting the assumptions on which anti-determinate interpretation is based. I will argue in the next chapter that in regard to texts having ideologies, an underdetermined account of biblical interpretation will want to avoid investing the text with such properties as ideologies. At the same time, however, Christians will need to attend to the question of how they can order their lives, practices, and their biblical interpretation with a sufficient vigilance to read scripture in such a way that they avoid sinful practices. Moreover, they will need to be well versed in the practices of forgiveness and reconciliation if they are to repent of sinful practices and the interpretations which underwrote them. In the next chapter I want to show how the ecclesial contexts in which Christians interpret the Bible need to, and occasionally have, provided resources which form Christians to be vigilant readers, open to their own sinfulness.

Chapter Three

VIGILANT COMMUNITIES AND VIRTUOUS READERS

Framing the Issue

The account of underdetermined scriptural interpretation I argued for in the previous chapter is underdetermined only in the sense that it is not governed by a full-blown theory of textual meaning (or a theory of textual anti-determinacy).[1] Rather, for Christians, scriptural interpretation should shape and be shaped by the convictions, practices, and concerns of Christian communities as part of their ongoing struggle to live and worship faithfully before God. At the end of the previous chapter I noted that my account of underdetermined scriptural interpretation was open to the charge that it provided no ways for Christians to avoid domesticating scripture so that scriptural interpretation would become simply an occasion to confirm and deepen corrupt and corrupting prejudices and practices already endorsed within a community of believers. I also indicated that the sharpest way of focusing this objection is, first, to note the ease with which Christians have interpreted scripture to underwrite some of their most sinful practices. Secondly, one would argue that because it gives up the regulatory force of a notion such as textual meaning, underdetermined interpretation has no resources for resisting this tendency. In this chapter I wish to address this objection.

To begin, however, it will be important to show where the force of this objection does and, more importantly, does not lie. There are different ways of

---

[1] One might argue that underdetermined interpretation is also a theory. If so, it is clearly of a different kind than either determinate or anti-determinate interpretation. One might cast this as the difference between a low-grade theory and a full-blown theory. A low-grade theory does not aspire to the epistemological and/or metaphysical comprehensiveness characteristic of a full-blown theory. I am grateful to Jim Fodor for helping me see this.

posing the objection that underdetermined biblical interpretation cannot counter Christians' tendencies to read the Bible in order to underwrite their own sinful habits and practices. These different ways of posing the question each entail the adoption of different theoretical stances and critical practices. They therefore call for different types of answers. In the first part of this chapter I will address the claim that the biblical texts themselves contain various insidious ideologies. This line of argument leads to the claim that any interpretive program which does not begin by exposing and rooting out the ideologies in the biblical texts will, generally, lead readers to become complicit in those ideologies.

Having addressed this objection, I will need to examine a different sort of objection to my account of underdetermined interpretation. This objection simply points to the numerous particular occasions where Christians have read the Bible to underwrite their own sin, arguing that this tendency is so pervasive that contemporary interpretive proposals must provide some ways of addressing it.[2] Further, this need points to, if not necessitates, a determinate theory of interpretation. I will begin, then, by addressing the objection that one must expose and resist the ideologies of the Bible.

Texts Don't Have Ideologies

Over the past couple of decades many of those who read the Bible from a feminist, Marxist, or liberationist perspective have noted that those who produced the biblical texts shaped them in the light of their own economic, ethnic, or gender-based interests.[3] It is not uncommon, then, for it to be claimed

[2] For a brief survey of some of these examples in regard to the way pauline texts have been read, see Neil Elliott's *Liberating Paul* (Maryknoll: Orbis, 1994), ch. 1. A major part of Elliott's solution to this problem is to argue that the pauline texts in question are not authentically pauline (see pp. 21–2). While such an argument may do something towards excusing the historical Paul, it is simply theologically inadequate. The texts are canonical, the apostle is not. Rather than ascribing a property to these texts, I am claiming simply that Christian identity depends on and is connected with an engagement with Christianity's canonical texts. Pseudonymity does not really matter unless it can be used as a basis for extracting those texts from the canon. I think this is unlikely to happen; hence, the claim of pseudonymity does not really move the argument forward.

[3] Obviously, noting that the biblical writers brought their interests to bear on their writing is not new. Redaction critics, and others before them, have long recognized this. What marks more recent "ideological criticism" of the Bible is the particular interest in the way ideologies shaped what was written. Ideology here is generally taken to refer to a constellation of beliefs, practices, and cultural formations.

that the racism, androcentrism, or elitism of the people who produced the text is a property of the text. Hence, the text has an ideology.[4] These neat steps are nicely summarized in the following comment: "The growing recognition of the ideological nature of all interpretation has led inevitably to the acknowledgment of the ideological nature of *the biblical text*."[5] This position calls for critical practices dedicated to exposing and combating these ideologies.

Without denying the obvious fact that Christians have interpreted the Bible to aid and abet various practices they ought to have named as sinful, I do want to take issue with the claim that the Bible contains ideologies.[6] Speaking of the Bible (or any text) as having an ideology introduces a whole range of conceptual confusions and fails to take seriously the varied history of biblical interpretation. Having made this rather bold claim, however, I must admit that I cannot demonstrate that texts don't have ideologies. Rather, I want to show that if one insists on speaking as if texts have ideologies, then one also has to hold to a range of other inelegant, awkward, or incoherent positions. Dropping the idea that texts have ideologies will allow questions related to the fact that Christians have interpreted the Bible to underwrite their sin to be reframed in more fruitful ways. This should further allow us to think more clearly about the relationships between biblical interpretation and Christian practice and about how one might transform those relationships.

In a manner analogous to that revealed in my discussion of meaning in the previous chapter, to think of texts as having ideologies is to think of an ideology as a property of a text. On this view, an ideology is seen as something

---

[4] This tendency is succinctly summarized by Itumeleng Mosala when he claims that the biblical texts, "as products, records and sites of social, historical, cultural, gender, racial and ideological struggles . . . radically and indelibly bear the marks of their origins and history. The ideological aura of the Bible as the Word of God conceals this reality" (*Biblical Hermeneutics and Black Theology in South Africa* (Grand Rapids: Eerdmans, 1989), p. 20). See also how easily Sandra Schneiders talks about the "ideology in that text" in *The Revelatory Text* (San Francisco: Harper Collins, 1991), esp. pp. 120–1 and ch. 7, which notes that "the biblical text itself is ideologically biased against women" (p. 181 *passim*).

[5] See Gerald West, "Some Parameters of the Hermeneutic Debate in the South African Context," *Journal of Theology for Southern Africa* 80 (1992), p. 4; emphasis in the original. I cite West here not only because of the clarity with which he has related this view, but because he is one of the most theoretically sophisticated commentators on these matters. See his *Biblical Hermeneutics of Liberation* (Pietermaritzburg: Cluster Publications, 1991).

[6] I first argued this point in "Texts Don't Have Ideologies," *Biblical Interpretation* 3:1 (1995), pp. 1–34.

hidden, inserted, or naturally occurring in a text.[7] Carrying the analogy with textual meaning further, one can see that without an agreement on the meaning of the term ideology, our conversations will tend to break down. Nevertheless, one might well argue that there are a sufficient number of well-articulated definitions of ideology such that a discussion need not be question-begging in the way accounts of meaning tend to be.[8] One simply needs to be clear about the definition of ideology one is using and then proceed in a consistent manner without ruling out other possible uses of ideology.

Even with an agreed definition of ideology, however, the more one presses the issue of an ideology being a property of a text, the less suitable such talk will become. In short, this is because, over its interpretive life, a text can be pressed into the service of so many varied and potentially conflicting ideologies that talk about a text having an ideology will become increasingly strained, resulting in alternatives similar to those I laid out in the previous chapter with regard to meaning.

Let me further explain what I mean by looking at the story of Abraham as it was read during various stages of its history. This will by no means be a comprehensive account. Nevertheless, this brief glimpse at the variety of ways the Abraham story has been read and the various interests which shape and are shaped by such readings should illustrate the conceptual difficulties with the notion that texts have ideologies.

According to our best scholarly guess, the story of Abraham initially was a discrete ancestral story which was favored by one segment within what came to be the confederation of Israelite tribes. Allegiance to this tribal story helped to mark one's separation from those members of other tribes who adhered to stories about Isaac or Jacob. The process of combining initially competing stories of Abraham, Isaac, and Jacob into one account helped serve to cement the Israelite intertribal confederation as they banded together to enhance their prospects for survival. The literary melding of these various stories reflected and enhanced the social and political union of the various tribes. As Norman Gottwald argues,

> The concerns and interests of the ancestor traditions are primarily of two kinds: (1) the arduous struggle to secure a viable community as expressed in the need for offspring and productive land; and (2) the repeated defense of the community against outside pressures to absorb or destroy it.[9]

[7] Interestingly, however, many of those who have claimed that texts have ideologies would never be so unsophisticated as to claim that the same text has a meaning.

[8] A. Giddens, "Four Theses on Ideology," *Canadian Journal of Political and Social Theory / Revue canadienne de théorie politique et sociale* 7 (1983), pp. 8–21.

[9] Norman K. Gottwald, *The Hebrew Bible: A Socio-Literary Introduction* (Philadelphia: Fortress Press, 1985), p. 175.

I am hardly competent either to defend or to dispute Gottwald's position. I will simply let it stand for the moment, with one qualification: I want to resist Gottwald's phrasing of the issue when he talks here about the "concerns and interests of the traditions" as if texts (or in this case traditions) have ideologies. What is clear from his account, however, is that the struggle to secure and defend the community is a concern and interest of the people who united the stories of Abraham, Isaac, and Jacob and ordered their social, material, political, and theological practices in relation to these stories. These concerns and interests are not properties of the stories themselves. In fact, these interests seem to be the exact opposite of those who initially produced the stories, and who seem to have been interested in excluding those devoted to Isaac or Jacob from the Abrahamic community. As one might expect, when the concerns and interests of readers of Abraham's story changed, they also interpreted and embodied the stories differently.

We can see a further example of such change when we look at Philo's (ca. 15 BCE – 50 CE) interpretation of Abraham.[10] Such a long historical jump will highlight the fact that Philo's social, political, material, and theological concerns and interests are very different from the concerns and interests of those who initially formed and interpreted Abraham's story.[11] Nevertheless, Philo shared with the early Israelites a commitment to the story of Abraham.

Mine will not be a comprehensive account of everything Philo says about Abraham. The entry under Abraham in the index to the Loeb edition of Philo runs to nine pages. In addition, Philo explicitly devotes two of his works to Abraham (*On Abraham* [*Abr.*]; *On the Migration of Abraham* [*Mig.*]). When it comes to reading scripture generally, and Abraham's story in particular, Philo, following his Alexandrian predecessors Aristobulus and Pseudo-Aristeas, views scripture as an allegorical composition. One has merely to plumb the allegorical depths of scripture to find that all wisdom has been encoded therein.

Given this approach, it is not surprising that Philo treats the human character Abraham primarily as an archetypal exemplar of wisdom, virtue, and piety.[12] Throughout *Abr.* Abraham is referred to as the Sage (ὁ σοφός). He is

---

[10] In my treatment of Philo and his social context I am deeply indebted to the excellent account given by David Dawson in his book, *Allegorical Readers and Cultural Revision in Ancient Alexandria* (Berkeley: University of California Press, 1992).

[11] Without jumping all the way to Philo we get some indication that the story of Abraham was used to support the competing interests of the exiles (Isa. 51:1–5) and those who remained in the land (Ezek. 33:23–4).

[12] Philo contrasts Adam, Enoch, and Noah, as those who yearn for virtue yet do not fully attain it, with the perfectly virtuous souls of Abraham, Isaac, and Jacob (*Abr.* 47–8).

the prototypical stoic who lives in conformity with nature (*Abr.* 6; *Mig.* 128) and in harmony with the will of God (*Legum Allegoriae* 3:197).[13] Abraham's movements, when read allegorically, are to be seen as those of a "virtue loving soul in its search for the true God" (*Abr.* 68); they are the movements of the soul from the image to the original, from opinion to knowledge and from appearance to reality (*Mig.* 1–14). It is important to remember, however, that although Philo sees the allegorical as superior to the literal, he by no means abandons the literal reading of scripture (see in particular *Abr.* 68, 88).

Clearly, the ideological interests which shape and are shaped by such a reading of Abraham's story are not those evident among the tribal confederation of Israel. The standard scholarly account is that within Alexandrian Judaism generally, and for Philo in particular, scripture was read as part of an overall strategy of universalizing the appeal of Judaism to non-Jewish Alexandrians. Recently, however, David Dawson has challenged this received opinion, arguing that Philo's allegorical strategy is actually designed to subordinate Hellenistic cultural ideals to scripture.[14] Rhetorically, this strategy of subordination focuses not so much on Abraham as on Moses, the one responsible for encoding the Pentateuch's allegorical meanings. Nevertheless, it seems reasonable that the interests and concerns which shape and are shaped by Philo's interpretation of Moses also work in regard to Abraham. As articulated by Philo, most of these allegorical meanings appear simply to rewrite the moral and philosophical achievements of Hellenistic culture. Yet, because Moses temporally precedes these Hellenistic writers, he is their superior; Dawson notes,

> By allowing Moses to rewrite the moral and philosophical wisdom of Hellenistic culture, Philo has in effect allegorically subordinated classical meanings and texts to scripture. Because Moses came before the classical authors, his rewriting paradoxically becomes original writing, and the classical writers become his weak imitators.[15]

The social and political context in which Philo offers his subversive allegorical readings gives some clue as to his ideological interests. The Alexandria of Philo's day was deeply stratified along both cultural and

---

[13] Further evidence of this is seen in the moderation Abraham exhibits in his grief over the death of Sarah (*Abr.* 255).

[14] Dawson, *Allegorical Readers*, p. 74.

[15] Dawson, *Allegorical Readers*, p. 112. I assume here that the same could be said of Philo's treatment of Abraham.

economic lines. Jews, especially community leaders such as Philo, often found themselves having to negotiate a path between the conflicting interests of the Greek citizens of Alexandria, non-Greek Egyptians who sought the cultural status and economic benefits of citizenship, and the Roman authorities. The Jewish community, which occupied a relatively prominent place in Alexandrian society, was also divided between a small hellenized elite, a large anti-Greek/ Roman group with revolutionary tendencies, and an orthodox group who sought, at the same time, social and political stability. Philo would have been a member of this last group.[16]

At various times and in various ways all of the major segments of Alexandrian society opposed the Jews. A number of anti-Jewish tracts were produced in Alexandria. Typical of such work was Apion's tract that tried to undermine Jewish claims to citizenship by offering a reading of Jewish history which argued that the Jews were simply Egyptians and therefore not eligible for citizenship in the Alexandrian *polis* with all of its social and material benefits. Such opposition posed a real threat to the orthodox identity and social status of the section of Alexandrian Jews whom Philo represented and for whom he wrote.

In response to this threat to Jewish identity and status, Philo combines his allegorical reading of the Pentateuch with an emphasis on "literal" obedience to its laws. The crucial text here is Philo's *Life of Moses*. As Dawson notes in this regard:

> In the *Life of Moses* Philo responds to Apion's challenge by showing that the highest Hellenistic ideals were first embodied in Moses and subsequently set forth in the specific form of Jewish laws. As a result, Moses emerges as the true philosopher-king, promulgating laws for a true *politeia*. In the process, Moses is far from being a mere occasion for the display of Greek ideals; Philo ties Moses' virtues to his specific deeds as the Septuagint or Jewish oral tradition records them. If the Greeks are Philo's audience, they seem to be invited by the *Life of Moses* to become Jewish. But the highly Hellenized Jews who are probably the actual audience are being told that the most authentic way to be Greek is to be authentically Jewish – which means, at minimum, obeying Jewish law.[17]

In this light, Philo's reading of Abraham would fit in as a part of a strategy of resistance to a series of social, political, and economic threats to his Jewish

---

[16] Dawson, *Allegorical Readers*, pp. 113–18.

[17] Dawson, *Allegorical Readers*, p. 118. Philo's criticism of his fellow Jews who allegorize their interpretation of the law without obeying the law can best be found in *Mig.* 89–90.

community in Alexandria. Clearly, the ideological interests which shape and are shaped by Philo's reading of Abraham are different and remote from those operating among the early Israelites. As I will note later, this difference only poses problems if one wants to talk about texts having ideologies. Before this, however, I want to look at two other readers of Abraham's story, Paul and Justin Martyr.

In chapter 5 I discuss in some detail Paul's reading of the Abraham story as found in Galatians. Here I will simply lay out the basic structure of his reading. My present aim is to show the differences between Paul's reading and that of someone like Philo and how, by the time of Justin Martyr, the story of Abraham could be read in a different way to support very different interests.

In Galatians Paul offers an interpretation of certain crucial aspects of the Genesis account of Abraham in order to oppose the seemingly ascendant interpretation held by at least some Galatian Christians.[18] Given the context of the epistle, it is clear why an ability and the power to give a persuasive account of the relevance of Abraham to the Galatians would be such an important issue to Paul and his opponents. This is because, at its root, the controversy is about how the Galatian Christians are to live in continuity with those who look to the God of Abraham, Sarah, Isaac, Jacob, and Jesus as their God. Paul and his opponents seem to share a great number of views about Jesus, about the followers of Jesus being the renewal and continuation of Israel, and about the inclusion of the Gentiles in this renewed people of God. The dispute between them is not whether Gentiles can be children of Abraham, but how.

For Paul's opponents, the conventional reading of the story of Abraham indicates that Gentile believers must be circumcised (cf. Gen. 17:9–14), observe a range of Jewish rituals, and take on a general attitude of obedience and service to Torah. Paul confronts this view with a counter-reading of crucial aspects of the Abraham story in Gal. 3–4. Throughout these two chapters Paul offers a reading of Abraham's story designed to resist the claims

---

[18] I have no great desire to manufacture a full picture of Paul's opponents in Galatia. As John Barclay has ably shown, there are numerous pitfalls in such an enterprise. See "Mirror-Reading a Polemical Letter: Galatians as a Test Case," *Journal for the Study of the New Testament* 31 (1987), pp. 73–93. On the other hand, the story of Abraham seems to run so strongly against Paul's argument that the best way to account for its presence in the epistle is that it was a text on which his opponents relied. One of several to make this point is C.K. Barrett, "The Allegory of Abraham, Sarah and Hagar in the Argument of Galatians," in *Essays on Paul* (Philadelphia: Westminster Press, 1982), p. 159.

made by his opponents' more conventional interpretation. To do this, he couples a commitment to the hermeneutical priority of the Spirit (cf. 3:1–5) with a range of figurative interpretations (e.g. 4:21–31). This counter-reading both resists the claims of those wanting the Galatians to adopt the law and supports Paul's call for the expulsion of these "agitators" from the Galatians' midst. Paul's reading is shaped by his vision of that political body which he describes as the unified ecclesia of Jews and Gentiles. Further, he accounts for the Galatians' material experiences in such a way that their experience becomes the lens through which Paul insists they read the story of Abraham.

Here, as with Philo, we find a reading of Abraham's story which reflects and is related to a whole range of ideological interests and concerns. As in the case of Philo, however, these interests are remote and discontinuous from those which operated in early Israel. Before moving on to examine the implications of these various readings of Abraham's story, I want briefly to examine Justin Martyr's *Dialogue with Trypho*.

Although written less than a hundred years after Galatians, Justin's *Dialogue* shows a profound shift in Christian interpretation of Abraham's story. Paul's reading of Abraham supports his contention that Gentiles are to be included with the Jews in the "Israel of God" without first being circumcised and otherwise obeying Torah. Alternatively, Justin's reading of Abraham's story supports his view that Christians (now almost exclusively Gentile) have supplanted the Jews as the people of God and that the Jews are now excluded from God's promises.

> ... Justin uses Abraham to render the Jews orphaned, without legitimate claim to Abraham as their father in any meaningful way. The Jews do not have a future, nor do they have any true past. Justin uses the very Abrahamic heritage that the Jews claim in order to show that they are not children of Abraham; he thus leaves them abandoned and disinherited.[19]

The most succinct summary of Justin's view of Abraham comes in *Dialogue* 119:3–6. Here Justin summarizes his first day's discussion with Trypho for Trypho's friends. In this passage Christ is presented as the one who calls Abraham, promising to make him a great nation. Since, then, Christians are also called by Christ, they are the true children of Abraham:

---

[19] This is the judgment of Jeffrey S. Siker in *Disinheriting the Jews: Abraham in Early Christian Controversy* (Louisville: Westminster/John Knox Press, 1991), p. 163. I am largely indebted to Siker's work for the account I offer here.

And we [Christians] shall inherit the Holy Land together with Abraham, receiving our inheritance for all eternity, because by our similar faith we have become children of Abraham. For just as he believed the voice of God, and was justified thereby, so have we believed the voice of God (which was spoken again to us by the Prophets and the Apostles of Christ), and have renounced even to death all worldly things. Thus, God promised Abraham a religious and righteous nation of like faith, and a delight to the Father, but it is not you [Jews], "in whom there is not faith" (Deut. 32:20).[20]

Justin's argument that Christians are children of Abraham because they share in the faith of Abraham is in certain respects not unlike Paul's argument in Rom. 4. The added move that Christians have supplanted the Jews as the people of God, however, is precisely the point Paul argues against in Rom. 9–11. In regard to circumcision, Paul and Justin agree that it is not required of Gentiles. Paul, however, struggles to maintain the importance of circumcision in God's plan of salvation in Rom. 3:1–2. Justin moves in the opposite direction, claiming that circumcision sets the Jews apart for God's judgment (see *Dialogue* 16:2).[21]

In relation to Paul, it is clear that a very different set of social, political, material, and theological interests inform and are informed by Justin's reading of Abraham. Siker, for example, lists four factors to account for this shift:[22] (1) The diminishing emphasis on eschatology led to a concomitant diminishing of the pauline version of a unified ecclesia of Jews and Gentiles in which "all Israel will be saved" (Rom. 11:26). The Jews did not come to Christ in large numbers. When this is coupled with a decreased emphasis on eschatology, it led Christians to view Jews as opponents rather than as potential converts or as those who share in God's salvation. (2) By the time of Justin the church was almost exclusively Gentile. These Gentiles came to see Gentile Christianity as the true Israel. "And so a century after Paul reprimanded the Gentile Christians in Rome for their presumption that they had replaced the Jews as God's people (Rom. 11:25), Justin Martyr could assume that God's people are Gentiles not Jews."[23] (3) The diminished presence of Jewish Christians also fueled theological questions about the status of the Jews. This questioning was intensified by the increasing alienation and outright hostility between synagogue and church by the end of the first century. (4) Finally, this hostility was

---

[20] *Dialogue* 119: 5–6, cited in Siker, *Disinheriting the Jews*, p. 164.
[21] Justin here alludes to the defeat of Bar Kochba by Hadrian, a judgment which Justin links to the Jews' responsibility for the death of Jesus.
[22] See Siker, *Disinheriting the Jews*, pp. 194–5.
[23] Siker, *Disinheriting the Jews*, p. 195.

given more force and precision by the increasingly uniform nature of Judaism after the destruction of the Second Temple.

While this is by no means a comprehensive look at the various ways the story of Abraham has been read over the centuries, it is comprehensive enough to point out the difficulties one encounters if one persists in talking about a text having an ideology.[24] The chief difficulty in continuing to talk about the ideology of the Abraham story in Genesis is that of answering the question, "Which of these (or other) ideologically loaded interpretations of Abraham is the ideology of the text?" It seems clear that all of the answers one might give to this question will be inadequate.

In a manner analogous to that found in discussions of textual meaning, one could argue that the ideological interests and concerns at work in the production of a text count as the ideology of the text. Such an emphasis will focus primarily on the author(s) of a text. While such a view is clear, it is not particularly satisfying. I do not know of any persuasive argument one might give to support the valorization of this particular point in a text's history.

In addition, there are a host of conceptual difficulties that would need to be addressed in any attempt to make the initial phase of a text's production the source of that text's ideology. For example, with a composite text such as Genesis it becomes difficult to determine who counts as the author, much less what purposes that author sought to advance. Is the author(s) of Genesis the person(s) who produced the Abraham story in opposition to stories of Isaac and Jacob? Or is it the person(s) who melded the three stories together as a way of solidifying the Israelite tribal confederacy?[25] Further, it is often very difficult to read back from an ancient textual artifact to the ideological interests behind its production. Such interests can get muted, disguised, or ironically displaced beyond recognition.

Most importantly, aside from the arbitrary nature of focusing on the phase of a text's production, one is also left trying to account for the various and incompatible ideological uses of a text over time. What does one say about Philo, Paul, or Justin? Have they misunderstood the ideology of the Abraham story in Genesis? Have they subtly been taken over by the text's ideology? Have they distorted or violated it?

---

[24] The use of the Abraham story to set up the boundaries of one's community continues long after Justin. See, for example, R. Firestone, "Abraham's Son as the Intended Sacrifice: Issues in Qu'ranic Exegesis," *Jounal of Semitic Studies* 34 (1989), pp. 95–131.

[25] I realize this is a somewhat simplistic account of textual production, but a more complex (but less illustrative) account would simply serve my argument better, rather than counter it.

Clearly, Philo, Paul, or Justin would have been unaware of the various redactional theories surrounding critical study of Genesis. Further, the term "ideology" would have been foreign to them. Alternatively, they all understood that one can read the story of Abraham in ways that support or undermine the various social, political, and theological aims they sought to advance. These ends, however, were very different from those of the person(s) who put together the Abraham story in Genesis. Had Philo, Paul, or Justin become complicit in those ideological struggles? Probably not; at least not in the sense that they were either continuing or opposing the same struggles which led to the Abraham story being written and read as it was initially. These struggles were long over, and the ideological purposes which the text of Genesis initially served were no longer significant in the lives of Jews in Alexandria, the Christians of Galatia, or Justin's audience in Ephesus.

Had these characters violated or distorted the ideology of the text? If the ideology of the text is simply the ideological aims of the text's author, then one has to say yes. This, however, is not a very interesting claim to make. It is simply a judgment based on the arbitrary decision to privilege one phase in the interpretive history of a text. Indeed, such a privileging will tend to render the vast majority of a text's interpretive history as a history of distortion or violation of its original ideological aims. Of course, changing one's time-frame and privileging another of the text's ideological uses will run into variants of the problems noted above.[26]

Without question, the production and interpretation of texts are part of the means by which various individuals and groups can try to further their social, political, and theological interests and concerns. This is particularly the case when a community seeks to order its practices and beliefs in accordance with a recognized canonical text. The writer(s) of Genesis, along with Philo, Paul, and Justin, all operated in this sort of context. They all managed to use

---

[26] As an alternative strategy one might claim that texts have ideologies and it is simply the case that each of these interpretations of Abraham is a different text. There is no one text of Genesis. Each interpretation of Genesis is its own text and such texts clearly have ideologies. An adherent of Stanley Fish's views about the role of interpretive communities might well want to say that the interests and aims of the various groups reading the story of Abraham are so specific to each group that one might as well say they are reading different texts, each text having its own ideology. See Stanley Fish, *Is There a Text in This Class?* (Cambridge, MA: Harvard University Press, 1980). Conceptually this is much clearer, but it is a curious notion to propose. Having already shifted the locus of the production of meaning from texts to interpretive communities, as Fish wants, why try to obscure the community's ideological interests by imputing them to the text?

Abraham's story to support their specific ideologies in ways we can display with varying degrees of certainty. These ideologies (not all of which are compatible) are not things they inserted into the text in the course of writing. Instead, they wrote/read Abraham's story in ways that were both shaped by and helped to shape the various social, political, and theological contexts in which they found themselves. In all of these cases there is no explanatory gain, and much conceptual confusion is introduced, in talking about the ideology of the text.

I have tried to make this argument in some detail because my arguments in favor of underdetermined biblical interpretation are open to the objection that they provide no counter to Christians' widely manifest tendencies to read the Bible in ways that underwrite sinful beliefs and practices. By showing the pitfalls of the notion that the biblical text itself contains pernicious ideologies which ensnare readers, making them complicit in those ideologies, I have not answered the objection. Rather, I have indicated that this way of talking about the issue is going to lead to more problems than it solves. Making this point, however, helps to clear the way to show where the force of the objection lies and how it might be addressed.

As I have already argued, the relationships between the biblical texts and their interpretation and embodiment by specific Christian communities in particular contexts will always be a complex affair. No theory of meaning can specify in advance and in a determinate manner the ways these interactions should operate. This means that I cannot produce a method that will, if properly followed, rule out Christians from interpreting the Bible to confirm and underwrite their sinful practices.[27] At the same time, anyone who would argue that a determinate theory of meaning can effectively rule this out will also have to account for the numerous examples where people with a determinate theory of meaning have read and embodied scripture in corrupt and corrupting ways. It is clear that what must be addressed are ingrained habits of perceiving and living in the world that cannot be changed by any theory of textual meaning.

Instead, what I can offer is an account of how Christian convictions about sin should play a role in their scriptural interpretation, enjoining them to maintain a certain sort of vigilance over their interpretation. Further, I argue that such an account entails that Christian communities maintain the practices of confession, forgiveness, and reconciliation in good working order. Finally,

---

[27] Of course the history of this type of reading indicates that even with such a method, it would not counter an ingrained habit such as reading Gen. 9 to justify the enslavement of dark-skinned people.

the good working of these practices will aid in the formation of virtuous readers who can exercise interpretive charity in the midst of interpretive disputes. The manifestation of interpretive charity will not eliminate disputes. It will, however, help them to be resolved in ways that enable Christians to live truthful, faithful lives. I will begin, then, by offering an account of the sort of vigilance Christians are called to exercise.

Vigilant Communities

"Your eye is the lamp of your body; when your eye is single ἁπλοῦς then your body is full of light; but when it is not sound πονηρός, then your whole body is full of darkness. Therefore, be vigilant lest the light in you (prove to) be darkness" (Luke 11:34–5). Jesus offers this admonition after he has been accused in 11:14–26 of casting out demons by the power of Satan. In response to this accusation, he notes, first of all, that a kingdom divided against itself cannot survive (11:17–18). The implication of this is that if Jesus is casting out demons by God's power ("by the finger of God"[28]), then these exorcisms serve as a sign of God's inbreaking rule (11:20). This sign calls for a singular response – follow Jesus, the stronger man of v. 22. Any other response is taken to be a form of opposition (11:23). After this episode, a woman interjects "Blessed is the womb that bore you and the breasts which you sucked!" Jesus corrects this assertion, noting that the response he seeks is not admiration of himself (or his mother), but "keeping and doing the word of God."[29] Again, there is an emphasis on the appropriate, single-minded response Jesus demands as he marches to Jerusalem.[30] Immediately following this, Jesus addresses the crowd from which the woman in v. 27 shouted to him. He criticizes them both for seeking a (further?) sign from him. Because they have not perceived and responded to wisdom greater than Solomon's and preaching greater than Jonah's, they will be judged. The crowds here suffer from a sort of blindness (or deafness) which renders them unable to understand Jesus and respond appropriately. Moreover, as vv. 34–6 make clear, they are responsible for this blindness because they are responsible for keeping their eye "sound" or well focused.

[28] The allusion here must be to Ex. 8:19 when, after matching Moses and Aaron sign for sign and plague for plague, the magicians of Egypt are forced to admit, when they cannot summon up gnats, that "this is the finger of God."

[29] See Luke Johnson, *The Gospel of Luke* (Collegeville: Michael Glazier, 1991), p. 186.

[30] Jesus' journey to Jerusalem begins with a similar set of encounters stressing the need for a singular, single-minded response to his proclamation of the rule of God (9:57–62).

The term used to characterize the sort of vision one should have is ἁπλοῦς. This word normally is used to mean "single" rather than, say, "double." This reading, however, is not particularly informative as an account of human sight. Susan Garrett, following Conny Edlund, has persuasively argued that in this context keeping one's eye ἁπλοῦς has to do with focusing one's attention on God alone. "The expression would have conveyed the notion that a given individual *focuses his or her eye on God alone.* No worldly pleasures, no competing masters, no evil spirits can cause a person of 'the single eye' to compromise his or her integrity toward the Lord."[31] Garrett bases her view on a study of the ways ἁπλοῦς and its related nominal and adverbial forms are used in the LXX and the *Testament of the Twelve Patriarchs.* Of particular interest is the use of ἁπλότης to designate the virtue of integrity. Perhaps the key text here is T. Iss. 4:1–6 where there are several occurrences of ἁπλότης which link integrity as a virtue whose practice is tied up with one's vision. For example: The single-minded person ὁ ἁπλοῦς "lives his life straightforwardly, and views all things single-mindedly not admitting with the eyes evils that come from the world's error, lest he look perversely upon any of the Lord's commands."[32] Garrett further, notes that in the *Testament of the Twelve Patriarchs* Belial strongly opposes the practice of ἁπλότης.[33] This is particularly interesting in the light of the dispute regarding Jesus' relationship to Satan at the beginning of Luke 11.

Given this way of reading ἁπλοῦς (I will use the English "single" from here on), in Luke 11:34 Jesus appears to be expanding his specific critique of the crowds' moral and spiritual blindness in 11:29–32 into a more general admonition.[34] The eye comes to stand, synecdochically, for all of one's powers of perception and judgment. If these powers are single-mindedly focused on Jesus, then one is full of light. An absence of such single-minded attention on Jesus is the sign of an defective, πονηρός, eye, resulting in spiritual darkness. This is followed in 11:35 by a warning. One must beware lest the "light" in you be darkness. This seems to be a warning against being deceived (by Satan,

---

[31] See S. R. Garrett, " 'Lest the Light in You Be Darkness': Luke 11:33–36 and the Question of Commitment," *Journal of Biblical Literature* 110:1 (1991), p. 99.

[32] See the discussion in Garrett, " 'Lest the Light in You be Darkness'," pp. 96–9. Also T. Iss. 3:4 where Issachar tells his children that he lived his life with a "singleness of vision" ἐν ἁπλότητι ὀφθαλμῶν.

[33] Garrett, " 'Lest the Light in You be Darkness'," p. 99; also T. Iss. 6:1; 7:7; T. Ben. 6:7; and T. Job 26:7–8.

[34] "I suggest that Luke included the sayings about 'light' and 'eyes' at just this point because of a notion that the onlookers' testing pointed to the *absence* of a ἁπλοῦς eye or heart" (Garrett, " 'Lest the Light in You be Darkness'," p. 102).

or by someone else, or by oneself) into thinking that one is full of light when in fact one is in darkness. Such deception would come about by diverting one's single-minded attention from Jesus.[35] The admonition of 11:34–5 argues that being able to make an appropriate response to an encounter with Jesus requires that one pay attention to the state of one's "eye." This is because keeping the body illuminated with true light requires maintaining the eye as a single-minded instrument focused on God.[36] This task requires ongoing attention; it is not a once-for-all achievement. Indeed, as 11:36 cryptically notes, this task will be completed at the eschaton when all darkness will be removed from those with a single eye.[37]

Those who follow Jesus, then, are enjoined to attend to the character of their eye. That is, they are to attend to the faculties by which they come to perceive Jesus and make judgments about him. To perceive Jesus properly, to judge rightly about him, requires one to maintain a single-minded focus on him. Failure in this regard is to open oneself to darkness. As 11:35 indicates, the most dangerous type of failure in this regard is to fall into that deception by which one comes to think that darkness is light. That is, one's eye can become so distorted that it confuses darkness with light. This type of failure is particularly poignant because it can only befall those who are seeking to be filled with light. It is just this type of failure which is relevant for my argument here. It precisely describes the sorts of situations that are the focus of this chapter. When Christians have, for example, read scripture to underwrite the kidnapping and enslavement of Africans, the murder of Jews, or the structures and practices of apartheid they have succumbed to just this type of deception. They do not claim to be enacting evil – just the opposite. They confuse darkness with light.

This passage presents images which are particularly crucial for understanding how a body of believers is to read and perform scripture in ways that do

---

[35] My reading here is consonant with Garrett's, p. 101. She, however, really only allows that Satan is the agent who diverts or corrupts one's "single" eye.

[36] In this respect, Jesus' admonition here can be read as a gloss on Deut. 6:4 where the singular character of The LORD, calls forth and demands a single-minded response from Israel (6:5). Jesus mentions Deut. 6:5 in Luke 10:27. Michael Wyschogrod discusses this in "The One God of Abraham and the Unity of God in Jewish Philosophy," a paper delivered to the Society for Scriptural Reasoning, New Orleans, Nov. 1996; see also his "The 'Shema Israel' in Judaism and the New Testament," in *The Roots of Our Common Faith*, ed. H.-G. Link (Geneva: WCC Faith and Order Paper 119, 1983).

[37] See Garrett, " 'Lest the Light in You be Darkness'," p. 103, who follows F. Hahn, "Die Worte vom Licht, Lk 11, 33–36" in *Orientierung an Jesus: Zur Theologie der Synoptiker*, ed. P. Hoffmann et al. (Freiburg: Herder and Herder, 1973).

not simply underwrite and replicate sinful actions. Rather than urging a more developed theory of meaning, this passage calls followers of Jesus to a life of vigilant self-reflection, ever seeking to keep their "eye" single-mindedly focused on Jesus. Unlike those who vigilantly seek to display the ideologies of the biblical text, however, the vigilance advocated here is to enable believers to focus their attention on God.[38]

For contemporary Christians, the reading and embodiment of scripture is a constitutive part of keeping their attention focused on God in the single-minded way Jesus demands here in Luke. Christians are, then, enjoined to read scripture as part of a discipline directed at keeping their "eye single." At the same time, since the reading and embodiment of scripture can be an occasion for sin, Christians must vigilantly struggle to read with an eye that is already single as the best way of avoiding their well-documented tendency to read scripture to underwrite sinful activity. Since having an eye single-mindedly focused on God is an ongoing activity ultimately perfected at the eschaton (see 11:36), these two demands work together interdependently. Of course, this also means that when this process of keeping one's eye single breaks down at some point, then this effects further reading of scripture to maintain a single eye and further attempts to read with a single eye.

Thus far I have argued that, like those who subscribe to the view that texts have ideologies, Christians must read scripture with and in the light of a certain type of vigilance if their interpretation is not to lead to sinful practice. Unlike those who think that texts have ideologies and who focus their attention on uncovering the ideologies in the text as a way of combating them, I have argued that the vigilance required to resist the temptation to read scripture in order to underwrite sinful practices is a vigilance that keeps Christians' attention single-mindedly focused on God after the manner Jesus prescribes in Luke 11:34–6.[39] So far, however, I have left issues concerning the character of that single-minded attention, and the ways to attain and maintain it, undeveloped. I now want to return to Luke's gospel as a way of developing those issues further. In doing this I will try to show that keeping one's eye single-mindedly focused on God implies a second sort of vigilance, a vigilance directed at oneself. The vigilance to which Christians are called, then, has a

---

[38] Although this lucan text is not quoted, there is an analogous saying attributed to Abba Bessarion: "Abba Bessarion, at the point of death, said, 'The monk ought to be as the Cherubim and Seraphim: all eye'." from *The Sayings of the Desert Fathers,* trans. B. Ward (Kalamazoo: Cistercian Publications, 1975), p. 35 n.11.

[39] Presumably, this is one way of characterizing the role of the Rule of Faith in biblical interpretation.

twofold nature. On the one hand, vigilance is to be directed at oneself and one's community. This will entail truthful, critical self-reflection. On the other hand, this vigilant attention to oneself is not an end in itself. It must result in believers becoming better able to attend to God. This, of course, should enable further, more truthful self-reflection.

Luke's gospel displays numerous characters who either succeed or fail decisively in exercising the single-minded vision called for in 11:34–6. An examination of some of them may help to display the character of the vigilance called for here. In 18:9–14 we find a brief parable told to those who "are confident of their own righteousness (δίκαιοι) and who scorned others."[40] This passage, which relates the prayers of a Pharisee and a tax collector, may well be the most explicit narrative example of the issues addressed in 11:35. The Pharisee's prayer is a thanksgiving for all of the ways he is filled with "light." His prayer does not so much thank God for granting him such virtue as it boasts that he had attained it (unlike others).[41] The tax collector is simply able to identify himself as a sinner and to ask God for mercy. This passage recalls both 7:36–50 and 16:14–15 where Jesus upbraids the Pharisees for their failure both to see themselves properly and rightly to identify God's desires for sinful people. It is not surprising that Jesus offers the judgment that it is the tax collector who is justified when he leaves justified (δεδικαιωμένος).

The story of the rich ruler found in 18:18–24 can also be read as an example of failure to develop and maintain a single eye. This becomes clearer when this story is contrasted with the single-minded focus on Jesus demonstrated by Zacchaeus in 19:1–10.[42] The ruler comes to Jesus wanting to know how he might inherit eternal life (18:18). He admits to having observed the commandments from his youth (18:21). According to Jesus, the only thing remaining for him to do is to sell all he owns, give the money to the poor, and become a disciple (18:22). At that point the ruler goes away. He does not dispute the truth of what Jesus says. Rather we get the clear impression that he is unable to do the one thing that would provide him with the life he sought.

---

[40] David Neale points out that this is not an attempt to identify a specific historical group of people. Rather it is an "assessment of the intended target audience." See *None But the Sinners* (Sheffield: Sheffield Academic Press, 1991), p. 169.

[41] The ambiguity about whom this prayer is actually addressed to is nicely shown by the use of the preposition πρός. On this see Johnson, *Luke*, p. 271.

[42] I have argued elsewhere that these two stories might be read together as examples of failing and succeeding in receiving the kingdom of God as a child. Most of what is related here replicates the points made there in more detail. See "Receiving the Kingdom as a Child: Children and Riches in Luke 18:15ff.," *New Testament Studies* 39 (1993), pp. 153–8.

Zacchaeus, on the other hand, merely wants to see Jesus (19:3). He ends up finding salvation, σωτηρία (19:9), the very thing sought by the rich ruler. Zacchaeus, the rich tax collector, makes that difficult move into the kingdom which seemed so impossible to the ruler. Based on his observance of the commandments (18:20–1) the ruler, presumably, considered himself a child of Abraham. His encounter with Jesus, however, leaves us in doubt of this. Zacchaeus, a widely recognized and self-confessed sinner (19:7–8),[43] alternatively turns out to be a "son of Abraham" based on the manner in which he receives Jesus. The ruler fails to attain that which he sought because he is unable to do the one final thing Jesus asked of him – give up his riches. Zacchaeus, with no prompting from Jesus, cannot seem to get rid of his riches fast enough. The rich ruler is too hesitant, too circumspect. Zacchaeus, rather, presents a picture of one who single-mindedly abandons anything which previously might have kept him from finding salvation. The story begins with him wanting to see Jesus. He does so in a way that shows that his eye is single. The ruler demonstrates that very dangerous position of mistaking darkness for light and, lacking a single eye, he fails to embrace a new type of light when it is offered to him.

Consider also the story of the "woman who was a sinner" and Simon the Pharisee in 7:36–50. The sinful woman's single-minded attention to Jesus focuses on washing and anointing his feet (7:37–8). Simon also has an interest in Jesus, but it is of a different sort.[44] He seems more interested in determining whether or not Jesus is a prophet (7:39) than in attending to him in the way

---

[43] The traditional view of 19:8 is that Zacchaeus is committing himself to a future course of action as an implicit sign of repentance. There is a recent body of interpretation, however, which reads 19:8 as Zacchaeus' defense to Jesus against the crowd's complaint that he is a sinner. (A recent advocate of this view is A. C. Mitchell, "Zacchaeus Revisited: Luke 19:18 as Defense," *Biblica* 71 (1990), pp. 153–76.) On this view, Zacchaeus is not pledging a change in his behavior. Rather, he is referring to his usual custom as a sort of *apologia*. I am not sure that my reading depends on taking a side in this debate. Nevertheless, it seems that the logic of the story leads one to read 19:8 in the traditional manner. For example, if Zacchaeus is in the regular habit of giving half his goods to the poor, he could hardly qualify as "rich" (19:2). Secondly, Jesus' claim to have come to seek and save the lost in 19:10 seems to draw its force from the fact that Zacchaeus really was in some sense lost. For a recent defense of this traditional view see D. Hamm, "Luke 19:8 Once Again: Does Zacchaeus Defend or Resolve?," *Journal of Biblical Literature* 107 (1988), pp. 431–7. Neale, *None but the Sinners*, pp. 185–8, also defends this traditional view.

[44] "The contrast between the sinful woman and Simon is a profoundly ideological one: The true and godly sentiment of repentance encounters the ultimate in self-righteousness . . ." (Neale, *None but the Sinners*, p. 144).

a more hospitable host might have done (7:44–6). Again, the "sinner" manifests the single eye.[45]

What is striking about those who fail to demonstrate the sort of single-minded attention required of those who would be filled with light is that they are all interested in Jesus. It is not the case that they are ignorant of or indifferent to him. Rather, they are not attentive in the appropriate way or to a sufficient degree. Moreover, they lack the self-knowledge shown by those who respond to Jesus appropriately. In Luke's gospel, those who respond best to Jesus are those who can identify themselves as sinners. In fact, it would seem that to keep one's eye single-mindedly fixed on Jesus requires the ability to see oneself as a sinner whose only redemption is through a single-minded attention to Jesus.

The account I have offered here makes clearer the importance of coming to recognize oneself as a sinner. This recognition orients one in such a way that it is possible to begin that process of keeping one's eye single and of redirecting one's eye on those occasions when one begins to confuse darkness with light. This, then, becomes a primary and necessary element which an underdetermined account of biblical interpretation will invoke as a way to counter the habit of reading scripture in ways that underwrite sin. If Christians are to read and embody scripture in ways that result in lives lived faithfully before God, they will need to recognize themselves as sinners. Moreover, they will need to train and form new members so that they, too, can identify themselves in this way.[46]

---

[45] See also the story of Peter's first encounter with Jesus related in 5:1–11. After a fruitless night of fishing, Peter is instructed by Jesus to lower his nets in a particular place. When Peter is confronted with a massive load of fish, a catch he clearly attributes to Jesus' intervention, his first response is "depart from me for I am a sinful man"(5:8). After being reassured by Jesus, however, Peter, along with James and John, leaves everything and follows Jesus (5:11).

[46] In *Reading in Communion: Scripture and Ethics in Christian Life* (Grand Rapids: Eerdmans, 1991) L. Gregory Jones and I argued for the importance of learning to read scripture "over against ourselves." We took this terminology from Dietrich Bonhoeffer. When it is situated in the life (and death) of Bonhoeffer, this way of putting the matter seems sufficient. Bonhoeffer uses this terminology after coming to the view that there were fundamental distortions in his life that needed to be addressed. Indeed, he goes so far as to claim that although he was at this time an accomplished theologian and Lutheran minister, he was not yet a Christian. Bonhoeffer came to see himself as a sinner, one who had read scripture "for himself" rather than "over against himself." His life nicely provides an example both of one who confused darkness with light and one who, by means of coming to know himself as a sinner and redirecting his eye in a single-minded way towards Jesus, comes to be filled with light. Apart from its context in the life of Bonhoeffer, however, the phrase "reading over against oneself" can seem somewhat abstract and unclear. It gives the

In terms of biblical interpretation, being able to identify oneself as a sinner injects a crucial element of provisionality into one's interpretive practices. This provisionality stems from the recognition that there may be something wrong in the ways a community of self-identified sinners interprets and/or embodies scripture. This recognition is part and parcel of the ongoing self-reflection that must characterize all those who struggle to keep their eye single. This should result in an individual's and/or a community's willingness to subject their interpretive practices to scrutiny and criticism. Even though a community and its members must ultimately be responsible for their own interpretive practices, their self-critical scrutiny may be directed and inspired by particular members within that specific Christian community, members of different Christian communities, or those outside any Christian community.[47] It is impossible to predict precisely where such prophetic insight might come. Therefore, those seeking to keep their eye single must always exercise a sort of vigilance that will enable them to hear and respond attentively to critical voices from wherever they might come. This is not to say that all criticism is equally important or even correct. Rather, my claim is that it must be attended to vigilantly because one cannot know exactly how to evaluate it in advance. The outsider may actually offer a truer account of ourselves and our interpretive practices than either we or those closest to us could offer. In other cases, outsiders may not have enough familiarity with Christian convictions and practices to offer a correct diagnoses of a community's struggles to embody scripture.

When Christians have read scripture to underwrite the practices of apartheid or the enslavement of Africans, for example, they had already abandoned (or ignored) those voices calling them to the critical self-examination of their interpretive practices that comes from recognition of oneself as a sinner. In this case, no change in interpretive method would bring about the needed transformations in their practices. In fact, those practicing different interpretive methods quite often ended up on the same sides in these debates. Alternatively, those on different sides in these debates often employed the same interpretive methods.

While recognition of oneself as a sinner is a necessary condition to keeping one's eye single and subsequently to reading and performing scripture

---

impression of being able to view oneself from afar in ways that can be quite problematic. By reflecting on the notion of the ἁπλοῦς eye and how its presence and absence is narratively displayed in a variety of characters in Luke, I am trying to give a more general and developed account of this process of learning to read over against oneself that does not potentially invoke the notion of a dual or split personality.

[47] See the chapter entitled "Listening to the Voices of Outsiders," in Fowl and Jones (eds), *Reading in Communion,* for a fuller account of this activity.

faithfully, it is not sufficient. Recognizing that one is a sinner must be done within the context of a community that engages in the practices of forgiveness, repentance, and reconciliation if that recognition is to result in lives manifesting single-minded attention to God. Further, recognizing oneself as a sinner is necessary but it must lead to growth in virtue, particularly growth in virtue as an interpreter of scripture. I will briefly discuss each of these issues in turn.

Sin, Forgiveness, and Reconciliation

In the previous section, I offered an interpretation of Luke's gospel which focused on the importance of keeping one's attention single-mindedly focused on Jesus. By looking at those in Luke who respond best to Jesus, those who most closely demonstrate a single eye, it appears that recognition of oneself as a sinner is a crucial first step in responding appropriately to Jesus. Moreover, those characters who fail to recognize themselves as sinners, tend also to be unable to respond appropriately to Jesus. Recognition of oneself as a sinner, however, cannot be the only step in maintaining a single-minded focus on God. Nevertheless, such recognition is a crucial step in transforming the alienating effects of one's sin into a life characterized by reconciled relationships with God and with others.

This point draws us back to Luke's gospel and its sequel, Acts. I have concentrated on the importance of recognizing oneself as a sinner for being able to respond appropriately to Jesus. It is equally important to note that a tremendous portion of Jesus' life and teaching in Luke is dedicated to displaying and describing God's forgiveness. From the very earliest stages of Jesus' public ministry he is engaged in forgiveness and controversy over how and under what conditions God forgives (cf. 5:17–26). Large portions of his teaching, particularly in relation to the Kingdom of God, focus on God's desire to forgive, God's gracious offer of forgiveness, and a call to his followers to forgive as God does (see, in particular, 7:40–50; 15–16). From his early encounter with the paralytic through his visit to Zacchaeus and his final controversy filled days in Jerusalem, to his words of forgiveness uttered on the cross (23:34),[48] Jesus claims both to have the authority to forgive sins and to offer that forgiveness without prior repentance. Moreover, Jesus both enjoins and empowers his followers to forgive (17:3; 24:44–9). The resurrection confirms Jesus' particular claims about God and God's desires for forgiveness

---

[48] Although this verse is missing in numerous important manuscripts, it closely fits a number of lucan themes. See also Johnson, *Luke*, p. 376.

and reconciliation. By the end of Luke (24:47) and into the early parts of Acts, the gospel of the crucified and resurrected one is closely tied to forgiveness and repentance (see Luke 24:47; Acts 2:38; 3:19; 5:31).

The ability to recognize oneself as a sinner is crucial for keeping one's eye single. This single-minded attention to Jesus, though, is not simply an occasion to dwell on one's sin. As Luke–Acts makes clear, the recognition of one's sinfulness is simply a step in being drawn into God's abundant forgiveness, which issues forth in loving repentance and, ultimately, reconciled relationships with God and others. Recognition of oneself as a sinner must lead one to become situated in a network of practices of forgiveness, repentance, and, ultimately, reconciliation, if sin is not to be the first and last word on one's life. The point of these practices is to help us unlearn the habits and escape the patterns of sin in which we have become complicit. Further, these practices are part of the process by which the sin which marks our relationships can be truthfully addressed, forgiven, and repented of with the aim of transforming sin-scarred relationships into reconciled relationships. This process is to result in relationships with both God and others that more closely resemble the relationships of self-giving love characteristic of the triune life of God. As L. Gregory Jones states, "Most fundamentally, then, forgiveness is not so much a word spoken, an action performed, or a feeling felt as it is an embodied way of life in an ever deepening friendship with the Triune God and with others."[49]

When Christians' convictions about sin and their practices of forgiveness, repentance, and reconciliation become distorted or inoperative, then Christians will also find that they cannot read and embody scripture with a single eye. Rather than shaping and being shaped by faithful living, scriptural interpretation is most likely to underwrite sinful practices. In such situations, Christians will have damaged their abilities to distinguish light from darkness. Indeed, they will be in the prime position to confuse darkness with light. Further, as 11:34–6 indicates, this situation will tend to build upon itself, since one's abilities to distinguish between light and darkness are dependent upon keeping one's eye single. In this situation simply having more interpretation along the same lines is not likely to help. Consider, for example, the numerous accounts of runaway slaves who, upon being returned to their masters, were charged in civil courts with having stolen property (themselves) from their masters. When some of these same slaves inquired why it was not a violation of Ex. 20:15 when they were taken from their country and enslaved, they were told that the slave trade did not involve stealing; it was a business.[50]

---

[49] L. Gregory Jones, *Embodying Forgiveness* (Grand Rapids: Eerdmans, 1995), p. xii.
[50] I owe this example to Michael Cartwright.

Noting the ideological interests involved in the production of Exodus would not really address this issue. One has to address the sinful ideology which shapes and is shaped by the scriptural interpretation of a particular community that has lost the ability to distinguish darkness from light. The doctrines and practices best suited to this are related to sin, forgiveness, repentance, and reconciliation.

Thus far, I have tried to address the argument that the underdetermined scriptural interpretation I advocated in chapter 2 is not capable of addressing those situations in which Christians interpret the Bible to underwrite their most sinful practices. One common way in which some scholars have approached this problem is through vigilantly attending to and exposing the ideologies of the biblical texts. Exposing these ideologies in the text can then direct one in resisting the workings of those ideologies.

In response I have argued that thinking of ideologies as properties of texts is conceptually confused. Further, by examining the Abraham story at various stages of its reception I tried to show that textual interpretation can shape and be shaped by an unpredictable variety of interests and concerns as different communities engage that particular text in the various contexts in which they find themselves. Therefore, if Christians are to combat their well-documented tendencies to read scripture to underwrite their sin, then they must attend to themselves. That is, they must primarily be concerned with their own common life, with the role of scripture in that common life, and with the voices of those both inside and outside the community which offer words of prophetic critique of the community and its interpretive practices.

I have used the notion of keeping one's eye single from Luke 11:34–6 to describe the character of this attentiveness which Christians are to demonstrate. Further, by situating this notion within the larger context of Luke's gospel, it becomes clear that the ability to direct one's attention single-mindedly towards God in the manner characteristic of one having a single eye, depends on being able to recognize oneself as a sinner. If this recognition, however, is to develop in faithful ways, it must be connected to practices of forgiveness, repentance, and reconciliation, so that our interpretive practices, and our lives more generally, are directed to deeper communion with the triune God and with others. In the absence or disruption of these convictions, recognitions, and practices, no amount of interpretive theory, no amount of ideological criticism, will help.[51]

---

[51] In a discussion of 2 Cor. 3, Richard Hays makes some similar remarks: "Where God's spirit is at work the community is being transformed into the image of Christ and liberated to see, when they read Scripture, that the old covenant prefigured precisely this transformation. Where this transformation is not occurring in a community of the faithful, no

At this point, I now want to explore how the growth in virtue which attends deeper communion with God will also affect scriptural interpretation. Ultimately, however, this growth in virtue will not act as a determinate theory of interpretation to eliminate interpretive disputes among Christians. Rather, it will shape the character of those disputes in ways that will be explored further in subsequent chapters.

Growth in Virtue: Charity in Interpretation

When Christians' convictions and practices regarding sin, forgiveness, repentance, and reconciliation are in good working order, the recognition of oneself as a sinner works towards keeping one's eye single. Further, this recognition draws one into a collection of practices designed to restore, reconcile, and subsequently deepen one's communion with God and others.[52] As a result, Christians will find themselves transformed by the Spirit to conform more nearly to the image of Christ (cf. 2 Cor. 3:18). Traditionally, this transformation has been (and still is) characterized as growth in virtue.[53] As one might expect, growth in virtue will demonstrate itself in scriptural interpretation as well.

Indeed, it is ultimately through the formation of virtuous interpreters of scripture that Christian communities can combat the temptation to read

---

interpretation, however careful and learned, can penetrate the veil that lies over the text." *Echoes of Scripture in the Letters of Paul* (New Haven: Yale University Press, 1989), p. 152.

[52] As Bernard of Clairvaux remarks, ". . . I must confess that I am not entirely satisfied with the first grace by which I am enabled to repent of my sins; I must have the second as well, and so bear fruits that befit repentance, that I may not return like a dog to its vomit." *On the Song of Songs,* trans. K. Walsh (Kalamazoo: Cistercian Publications, 1981), sermon 3:3, p. 18.

[53] In the same sermon mentioned in n. 52 above, Bernard goes on to note, "On receiving such a grace [the "second grace" which leads one to desire to bear fruit that befits repentance] then, you must kiss his [Christ's] hand, that is, you must give glory to his name, not to yourself. First of all you must glorify him because he has forgiven your sins, secondly because he has adorned you with virtues." *On the Song of Songs*, sermon 3:4, p. 19. In book 1, para.10 of *On Christian Doctrine* Augustine (using images very similar to Luke 11) makes a similar point when he says, "Therefore, since that truth is to be enjoyed which lives immutably, and since God the Trinity, the Author and Founder of the universe cares for His creatures through that truth, the mind should be cleansed so that it is able to see that light and to cling to it once it is seen. Let us consider this cleansing to be as a journey or voyage home. But we do not come to Him who is everywhere present by moving from place to place, but by good endeavor and good habits" (from the translation by D. W. Robertson (New York: Macmillan, 1958)).

scripture in ways that underwrite sinful practices. This is not because virtuous interpreters will always agree with each other. Short of the eschatological completion of the promises of Jeremiah 31 and 1 Cor. 13, texts which promise interpretive clarity (and, in the case of the completion of Jer. 31, obviate the need for texts at all), Christians will need to engage scripture in the recognition that they will disagree with each other. Christians ought to expect that their scriptural interpretation will be marked by sustained disagreements about how best to interpret and embody scripture in any particular context. In fact, the absence of such arguments would be a sign of a community's ill health.[54] The exercise of virtue in scriptural interpretation, therefore, is not primarily a way to eliminate disagreement. Rather, it provides part of the context in which disagreements can best be articulated, debated and, at least provisionally, resolved, so that Christians can live and worship faithfully in the situations in which they find themselves. Much of the rest of this book will be devoted to displaying further doctrines and practices that comprise the context in which Christians can best interpret scripture. As a way of concluding this chapter, I wish to explore what the exercise of the virtue of charity in interpretation might look like.

Of course, there is no way to specify precisely what the exercise of any virtue will look like in particular situations. I will, however, lay out some of the central dispositions and habits of charitable interpretation, keeping in mind that these will need to operate in particular contexts and in conjunction with other convictions and practices of scriptural interpretation.

It is well known that Augustine argued that all proper biblical interpretation must work to build up charity in believers.[55] While I agree with this, I am not here so much interested in how biblical interpretation might build charity, as in how the development of charity might manifest itself in biblical interpretation. In fact, I will return in a moment to look at Augustine as an example of a charitable interpreter. Before that, however, I want to display some of the particular interpretive habits and dispositions a charitable interpreter will bring to interpretive disputes.

[54] My claim here is analogous to Alasdair MacIntyre's claims about the importance for the health of a tradition of argument and debate. He goes so far as to characterize a living tradition as "an historically extended socially embodied argument, and an argument precisely in part about the goods which constitute the tradition." *After Virtue*, 2nd edn (Notre Dame: University of Notre Dame Press, 1984), p. 207 and ch. 15 more generally.
[55] See *On Christian Doctrine*, book 1, paras 39–44, and especially the beginning of para. 40, "Whoever, therefore, thinks that he understands the divine Scriptures or any part of them so that it does not build the double love of God and our neighbor does not understand it at all."

Initially, a charitable interpreter will both recognize interpretive differences and refuse temptations to reduce or rationalize those differences and disputes away.[56] In regard to any particular dispute, the charitable interpreter will want to avoid certain extremes. One extreme presumes that the parties to the dispute inhabit such different conceptual worlds that they cannot speak to each other, that they do not even speak the same language. Thus, there is no way of rationally evaluating their differing views. One must simply choose on the basis of personal preference, a choice which is thereby not open to criticism. Another extreme presumes that all disagreements are basically reducible to single solutions which only the irrational or the perverse will refuse to accept.

For a philosophical counter to these extremes, one has recourse to Donald Davidson's notions about interpretive charity. Davidson's position is difficult to reproduce in all of its subtlety. My aims here are limited to discussing Davidson's arguments against certain forms of conceptual (or interpretive) relativism. Davidson initially articulated what he came to call a principle of interpretive charity in his essay "On the Very Idea of a Conceptual Scheme."[57] In this essay Davidson is primarily interested in undermining a version of conceptual relativism, the view that some people's conceptual schemes are so different from our own that one might say that they actually inhabit a different reality.[58] Conceptual relativism moves from the recognition that all knowledge is relative to the conditions, perspectives, prejudices, and assumptions of the knower to the claim that at least some of these perspectives or schemes are sealed off from each other in such ways that they are unintelligible and untranslatable to those who inhabit other schemes.[59]

---

[56] In addition to recognizing interpretive differences in the present, charitable interpreters will need to eschew "Whiggish" accounts of the history of interpretation. These accounts optimistically regard biblical interpretation as a steady, if not uninterrupted, progression of ever-improving interpretations, moving away from the errors of the past and ever closer to the promised land of meaning.

[57] This essay first appeared in *Proceedings and Addresses of the American Philosophical Association* 47 (1974). It was later reprinted as a chapter in *Inquiries into Truth and Interpretation* (Oxford: Oxford University Press, 1984), pp.183–99. Davidson developed some of his views in this essay in several subsequent works, most notably in "A Coherence Theory of Truth and Knowledge," in *Truth and Interpretation,* ed. E. LePore (Oxford: Blackwell, 1986).

[58] As Davidson describes it, conceptual schemes are "ways of organizing experience; they are systems of categories that give form to the data of sensation; they are points of view from which individuals, cultures or periods survey the passing scene." *Inquiries into Truth and Interpretation*, p. 183.

[59] Variations on this type of relativism can be found in the work of B. L. Whorf in

Davidson shows that views about such extreme differences between ways of organizing reality (or ways of interpreting texts) are incoherent. He does this by noting that once we grant that those who differ from us speak a language, then we have no way of making sense of the claim that something is so different from us that we cannot *in principle* make sense of it. The claim of such difference presupposes enough knowledge of the object under discussion to render the claim false. We can never be in a position to judge that others have beliefs and concepts so radically different from our own.[60] If there were absolutely no parallels between one group's expressions and practices and our own, we would lack sufficient reason for ascribing the term language to their expressions. We would not have good reason to call their actions purposeful as opposed to random.

Davidson demonstrates that radical impenetrable difference in interpretive practice or anything else is an incoherent notion.[61] This does not mean, however, that at any point in time, those holding strongly opposed views will be able to make sense of each others' claims. Initially, it may be extremely difficult to make sense of the claims of others, particularly those most different from us. This, however, is a contingent problem which can be addressed through hard work and patience. Rather than assert that such differences render conversation and debate impossible, the charitable interpreter will begin the slow, often tedious process of learning the presumptions, conventions, and idioms needed to make others' views intelligible. Charitable interpreters will resist the move to close off this activity prematurely; they will always recognize the provisionality of their work. That is, interpretive charity entails both a willingness to listen to differences and a willingness to hear those differences in their fullness.

---

linguisitics and Dennis Nineham in biblical studies. Some of Stanley Fish's recent rhetoric comes close to this point of view. The initial relativist villain whom Davidson seems to have had in mind is Thomas Kuhn. Jeffrey Stout, however, in *The Flight from Authority* (Notre Dame: University of Notre Dame Press, 1984), pp. 163ff. gives a "charitable" reading of Kuhn which indicates that he is not a conceptual relativist of this sort.

[60] This is well illustrated by Davidson's comments regarding Whorf and Kuhn. "Whorf, wanting to demonstrate that Hopi incorporates a metaphysics so alien to ours that Hopi and English cannot, as he puts it, 'be calibrated', uses English to convey the contents of sample Hopi sentences. Kuhn is brilliant at saying what things were like before the revolution using – what else? – our post-revolutionary idiom." *Inquiries into Truth and Interpretation*, p. 184.

[61] For a fuller account of this position in regard to the work of Alasdair MacIntyre and Jeffrey Stout see my essay, "Could Horace Talk with the Hebrews? Translatability and Moral Disagreement in MacIntyre and Stout," *Journal of Religious Ethics* 19 (1991), pp. 1–20.

If the very idea of a conceptual scheme radically different from our own is unintelligible, does this mean that all differences between interpreters are really chimera? Davidson would clearly answer no:

> It would be wrong to summarize by saying that we have shown how communication is possible between people who have different schemes, a way that works without the need of what there cannot be, namely a neutral ground, or a common coordinate system. For we have found no intelligible basis on which it can be said that schemes are different. It would be equally wrong to announce the glorious news that all mankind – all speakers of language, at least – share a common scheme and ontology. For if we cannot intelligibly say that schemes are different, neither can we intelligibly say they are one.[62]

Having avoided extreme approaches to interpretive disputes or differences, the real questions facing the charitable interpreter concern how to address differences in interpretation. The first step is to note that all differences, all disagreements, are only intelligible against a background of similarity and agreement. If these agreements were not already in place we would have little hope of finding a common subject-matter about which to disagree.[63] Agreement may not be easy to display. For example, such things as the use of a common vocabulary might actually obscure real differences and agreements. Charitable interpreters, then, may need to begin to address an interpretive dispute by exposing the nature and types of agreement lying beneath its surface. By doing this one sharpens and thereby clarifies the nature and type of a disagreement. We should not expect that this aspect of interpretive charity will eliminate differences between interpreters. Such charity will, however, separate the real from the apparent differences. It will also provide a shared background of assumptions to which recourse can be made in debating a disagreement.

A related habit of the charitable interpreter is the practice of maximizing the reasonableness of those with whom one differs. Or, alternatively, a charitable interpreter ought to avoid ascribing irrationality wherever possible. I have no great stake here in adjudicating philosophical debates about rationality. Rather, I am using the term in a limited, non-technical, sense of attributing rationality to someone when they have (or had) good reasons for holding their views. "That is, the rationality of a given person's beliefs or actions is relative to the reasons or reasoning available to that person. And

---

[62] *Inquiries into Truth and Interpretation*, p. 198.
[63] See also the discussion of this point in ch. 2 above.

the availability of reasons and reasoning varies with historical and social context."[64]

To be a charitable interpreter one must develop the dispositions, habits, and abilities which enable one to show how a sensible person could hold views with which one differs without being considered irrational. In other words, the charitable interpreter presumes that those who differ hold their differing views for good reasons and tries to display what those reasons are or were.[65] It is important to note, however, that charitably seeking the reasons for the beliefs and actions of those with whom one differs is not the same as presuming that such people are correct about whatever points happen to be at issue. Interpretive charity simply presumes that by illuminating points of agreement and by minimizing ascriptions of irrationality one can better account for the words and deeds of others, not that one has to agree with them. Interpretive charity need not lead to a watering down of one's own convictions in the process of presuming and displaying the rationality of others' positions. Nevertheless, in any interpretive conflict of importance, one's ability to give a charitable account of a differing position is crucial to developing a superior position. As Alasdair MacIntyre has argued, in any interpretive conflict which is rationally resolved, the position which prevails will be the one that can show how it accounts for the strengths in alternative positions while avoiding or resolving the weaknesses in those alternatives.[66]

An Example of Interpretive Charity

As one example of interpretive charity I want briefly to examine Augustine's (354–430 CE) 5th and 6th tractates on John's gospel. These sermons take John 1:33–4 – John the Baptist's testimony about Jesus which follows Jesus' baptism – as their text. Augustine employs this text in a larger argument against the Donatists and their views on baptism. It may seem odd to take one of

---

[64] See Stout, *The Flight from Authority*, p. 168 and the discussion beginning on p. 166.

[65] This entails that a charitable interpreter should deal with the strongest versions of opposing arguments. This may even require the charitable interpreter to recast opposing views to make them as strong as they can be. For a scholarly example of this see M.G. Brett's recasting of Childs' canonical approach in *Biblical Criticism in Crisis?* (Cambridge: Cambridge University Press, 1991).

[66] MacIntyre first laid out the structure of this argument in "Epistemological Crises, Dramatic Narrative and the Philosophy of Science," *The Monist* 60 (1977), pp. 453–72. This strategy is then put in practice in *After Virtue; Whose Justice? Which Rationality?* and *Three Rival Versions of Moral Inquiry*.

Augustine's anti–Donatist writings as an example of interpretive charity. I have several reasons for doing this. First, it points to the fact that interpretive charity is not the same as being nice. Secondly, it shows that one can extend interpretive charity to one's opponents without necessarily having to water down one's convictions about the truth of the matters at stake.[67] Thirdly, the disputes between Donatists and Catholics show how much overlap there is in their two positions: They largely believed the same things; they read the same scriptures; to the extent we know about them, their liturgies were remarkably alike.[68] Hence, there is ample opportunity for a charitable interpreter to show the points of agreement as a way of clarifying the disagreements, to maximize the rationality of those who hold differing views, and to elaborate a position that recognizes the strengths of opponents' views while avoiding their weaknesses. In these particular tractates, Augustine is able to show the points at which he agrees with Donatist claims about baptism, even granting the sacramental validity of Donatist baptisms. At the same time, he argues that the truth of their claims does not, and should not, lead to their conclusions and their separation from the church. Moreover, his argument is from the outset shaped by scripture, including his engagements with scriptural texts used by his opponents.

The johannine text which forms the basis for these two tractates relates John the Baptist's testimony that he did not know who Jesus was. Rather, he had been told by God that the one on whom the Spirit descended in the form of a dove is the one who will himself baptize with the Holy Spirit. Early in tractate 5 Augustine draws a distinction between John the Baptist's baptism and the baptism Christ commands his followers to perform. John's baptism is uniquely given to him directly as a gift (5.4).[69] Christ's baptism, the baptism performed by the church, is always still Christ's baptism. It is never given to another in the way John's baptism is given to him: ". . . the Lord Jesus Christ did not wish to give his baptism to anyone, not that no one should be baptized with the Lord's baptism, but that the Lord himself must always be baptizing" (5.6). Obviously, the baptism is performed by Christ's human servants, but it is not their baptism (cf. 1 Cor. 1:10–17). "For the quality of the baptism is commensurate with the quality of the person by whose power it is given, not with the quality of the person through whose ministry it is given" (5.6). The Donatist position rejects

---

[67] Of course, in some instances interpretive charity demands that we revise our convictions about the truth of the matters at issue.

[68] See W. H. C. Frend, *The Donatist Church*, 2nd edn (Oxford: Clarendon Press, 1985), pp. 2–3.

[69] "He alone received such a gift; there was no just man before him, none after him, to receive such a gift" (5.4).

the baptism of *traditores* on the basis of their sinfulness. Augustine will agree that there is a relation between the character of the baptizer and the quality of the baptism. He further indicates that he has no stake in defending the character of *traditores* or any other minister for that matter.[70] He argues, however, that since the baptism is Christ's alone and given to no one else, then the quality of the baptism is assured. The Donatist mistake is in failing to see the distinction between the ministers of baptism and the one whose baptism it truly is.[71] Indeed, if the character of the minister is the primary concern, then who really can baptize? Or will there be a sliding scale of baptismal quality based on the righteousness of particular ministers? (5.17–20; 6.6).

In the middle of this tractate (paras 8–11) Augustine returns to a point raised at the beginning. Here his argument picks up the anomaly of John confessing that he did not know the Lord in 1:33 and the obvious fact that John must have known the Lord (cf. John's claim in 1:30 that Jesus is the Lamb of God who takes away the sins of the world). Augustine argues that what John learns that he did not previously know is that Christ would retain his baptism for himself. This is testified to by the Spirit who descends as a dove and confirms that Jesus is the one who will baptize with the Holy Spirit.[72]

The image of the dove provides a polyphonic focus for Augustine's arguments in the rest of tractate 5 and into tractate 6. On the one hand, the dove is the Spirit who descends on Jesus at baptism. This image is developed more fully in tractate 6. On the other hand, the dove is also the church.[73] In regard to this use of dove Augustine cites Song of Songs 6:8, "One is my dove," to make a point about the unity of the church. Any who destroy the unity of the dove can only be hawks or falcons, birds of prey. Donatists who claim to be the true church by virtue of having suffered persecution are, ironically, the arch persecutors of the church because they tear at its unity as a hawk shreds its victims (5.12).[74]

As tractate 6 begins, Augustine continues to build on the image of the dove. He distinguishes between the dove and the raven which Noah sent out from the ark. The ark, being the church, contains both raven and dove (6.2,4). He

---

[70] See 5.7, 8, 11.

[71] "What does a wicked minister do to you when the Lord is good?" (5.11).

[72] At the beginning of the tractate Augustine had already laid out the argument about the unity of trinitarian activity.

[73] This allows Augustine to say things like "Let the dove teach the dove"(5.10), and "Dove, acknowledge what dove taught" (5.11).

[74] Although he does not use this verse, presumably Augustine would find the Donatists to be perfect examples of those who confuse darkness with light. As a result, they are much more dangerous to the church than pagan persecutors (5.13).

then returns to the dove as the Spirit, contrasting the single dove that descends on Jesus with the many tongues of fire which descend on the disciples at Pentecost. The singularity of the dove provides unity amidst a diversity of tongues. "Tongues differ from one another, but the difference of tongues does not constitute schisms. In parted tongues, fear not disintegration; recognize unity in the dove" (6.3,5).[75] The doves also are used to characterize believers. They, like doves, are innocent, simple, and full of true peace. This stands in contrast to the ravens who also inhabit the ark. Ravens lacerate, devour, and bring false peace.[76]

Augustine recognizes that the Donatists would agree there is one dove, one true church, and one Spirit. The question then concerns how to adjudicate conflicting claims to represent the dove (6.12). Augustine recognizes that there are good and evil people on both sides, so this cannot be the determinant. Nevertheless, the dove is simple, peaceful, and innocent. Those that would split off cannot manifest the characteristics of doves; they are, rather, ravens (6.12).[77]

As a way of further developing this point, Augustine returns to baptism. Augustine rejects the Donatists' demand that those joining them be re-baptized. Moreover, he grants the sacramental validity of Donatist baptisms. Therefore, those Donatists who become Catholic are not to be re-baptized. In terms of its sacramental validity, Augustine clearly, if reluctantly, recognizes Donatist baptism – as long as it is not re-baptism (6.15). If their baptism (and other sacramental acts) is valid and in other respects similar to the practice of the Catholics, why does Augustine see the Donatists as such a threat? What is it that they lack (6.15)? While their baptism is sacramentally valid, Augustine also notes that Donatist baptism is not beneficial to them. This is because their baptism does not produce charitable people. The Donatists do not have love, therefore, their baptism is not beneficial to them. "But, you will say, I have the sacrament. You say the truth. The sacrament is divine; you have baptism, and I admit it. But what does the same Apostle say? 'If I know all the sacraments and have prophecy and faith so as to move mountains,' perhaps to prevent you from also saying, 'I have believed and this is enough for me'. Faith is great, but it gives no benefit at all if it should lack love" (6.21).[78]

---

[75] Also, "In the dove is unity; in the tongues of the nations is community" (6.9).

[76] Augustine likens the Donatists' call for rebaptism to the cry of the raven (6.11).

[77] In an earlier passage, Augustine also implies that if the Donatists were correct and not schismatics, then one would have expected donatism to have spread beyond a rather small part of Africa (6.10).

[78] Also, "Do not boast about your baptism because I say it actually is [baptism]. Look, I say it actually is. The whole Catholic church says it actually is. The dove perceives and acknowledges and moans because you have it outside" (6.17).

How does Augustine justify his claim that the Donatists lack love? They break the unity of the church. Baptism outside the dove tears at the body of the dove and brings ruin on those ravens who feast on the body of the dove. Throughout this part of the tractate, Augustine quotes passages from 1 Cor. 13:1–3, situating the Donatists (usually by means of their own claims) with those who have all knowledge and power, those who are eloquent, and those who give themselves over to suffering, but who gain nothing because they do not have love.

Is it the case that Augustine thinks that the church has only ever only held one view about baptism? No, he clearly recognizes that there have been disputes about baptism in the past. He quotes Phil. 3:15 to support the view that there have been and can be disagreements over a matter. The church can even tolerate erroneous views as long as there is opportunity for debate and correction. By setting themselves apart from the dove, the church, the Donatists have excluded themselves from the conversation (5.17). They are therefore not in a position where they can either be corrected or offer correction.

Ultimately, one may well argue that Augustine's *actions* against the Donatists not only lacked charity but were simply theologically mistaken. In these tractates, however, I have tried to show that, at least in this point in the dispute, Augustine exemplifies the characteristics of a charitable interpreter outlined above. He agrees with the Donatists that certain ministers of Christ's baptism were and are corrupt. He even recognizes the sacramental validity of their baptism. From this base of agreement, however, he argues that the Donatist position is mistaken in failing to note that baptism belongs to Christ, not to the minister. Further, by dividing the church, the Donatists render their sacramentally valid baptisms powerless to help form charity in the baptized. This is because these baptisms are occasioned by what Augustine sees as a great act of violence, the tearing apart of the body of the dove, the church. In these tractates Augustine aims to show the proper concerns of the Donatist position, while incorporating those concerns into his own superior position.

Conclusion

I began this chapter by addressing the criticism that the underdetermined interpretation I advocated in chapter 2 was unable to help Christians withstand their tendency to read scripture in ways that underwrite sinful practices. One way of addressing this tendency is through a sort of ideological criticism which argues that the texts of the Bible contain various ideologies which must be vigilantly exposed and resisted. While I agree that Christians must exercise a certain sort of vigilance if they are to avoid reading scripture to support their own sinful habits and practices, I also argued that texts do not have ideologies. Hence, the vigilance that should characterize Christian interpretation of scripture should not be directed at scripture, but at the individuals and communities interpreting scripture.

This sort of vigilance is best characterized by the notion of the single eye found in Luke 11:34–6. Further, by setting this passage in the wider context of Luke's gospel, it appears that an essential step in keeping and maintaining a single eye is the recognition of an individual's and community's sinfulness. This recognition is a necessary step; it is not, however, sufficient to help Christians resist the temptation to read scripture to support their sin. Rather, the recognition of sinfulness must lead one into the practices of forgiveness, repentance, and reconciliation. Unless these practices are in good working order, the recognition of our sin will be the first and last words on our lives. In such a situation, simply carrying on the same interpretive practices and habits will not help.

Recognition of sin and engagement in the practices of forgiveness, repentance, and reconciliation are themselves elements in the process of growing into deeper communion with the triune God and with others. This growth (as opposed to a theory of meaning) is ultimately the only real counter to Christians' manifest tendencies to read the Bible in ways that underwrite sin. Further, this growth in communion with God and others enables our own growth in the virtues, chief of which is charity. I conclude the chapter by examining some of the characteristics of a charitable interpreter. It is important to note, however, that the presence of interpretive charity will not necessarily reduce interpretive disputes. Christians must recognize that such disputes are constitutive of being part of a living tradition of people reading scripture in order to live holy lives and to worship God truthfully. Rather, interpretive charity is one element which shapes the ecclesial contexts in which we might then expect interpretive disputes to result in faithful living and truthful worship. In the chapters which follow, I will address some of the other elements that need to shape an ecclesial context in which scripture is read in the way Christians need to read it.

Chapter Four

HOW THE SPIRIT READS AND HOW TO READ THE SPIRIT

Introduction

In the previous chapter I addressed the objection that my account of underdetermined interpretation left Christians with no resources for resisting their tendency to read scripture in ways that supported their own sinful beliefs and practices. I argued that the resources for resisting this tendency lie not in theories of textual meaning, but in Christians' abilities to exercise a particular sort of vigilance and to engage in practices of forgiveness, repentance, and reconciliation which will themselves lead Christians to grow in virtue. It is important to remember, however, that, in and of themselves, these resources will not work to eliminate interpretive disputes among Christians. Indeed, this side of the kingdom an absence of interpretive dispute is not necessarily a desirable result. Rather, because no particular scriptural passage is self-interpreting, Christians will always need to debate with each other over how to interpret and embody scripture in the various contexts in which they find themselves. In this situation of ongoing debate, argument, and struggle, the resources displayed in the previous chapter will do more to direct these debates, arguments, and struggles towards generating faithful living and worshipping than theories of textual meaning.

This, however, is but one of the ways in which Christians' convictions and practices need work to determine their interpretation of scripture. Clearly, there is a vast array of convictions and practices which should shape and be shaped by Christian interpretation of scripture. Further, these convictions and practices should not be taken to operate in isolation from each other. Rather, they should work together in ways that enhance and illuminate each other. In this book I am simply pointing out some, but by no means all, of the important convictions and practices which should play a role in Christian interpretation of scripture. In part, the selection of issues in this book reflects my views that these topic are particularly in need of attention. In this light, the current chapter will turn to explore how Christian convictions about the Holy Spirit bear on issues of interpretation.

I will begin by looking at John's gospel to make some general comments about the role of the Spirit in scriptural interpretation. These comments will indicate that the Spirit's intervention and interpretive work is crucial if the followers of Jesus are faithfully to carry on the mission Jesus gives them. This is because the Spirit enables believers to understand the words of Jesus in the light of his death and resurrection. Further, because the Spirit speaks in unison with the Father and Son, all Spirit-directed actions will also conform to God's will. These considerations will provide a trinitarian grounding to my discussion about the role of the Spirit in interpretation. The aim of this is to keep the Spirit from seeming to be a free-floating entity operating in distinction from the other persons of the Trinity.[1]

I will then move to a closer examination of Acts 10–15 and the issues surrounding the inclusion of Gentiles in the church. Here the Spirit plays a decisive role in a particular set of disputes involving scriptural interpretation. What is striking about this passage is that the characters demonstrate a remarkable facility for recognizing, interpreting, and acting upon the work of the Spirit. I argue that this facility is underwritten by two interconnected elements. The first is the ability to bear witness to the work of the Spirit in the lives of others. The second is the way that this ability is sustained by the particular friendships that these Christians are able to form.

I then conclude by looking at two arguments for reading the contemporary disputes over the role of homosexuals in the church as an analogous extension of the disputes over the inclusion of Gentiles in the church in Acts 10–15. To even be in a position to debate, and perhaps enact, this type of analogical extension, Christians will need to begin by opening themselves to the sorts of friendships with homosexuals that would enable them to testify about the

---

[1] I do not say a great deal about scripture and the Trinity here. I presume the persuasiveness of David Yeago's account which shows the connection between scripture and the trinitarian doctrines of Nicea. See "The New Testament and Nicene Dogma," in *The Theological Interpretation of Scripture: Classic and Contemporary Readings,* ed. S. E. Fowl (Oxford: Blackwell, 1997), " . . . the Nicene *homoousion* is neither imposed *on* the New Testament texts, nor distinctly deduced *from* the texts, but, rather, describes a pattern of judgments present in the texts, in the texture of scriptural discourse concerning Jesus and the God of Israel" (p. 87).

work of the Spirit in the lives of their friends. Without this step, Christians will neither be able to read the Spirit nor read with the Spirit. I will begin by looking at the promise of the Spirit in John.

The Promise of the Spirit

Jesus' farewell discourse in John 13–17 provides the most extensive account of the role of the Spirit in the New Testament. Even here, however, there is not a great deal of detail. In this section the primary role of the Spirit is to enable the disciples to carry on as faithful followers of Jesus after his "departure" – his death, resurrection, and ascension (14:18). As the obedient Son is to return to his rightful place with the Father who sent him, the Spirit will "bring to your remembrance all that I have said to you" (14:26). Further, Jesus indicates that he has more to say that the disciples simply cannot bear yet. The Spirit will make this known to them, too (16:12–15). These new words which the Spirit will speak are trustworthy because the Spirit speaks in unison with the Father and the Son (16:13). Reminding and speaking of what is "more" are activities of the Spirit that enable the followers of Jesus to continue the mission Jesus started and which they are to continue. The Spirit will guide and direct the followers of Jesus into the future, while, at the same time, enabling them to "abide in the true vine" (15:1–11).

If John's gospel is anything to go by, even the "remembering" of Jesus' words is not strictly a feat of Spirit-enhanced memory.[2] In 2:22 and 12:16 we may get two glimpses of the sort of remembrance Jesus speaks of in 14:26 as a work of the Spirit.[3] In 2:13–25 we read of Jesus going up to Jerusalem for Passover. When he enters the temple, he overturns the tables of the money-changers and drives out those selling sacrificial animals. This act in itself inspires the disciples to "remember" Ps. 69 (68):10. When asked to show by what authority he did these actions, Jesus responds, "Destroy this temple, and in three days I will raise it up" (2:19). Although at the time

[2] As J. D. G. Dunn notes, " . . . the teaching function of the Spirit for John is *not* limited to recalling the *ipsissima verba* of the historical Jesus. But neither does the inspiring Spirit create wholly new revelation or portray a Jesus who is not in substantial continuity with the once incarnate Jesus. There is *both freedom and control* – liberty to reinterpret and remould the original kerygma, but also the original kerygma remains as a check and restraint." See *Jesus and the Spirit* (London: SCM, 1975), p. 352.

[3] C. K. Barrett is one of the few modern commentators on John to link the remembering in 2:22 and 12:16 with the promises about the Spirit in 14:26. See *The Gospel According to St. John,* 2nd edn (London: SPCK, 1975), p. 201.

nobody seems to understand what Jesus means, in 2:22 we learn, "When, therefore he was raised from the dead, his disciples *remembered* that he had said this; and they believed the scripture and the word which Jesus had spoken."

In chapter 12, there is an even more interesting example. As Jesus enters Jerusalem for the final time there is great cheering and the crowds lay palms before him and proclaim him "King of Israel" (12:13). In response to this, Jesus sits upon a small donkey. This leads John to make reference to a passage largely drawn from Zechariah 9:9.[4] In 12:16 we read, "His disciples did not understand these things at first; but when Jesus was glorified, then they remembered that these things had been written of him and had been done to him." What is striking here is that Jesus does not actually speak the words of Zechariah 9:9. In fact, no one speaks these words; the citation is to be John's interpretive mark on this event.[5] This passage, with all of its allusions, brings out the true nature of Jesus' kingship in contrast to the crowds who want to make Jesus king after his raising of Lazarus (12:9–14).[6] What seems to be the case is that initially the disciples did not understand Jesus' actions. After his glorification (which is completed subsequent to the giving of the Spirit), the disciples (who cannot, then, be strictly limited to those present at the events related in ch. 12) are enabled both to understand the actions by means of the citation and to understand the citation in the light of Jesus' actions. The "remembering" here involves being able to connect an event (Jesus' entry into Jerusalem) with a scriptural text (Zech. 9:9) in ways that allow them to be understood in new and unanticipated ways. In each of these cases, the disciples only "remember" in the light of the resurrection. The act of remembrance that the Spirit enables here is not so much an exercise in recollection as an understanding of things said and done in the past from the perspective of the death and resurrection of Jesus.

The disciples' mission of abiding in the true vine and bearing fruit for the glory of God (15:8) cannot be achieved simply by a wooden repetition of what one has done in the past. Simply repeating the words of the past will not be sufficient to carry on as faithful followers of Jesus. There are two reasons for

---

[4] This citation also bears the influence of Zeph. 3:16; Isa. 40:9–10; 44:2, 6. For a good discussion of the sources and allusions in this passage see B. G. Schuchard, *Scripture within Scripture* (Atlanta: Scholars Press, 1992), pp. 71–84.

[5] Although he does not make reference to this verse, Dunn notes that the johannine account of the interpretive work of the Spirit leads John to "regard his own gospel as the product of the inspiring Spirit" (*Jesus and the Spirit*, p. 352).

[6] Schuchard, *Scripture within Scripture*, pp. 76–8, nicely points out this contrast.

this. First, as these two examples from John indicate, even the act of remembering must be accompanied and enabled by a Spirit-directed understanding of the past that views things from the perspective of the death and resurrection of Jesus. The past does not simply exist as an uninterpreted collection of sense data. The past is always a particular sort of remembering. In this context, this specific "past" only exists by means of the subsequent work of the Spirit. Secondly, even as our words and actions remain formally the same, our changing circumstances will mean that these words will be understood in new ways. As Nicholas Lash notes,

> If in thirteenth-century Italy, you wandered around in a coarse brown gown, with a cord around your middle, your "social location" was clear: your dress said that you were one of the poor. If, in twentieth-century Cambridge, you wander around in a coarse brown gown, with a cord around your middle, your social location is curious: your dress now says, not that you are one of the poor, but that you are some kind of oddity in the business of "religion." Your dress now declares, not your solidarity with the poor, but your amiable eccentricity.[7]

Here Lash is not attacking the Franciscans as much as he is pointing out that temporal and cultural change necessitates ongoing discussion and debate about how to continue a tradition. "Fidelity to tradition, in action and speech, is a risky business because it entails active engagement in a process of continual change."[8]

The Spirit's role is to guide and direct this process of continual change in order to enable communities of Christians to "abide in the true vine" in the various contexts in which they find themselves. In terms of John's gospel, this is the "more" which Jesus speaks to the disciples through the Spirit. Because the Spirit speaks this "more" in unison with the Father and the Son, believers can act in ways that are both "new" and in continuity with the will of God.

The Spirit at Work: Acts 10–15

So far, there is little that I have said about the role of the Spirit in scriptural interpretation that Christians would not widely recognize. As Christians have struggled both to interpret and to embody scripture in the various contexts in which they find themselves, they have traditionally made reference to the role

---

[7] Nicholas Lash, "What Authority Has Our Past?," in *Theology on the Way to Emmaus* (London: SCM, 1986), p. 54.
[8] "What Authority Has Our Past?," p. 55.

of the Holy Spirit in these struggles. Christians hope and expect that the Spirit will guide, direct, and confirm their readings of scripture as well as the practices generated and underwritten by such readings. In short, Christians presume that proper interpretation of scripture must be guided by the Spirit.[9] At this formal level I expect that there would be widespread agreement about the Spirit's role in interpretation.

It is more difficult, however, to account for the practical force of claims about the Spirit's role in scriptural interpretation. How, especially in the absence of miraculous and unambiguous signs, can an individual or a community distinguish Spirit-inspired interpretation and practice from more mundane varieties?[10] Are there particular exegetical methods that will generate Spirit-inspired interpretation? How might we know this? Are we left with a set of widely accepted convictions about the importance of the Spirit in interpretation without any way of giving force to those convictions in any particular act of interpretation? Are there ways of talking about the hermeneutical significance of the Spirit that do more in practice than pay lip-service to the role of the Spirit and then continue as normal?

One can, of course, take the long-range view. This view would note that over time one can distinguish Spirit-inspired interpretation and practice by its effects. Readings which lead to faithful worship, practice, and belief are retrospectively seen to have been Spirit-directed. Such a position tends to shift the question to how to construe faithful worship, practice, and belief and, thereby, tends to remain agnostic about the role of the Spirit in particular contemporary interpretive disputes.

There is much to be said for this view. In fact, it is narratively represented in Acts 5 by the advice Gamaliel gives to the Sanhedrin about how to deal with the proclamations of the first followers of the resurrected Christ. After noting the rise and fall of various characters who "claimed to be somebody," Gamaliel says, "So in the present case, I tell you, keep away from these people and let them alone; because if this plan or this undertaking is of human origin it will fail; but if it is of God, you will not be able to overthrow them – in that case you may even be found to be fighting against God!" (5:38–9). This form of patient discernment must be part of any attempt to account for the hermeneutical significance of the Spirit. I am, however, more concerned with what

[9] See, for example, the Westminster Confession (1646), which claims that "The Supreme Judge by which all controversies of religion are to be determined . . . can be no other but the Holy Spirit speaking in the Scripture" (ch. 1 art. x). In the Vatican II document *Dei Verbum* (par. 23) the church reading scripture is referred to as the "Pupil of the Holy Spirit."
[10] For a talmudic account of the unpersuasive nature of signs in a debate about *halachah* see *Baba Mezia* 59.

might be said, in a temporally more immediate way, about the role of the Spirit in interpretation. While specific decisions and resolutions of disputes within the church should be open to revision, Christian communities, like everyone else, must also make decisions and resolve disputes without the benefit of retrospective judgments. Can Christians in the midst of interpretive and practical disputes recognize, account for, and interpret the Spirit's work in more immediate ways? To answer these questions, we should look to Acts 10–15.

"For it seemed good to the Holy Spirit and to us . . . . " This is the way the substantive decisions of the so-called Jerusalem Council are introduced in Acts 15:26ff. The narrative leading up to these decisions runs from Acts 10 through chapter 15. In these chapters we read how the earliest followers of Jesus addressed one of the most significant theological, moral, and ecclesial issues ever to confront the church: how and under what conditions ought Gentiles to be admitted to this Jewish group of believers?

In the course of this narrative, the characters in these chapters make numerous explicit judgments about the work of the Spirit. In addition, there is a presumption that the Spirit generates their scriptural interpretation. Throughout this narrative the central characters show a remarkable facility for recognizing, interpreting, and acting upon the work of the Holy Spirit. In examining this passage, I wish to show that there are habits, practices, and dispositions narratively displayed here that are crucial for contemporary Christian communities as they struggle to read and embody scripture in the Spirit.

I will begin by addressing some particular objections to drawing any implications and analogies from Acts to contemporary Christian communities. Then I will move to discuss Acts 10–15, articulating some of the communal structures, habits, and practices that seem to facilitate the recognition and interpretation of the Spirit's work. I will then try to show how an absence of these structures, habits, and practices works to undermine contemporary American Christian communities' abilities to address a whole range of issues regarding the role and place of homosexuals within the church.

There are several objections one might raise to the prospect of finding guidance about the hermeneutical significance of the Spirit by looking to Acts. On the one hand, historical critics have raised numerous questions about the historicity of the events portrayed in Acts generally, and chapters 10–15 in particular. Without question, if one is interested in reconstructing a narrow historical record of the first generation of the Christian movement, then these chapters will simply be one piece of evidence that must be evaluated along with other pieces. Apart from this concern, it must be admitted that the narrative here has much to say about the role of the Spirit in the formation of theological, moral, and interpretive judgments. For my purposes, the pre-scriptive (and no doubt idealized) picture found in these chapters is more important than their historical accuracy.[11] Even if the actual making and enacting of decisions regarding Gentile inclusion in the earliest Christian communities was much more rough and tumble than Acts relates, the importance for contemporary Christians of how these decisions *should* have been worked out remains.

Secondly, one might object that Acts makes it clear that one way of discerning the work of the Spirit is through the presence of what the text calls "signs and wonders." One might then claim that these signs and wonders are the only reliable markers of the Spirit's activity. In the absence of such miraculous occurrences, we cannot do much more than carry on our present struggles over scriptural interpretation and practice, hoping in some general way that the Spirit will hover over our debates and discussions.

Clearly, one's interpretive position is enhanced if one can call down fire from heaven in the manner of Elijah in his dispute with the prophets of Baal. This, however, is a relatively rare event. Can we expect the Spirit to play a role in our struggles over how to interpret scripture so as to live and worship faithfully before God in the absence of such decisive and unambiguous divine interventions?

In this regard, it is important to recognize that the presence of miraculous signs is not a straightforward event. As the Corinthian correspondence makes very clear, what one takes to be a sign and how one interprets and evaluates those signs can be quite contestable matters. Reading the signs requires the work of the Spirit as often as it confirms the work of the Spirit. In short, we may well find that the issue of the presence or absence of miraculous signs is not, on its own, the determinative issue in detecting the work and will of the Spirit.

Relative to the rest of Acts, such miraculous verification of the Spirit's work is not a central element in the narrative of Gentile inclusion in chapters 10–15. Further, an examination of these chapters will indicate that the central characters are not credulous bumpkins, easily swayed by magic posing as miracle. Even when miraculous events are crucial, however, these events are not self-interpreting. Most obvious in this case is the vision Peter receives in chapter 10.

---

[11] This is the strategy Luke Johnson adopts in *Decision Making in the Church* (Philadelphia: Fortress Press, 1983). An expanded and revised version of this book was re-issued under the title *Scripture and Discernment* (Nashville: Abingdon, 1996) and the relevant pages here are pp. 70–5.

There are several very practical social structures, practices, and habits at work which enable the characters to recognize, interpret, and enact the work of the Spirit. My suggestion is that in the absence of these elements, no number of miracles will be able to account for the transformation in peoples' views which are related in these chapters. Having laid out my views regarding these two issues in interpreting Acts, I now want to look specifically at the relevant texts.

Much in the early chapters in Acts focuses on the eschatological reconstitution of Israel. This is displayed in chapters 1–7 by the transformations and restorations that occur in and around Jerusalem. Under persecution in Jerusalem, the gospel begins to spread to those on the margins of Israel, Samaritans (8:4–25) and an Ethiopian eunuch (8:26–40).[12] It seems only a matter of time before the gospel reaches Gentiles. Indeed, there have been numerous foreshadowings of this in Luke/Acts: These include the announcements of Simeon (Luke 2:32; cf. Acts 13:47) and John the Baptist (Luke 3:6), both drawing on Isaiah to proclaim that the gospel of Jesus Christ will inaugurate salvation to the "Gentiles"/"all flesh." According to the resurrected Christ, the scriptures themselves note that repentance and forgiveness of sins in Jesus' name is to be proclaimed to "all nations" (Luke 24:44–7). In addition, the resurrected Christ commissions the disciples to be "my witnesses to the ends of the earth" (Acts 1:8). What comes as no real surprise to readers of Luke/Acts, however, is cloaked in mystery to the central characters of the narrative, particularly Peter.

Chapter 10 relates the initial presentation of the Gospel to the Gentiles. We are introduced to Cornelius, a Roman centurion. Cornelius does much to tie himself to the people of Israel; he "fears God" and prays constantly. "Cornelius is clearly an uncircumcised Gentile (cf. 11:3), yet his piety parallels that of a

---

[12] There is some ambiguity regarding the status of this eunuch. Is he a Jew or a Gentile? This question is of some importance given the clear indication in chapters 10ff. that Cornelius is the first Gentile convert. The text notes that this eunuch was worshipping in Jerusalem (8:27) and that he possessed a scroll with, at least, part of Isaiah on it (8:28). This would indicate that he was a Jew. According to Deut. 23:1 a eunuch could not be a member of the assembly of the Lord. Alternatively, Isa. 56:3 (note that the eunuch is reading from Isa. 53) includes eunuchs who keep the sabbath and keep the covenant among those on the margins of Israel whom God will in no way cut off. Further, Isa. 11:1 mentions Ethiopia as one of the places from which God will gather the "remnant of his people." In the light of these prophetic allusions and given the pattern in Acts of moving out from Jerusalem to those on the margins of Israel, I agree with Luke Johnson (*The Acts of the Apostles* (Collegeville: Michael Glazier, 1992), p. 159) who says, "Whoever the 'historical Ethiopian' might have been, therefore, Luke clearly wants his readers to see him as part of the 'ingathering of the scattered people of Israel'."

devout Jew."[13] In a series of parallel episodes he and Peter are brought into contact.

Cornelius is given a vision as the result of his devotion (10:4). He is told to bring Peter from Joppa to his home in Caesarea. While Cornelius is responding to his vision, Peter is receiving another vision. Peter is clearly perplexed by the vision he receives (10:17). In part he seems to take the vision as a test of his fidelity to food laws. When the voice from heaven replies "What God has made clean you must not call unclean," however, it indicates that the issue here is not Peter's faithfulness. Rather the problem lies with his overly narrow understanding of the terms "common" (κοίνον) and "unclean" (ἀκάθαρτον).[14]

Even if Peter understood this much, it is by no means clear what he is to make of this vision. While he is pondering these things, the men from Cornelius arrive looking for him. Peter does not put this event together with his vision. Instead he has to be prodded by the Spirit not to make any dismissive or over-hasty judgment regarding these men.[15] In line with the Spirit's prompting, Peter welcomes them, shows them hospitality, and agrees to go with them. This welcome is paralleled by the one Cornelius extends to Peter and his companions. In v. 28 Peter makes it clear that by the hospitality he extended in Joppa and the hospitality he accepted at Cornelius' house he has managed, at least partially, to understand the thrust of the vision he saw.[16]

Following Cornelius' account of what God has told him (vv. 30–3), Peter begins his own account of the Gospel. Peter "truly understands" now that the boundaries of God's people are not constrained by racial or ethnic considerations, by human barriers of "clean" and "unclean." Nevertheless, Peter does give his message to this agent of the "pax Romana" an ironic bite, characterizing the gospel as God's message of "peace through Jesus Christ." Peter concludes his message by proclaiming that forgiveness of sins is granted to those who believe. No promises are made regarding the Spirit.

While he is speaking, however, the Spirit descends upon all those listening.

---

[13] See Robert Tannehill, *The Narrative Unity of Luke–Acts*, 2 vols (Minneapolis: Fortress Press, 1990), vol. 2, p. 133. Also F. F. Bruce, *The Acts of the Apostles*, 3rd edn (Grand Rapids: Eerdmans, 1990), p. 252.

[14] B. R. Gaventa, *From Darkness to Light: Aspects of Conversion in the New Testament* (Philadelphia: Fortress Press, 1986), p. 114, notes, "What is at issue between Peter and the voice is not whether Peter eats some particular item for lunch but how he applies the terms 'common' and 'unclean'. His practice is not the subject here, but his assumption that he knows what is clean and what is unclean!"

[15] See my further comments below regarding the use of μηδὲν διακρινόμενος in v.20.

[16] Indeed, I think Gaventa, *From Darkness to Light,* pp. 107ff., is right to indicate that the real conversion here is Peter's not Cornelius'.

They speak in tongues just as those early Jewish followers did in 2:1–4. The fact that even the Gentiles received the gift of the Spirit astonishes Peter's circumcised companions (v. 45). Luke seems to emphasize here that the amazement of those believers of the circumcision (ὁι ἐκ περιτομῆς πιστόι)[17] is focused not on the event of glossolalia but that "the gift of the Holy Spirit has been poured out even on the Gentiles."

It is not yet clear what the full implications of this will be, but it is clear both that God accepts Gentile believers and that God confirms Peter's practice in going to Cornelius. Not only does Peter baptize Cornelius and his household, he accepts their hospitality when they ask him to remain for several days. "Consistent with the entire narrative, this request suggests that the inclusion of Gentiles does not have to do merely with a grudging admission to the circle of the baptized. Including Gentiles means receiving them, entering their homes, and accepting hospitality in those homes."[18]

Indeed, as the story moves into chapter 11, the sticking point seems to be the fact that Peter accepted (and offered) hospitality to "uncircumcised men" (11:3). Ernst Haenchen argued that this emphasis on table fellowship is Luke's attempt to soften a comprehensively hostile reaction by some in Judea to including the Gentiles.[19] As Beverly Gaventa notes, however,

> . . . this interpretation fails to see the pervasive thread of hospitality that runs throughout this narrative. It also overlooks the fact that the inclusion of Gentiles and table-fellowship with Gentiles are inseparably related. To balk at eating with Gentiles is to balk at receiving them into the community.[20]

This emphasis on table fellowship will play a crucial role in my later discussion. It also foreshadows the concerns addressed in the "burdens" placed on Gentile believers in 15:28–9.

What is particularly interesting is the way this dispute is addressed and resolved in 11:2–18. The scene is set when Peter goes up to Jerusalem and is confronted by "those of the circumcision" (ὁι ἐκ περιτομῆς).[21] (Notice the

---

[17] Given the role of these witnesses in 11:2ff. it is more important that we know they are circumcised believers than that we learn their names.

[18] Gaventa, *From Darkness to Light*, p.120.

[19] Ernst Haenchen, *The Acts of the Apostles*, trans. B. Nobel and G. Shinn (Philadelphia: Westminster Press, 1971), p. 354.

[20] Gaventa, *From Darkness to Light*, p. 120.

[21] Just as Peter and John went out from Jerusalem to confirm what was happening with the Gospel in Samaria (8:14–15), here, too, Luke wants to see these events validated by the Jerusalem church (cf. also 11:22). See also Johnson, *Acts*, p. 197.

absence of the adjective πιστόι which is used in 10:45 to characterize "those of the circumcision" who go with Peter to Cornelius' house.) These characters "criticized him" (διεκρίνοντο πρὸς αὐτόν) for eating with un-circumcised men. Of course, διεκρίνομαι is the very thing the Spirit commanded Peter not to do in 10:20.[22] That is, these Jerusalemites are engaging in the very type of hasty and dismissive judgment that Peter was told to avoid.

In response to this judgment, Peter testifies to the things he has seen, both earthly and heavenly (11:4–17). He relates the vision of the sheet lowered down from heaven and the arrival of the men from Caesarea. He includes the Spirit's injunction not to dismiss this matter too quickly (μηδὲν διακρίναντα).[23] He notes that he had six witnesses with him as well. We already know that they are circumcised; their presence counters possible claims that Peter's account is idiosyncratic. Peter continues by relating Cornelius' vision. Without recounting the content of his preaching, Peter cuts to what is the decisive point for him, "And as I began to speak, the Holy Spirit fell upon them just as it had upon us at the beginning" (v. 16). Peter interprets this in the light of Jesus' words foretelling the coming of the Spirit. He then concludes that if God has given the Gentiles the "same gift he gave us when we believed in the Lord Jesus Christ, who was I to hinder God" (v. 17). For Peter, the pouring out of the Spirit upon the Gentiles takes this matter out of his hands. It is the decisive point which convinces him that this is God's doing. To disagree or criticize (διακρίνομαι?) would be hindering God. For Peter's audience, his testimony to the pouring out of the Spirit upon the Gentiles is convincing.

While this seems to settle the issue of whether Gentiles can be included in this body, an issue whose outcome was widely foreshadowed, the question of how and under what conditions Gentiles should be admitted to this Jewish group is left unaddressed.[24]

The Jerusalem community recognizes that the Gentiles have "been given the gift of repentance unto life", but the issue of relations has not been solved . . . . The question whether Gentiles must become Jewish before they can be part of

---

[22] "Luke exploits the polyvalence of *diakrinomai* in a fascinating way. What the Spirit forbade Peter to do toward the Gentiles, namely, 'debate/make distinctions/doubt' (10:20), these fellow Jews are now doing toward him." Johnson, *Acts*, p. 197.

[23] The NRSV translates this occurrence of the phrase as "not to make a distinction between them and us." This reads 11:12 in the light of the more explicit 15:9, which seems unjustified given the explicit use of "between us and them" in 15:9.

[24] As Bruce, *Acts of the Apostles*, p. 270 notes.

the people of God still remains. And if they do not, how can Jewish believers associate with them and still be faithful to God's revelation?[25]

It is not until chapter 15 that this issue is directly confronted. Following this rather intensive examination of one incident running from 10:1–11:18, the narrative advances quickly. The tribulation which began in chapter 8 and was focused in Jerusalem is rejoined. Likewise, this tribulation leads to a further spreading of the Gospel and the establishment of a primarily Gentile church in Antioch.

There seems to be a particularly intense relationship between Jerusalem and Antioch. Jerusalem sends Barnabas to Antioch (from whence he is subsequently passed on to other churches) to supervise and confirm what is going on there. Agabus (also from Jerusalem) predicts a famine, which leads those in Antioch (and elsewhere) to send food to Judea (including Jerusalem). While Jerusalem becomes the locus for persecution, Antioch becomes the locus of a spreading mission to Jews and Gentiles. Finally, having returned to Antioch from what becomes known as the first missionary journey, Paul and Barnabas encounter "certain individuals from Judea," later identified as from Jerusalem (15:24), arguing that Gentiles must be circumcised in order to be saved. Paul and Barnabas disagree so sharply with these unnamed characters that it is agreed that they should go up to Jerusalem to discuss the matter with the "apostles and elders" (15:2).

As they proceed up to Jerusalem they tell stories about the conversion of the Gentiles (15:3). These stories are greeted with great joy, and they remind us that the issue here is not whether Gentiles can turn to God, but whether or not they should be circumcised. As Peter welcomed the men from Cornelius, and was, in turn, welcomed by Cornelius, we read that those from Antioch are welcomed by the church in Jerusalem. What is striking here is that serious disagreement does not rule out hospitality.

At this point in the narrative the issue of whether or not Gentile believers need to be circumcised and keep the law is directly joined. From the perspective of a church made up almost exclusively of Gentiles for nearly two millennia, it may be hard to recognize the merits of the pro-circumcision argument. Nevertheless, it would be fairly consistent for a Jewish follower of Jesus both to recognize Gentiles as capable of receiving the Gospel and simply to assume that they would in other respects become Jewish.

These first followers of Jesus did not see their convictions about Jesus as in any way incompatible or discontinuous with their convictions about

---

[25] Johnson, *Scripture and Discernment*, p. 98.

being the reformed and reconstituted people of Israel. They quite rightly recognized that God was bringing Gentiles into Israel, not that they were going out from Israel to be joined with the Gentiles. Given these presumptions, it seems quite natural to expect Gentiles who join this group to be circumcised and observe the Law. While there are a few exceptional cases, the vast majority of Jews would have simply presumed that joining Israel implied circumcision, and that they had numerous good reasons for thinking this.[26] Further, these reasons are neither obviously nor necessarily negated by faith in Christ. In short, those who proposed circumcision and Torah observance for Gentile believers in Jesus had a strong case. It may even be that Luke considered the arguments here so self-evident that he did not have the characters rehearse them.

The demand for circumcision of Gentile converts in v. 5 starts off a long debate. This debate reaches its climax in three distinct speeches. Peter begins by giving an account of his encounter with Cornelius which focuses primarily on synthetic and systematic judgments rather than on the specific details of his visit to Cornelius.[27] Peter's testimony is, in fact, transformed into God's testimony in v. 8. God has borne witness to the acceptability of the Gentiles by sending the Spirit on them. God has not "discriminated" ($o\mathring{v}\theta\grave{\varepsilon}v\ \delta\iota\acute{\varepsilon}\kappa\rho\iota\nu\varepsilon\nu$) between "us and them." Finally, God has cleansed their hearts.[28] That is, as 10:15 indicated, God has made the Gentiles "clean." By its third telling, it is clear the Peter has caught the importance of the vision he first saw in Joppa. For Peter, the upshot of this is clear. Without requiring circumcision and Torah observance, God has poured out the Spirit on the Gentiles. The Spirit is the decisive marker of God's acceptance. Hence, the fact that the Gentiles have received the same Spirit as the Jewish believers apart from circumcision

---

[26] "Because of the way this story finally ends, it is easy to dismiss these 'legalists' and their position. For us to appreciate the decision that was made, however, it is important to recognize the force of their position. It was theologically respectable. If part of God's revelation consisted in the practice of circumcision as the symbol of entrance into the people (and it did); and if all the previous revelation by God had taught the necessity of keeping the Law to be a full part of the people and receive its blessing (as it surely did); then their statement is neither superficial nor silly. In fact, the weight of evidence would seem to be on their side" (Johnson, *Scripture and Discernment*, p. 101).

[27] Tannehill, *The Narrative Unity of Luke–Acts*, calls this a "distinctly theological" rather than a personal account (vol. 2, p. 184).

[28] In relation to the issue of circumcision, this comment may well echo texts such as Deut. 10:16; Jer. 4:4; Ezek. 44:7 where "circumcision of the heart" is more important than physical circumcision (cf. Col. 2:11). Of course, these texts would have also presumed physical circumcision as well (see also Philo, *Migr.* 92).

indicates that circumcision should not now be required of them. Indeed, he goes so far as to imply that those who do not see things this way are hindering God (v.10).

We are then briefly told about Pauls' and Barnabas' account of the "signs and wonders" God had accomplished among the Gentiles. This testimony confirms that Peter's observations, based on a single encounter with Cornelius, are repeated among the Gentiles more generally.

James then renders his judgment ($\kappa\rho i\nu\omega$) in 15:19. This judgment contrasts both with the hasty and unformed judgment Peter is urged by the Spirit to avoid ($\mu\eta\delta\grave{\epsilon}\nu\ \delta\iota\alpha\kappa\rho\iota\nu\delta\mu\epsilon\nu o\varsigma$) in 10:20, and with the negative judgment ($\delta\iota\epsilon\kappa\rho i\nu o\nu\tau o$) rendered on Peter's actions by "those of the circumcision" in 11:2. Further, in Peter's summary of this event in 15:7–11 he urges his audience to recognize that God does not discriminate ($o\dot{v}\theta\epsilon\nu\ \delta\iota\acute{\epsilon}\kappa\rho\iota\nu\epsilon\nu$) between "us and them." Thus, the only times that $\delta\iota\alpha\kappa\rho i\nu\omega$ appears in Acts are in relation to Peter's visit to Cornelius and subsequent discussions of its significance. The appearance of $\delta\iota\alpha\kappa\rho i\nu\omega$ in Acts ceases with James' use of $\kappa\rho i\nu\omega$ in 15:19, rendering the judgment to which the Spirit has been pointing at least from chapter 10.

James begins by making reference to how Simeon "has related how God first looked favorably upon the Gentiles, to take from them a people for his name." Although I cannot fully argue the point here, I think it is possible to take this reference to Simeon as polyvalent.[29] That is, it should be read as a reference to Simon Peter's comments in vv. 7–11. It also, however, alludes to the words of the prophet Simeon in Luke 2:32, that through Jesus God was causing a light to shine among the Gentiles. Further, James notes that the words written in the prophets agree with these testimonies.[30] This leads to a citation based on Amos 9:11–12.[31] This collocation of individual testimony and scriptural agreement leads James to issue his judgment that the Gentiles need not be circumcised.

James does, however, advocate sending an epistle to the Gentile congregations urging them to avoid certain things. This letter is often referred to as the

---

[29] I offered such a fuller account in "Simeon in Acts 15:14: The Voice of Simon Peter and Echoes of Simeons Past," read to the Literary Criticism and Biblical Criticism section of the Society of Biblical Literature annual meeting in 1995. I hope to publish this study soon.
[30] Johnson, *Scripture and Discernment*, p. 105 and *Acts*, p. 265 stresses that the Greek clearly has the prophets agreeing with the testimony ($\tau o\acute{v}\tau\wp\ \sigma\nu\mu\phi\omega\nu o\tilde{v}\sigma\iota\nu$).
[31] While the citation here is quite close to the LXX of Amos, Richard Bauckham has shown that there are a variety of allusions to other texts here. See "James and the Jerusalem Church," in *The Book of Acts in its Palestinian Setting*, ed. R. Bauckham (Grand Rapids: Eerdmans, 1995), pp. 453–5.

"decrees" of the Apostolic Council. Given that within Acts 15 this list of things to avoid appears three times, each time worded differently from the others, and given the diversity in the textual history of this passage, it seems clear that this "decree" was probably not a single definitive document.[32] Rather, the decree is accompanied by witnesses from both Jerusalem (Judas and Silas) and Antioch (Paul and Barnabas) who are to relate the council's decision "by word of mouth" (15:25–7). This may indicate that the testimony of Paul, Barnabas, Judas, and Silas involves more than mere repetition of a set form of words. There is, no doubt, some interpretive work to be done to apply the "spirit" of the decree in specific contexts.

Without necessarily pinning down the exact wording of the council's decision, there are several elements to be noted that are relevant to my present discussion. First, while it is James who articulates a judgment here, it becomes the basis for a communal consensus. Unlike the abortive moments of διακρίνω which appear earlier in the narrative, James' κρίνω "seems good to the Holy Spirit and all of us." While James' judgment becomes authoritative, it does so because it articulates for the community the sense of the Spirit's work. It is not authoritative simply because James, the leader of the church in Jerusalem, says so.[33]

Further, the constraints imposed on the Gentiles seem to have two functions. First, they enable Jewish and Gentile believers to enjoy a minimal degree of table fellowship without insisting that the Jewish believers funda-

---

[32] For a good summary of the textual and semantic differences here see Johnson, *Acts*, pp. 266–7; also Bruce, *Acts of the Apostles*, pp. 342–4. Recently Peder Borgen has argued that there was no specific decree coming from the Jerusalem council. Instead the upshot of the council was to delete requirements for circumcision from Christian appropriations of the ritual and moral demands of Jewish proselyte traditions. See "Catalogues of Vices, The Apostolic Decree, and the Jerusalem Meeting," in *Early Christianity and Hellenisitic Judaism* (Edinburgh: T. & T. Clark, 1996), pp. 233–51. I am not persuaded by this alternative. Borgen has not established the existence of this Jewish proselyte tradition as an independent entity. In fact, it can only be established by separating moral and ritual demands from the differing theological accounts of God's activity with Israel operative in Judaism and Christianity.

[33] "James makes judgment (*krino*, 15:9), but does not decide alone. The apostles and the elders must agree *with the whole Church* for that decision to be carried (15:22). In fact, it is not enough for the Mother Church to decide the issue unanimously; the local churches who are addressed must also 'rejoice at the consolation' and send the emissaries back 'in peace' for the decision truly to have been reached (15:31, 33). Not only the communication of a decision from on high, but the steady presence in the affected community of prophets who can console and strengthen, teach and preach the word of God, finish off this process of decision-making in Luke's idealized rendition (15:32, 35)." Johnson, *Acts*, p. 84.

mentally compromise their Jewish identity. Given the consistent role that hospitality has played in making this agreement possible, it seems both reasonable and important that any decision on these issues should enhance prospects for table fellowship within these communities of believers.[34] This is also significant, given the importance Paul places on a certain type of "agape" meal for Christian identity (cf. 1 Cor. 11:17–34; Gal. 2:11–14).

Secondly, James bases the conditions to be imposed on the Gentiles, which seem (in whatever form one examines) to draw on Lev.17–18, on the claim that "Moses has those who proclaim him in every city." The point seems to be that "Luke regards these conditions as rooted in Torah, and that Torah's own norms for proselytes and sojourners (Lev. 17:8, 10, 13, 15) would be known already to Gentiles close to the synagogue such as had converted."[35] Although they are not required to be circumcised, Gentile converts are not free simply to live as they please. The work of the Spirit, which sustains the decision not to require circumcision, does not imply that one can ignore scripture. In fact, the process of coming to a decision on this matter, which ultimately is articulated by James, reflects a complex series of interactions between interpretations of the Spirit's work and Spirit-inspired interpretation and application of scripture. Understanding these interactions will be essential for any Christian community if the Spirit is to play a significant role in the interpretation and embodiment of Scripture. It is to these matters that I now turn.

Reading the Spirit as Essential for Reading with the Spirit

Thus far I have relied on John's gospel to provide a trinitarian grounding for the importance of the role of the Spirit in interpreting and embodying scripture. My discussion of Acts 10–15 has presented a specific narrative example of the Spirit's role in a dispute among the earliest followers of Jesus. This dispute involved questions both about how to interpret scripture and about how to interpret the work of the Spirit in displaying the will of God. At this point I will try to state what the narrative only implies about how to recognize, interpret, and act upon the work of the Spirit.

[34] Even if Bauckham ("James and the Jerusalem Church," pp. 460–7) is right that the prohibitions of the "decree" arise out of a complex exegetical approach to Lev. 17–18 rather than pragmatic considerations, it is still the case that these prohibitions would have had the pragmatic result of enhancing the prospects for table fellowship.

[35] Johnson, *Acts*, p. 267.

As Luke Johnson has repeatedly stressed in regard to James' judgment, the interpretation of scripture is guided by the testimony about the Spirit's work, rather than the other way around.

> What is remarkable, however, is that the text is confirmed by the narrative, not the narrative by the Scripture. As Peter had come to a new understanding of Jesus' words because of the gift of the Spirit, so here the Old Testament is illuminated and interpreted by the narrative of God's activity in the present.[36]

As we will also later see with Paul, experience of the Spirit's work provides the lenses through which scripture is read rather than vice-versa. This is perhaps the most significant point the New Testament has to make about the hermeneutical significance of the Spirit; this point runs against the grain of modern interpretive presumptions. Nevertheless, we should not treat the pattern of the priority of Spirit experience to scriptural interpretation as an abstract hermeneutical rule. On the one hand, Johnson's observations – along with Richard Hays' parallel ones, which appear in the next chapter – are a useful corrective to the presumption that in the New Testament exegesis according to abstract principles shapes the way the work of the Spirit is understood. On the other hand, seeking to demonstrate the priority of either Spirit experience or exegesis is to bind oneself to false alternatives. The pattern of reading scripture found in Acts and elsewhere in the New Testament cannot be easily or profitably separated from the very specific types of ecclesial contexts in which that reading takes place. As my overview of Acts 10–15 has indicated, the Spirit's activity is no more self-interpreting than a passage of scripture is. Understanding and interpreting the Spirit's movement is a matter of communal debate and discernment over time. This debate and discernment is itself often shaped both by prior interpretations of scripture and by traditions of practice and belief. This means that in practice it is probably difficult, if not impossible, to separate and determine clearly whether a community's scriptural interpretation is prior to or dependent upon a community's experience of the Spirit. Experience of the Spirit shapes the reading of scripture, but scripture most often provides the lenses through which the Spirit's work is perceived and acted upon. Even here the notion of an "experience of the Spirit" should not be taken as a reference to an internal mental transaction, immediately perceived and understood by isolated individuals. I will say more about this in the next chapter.

The difficulty, if not impossibility, of clearly separating moments of scriptural interpretation from moments of interpretation of the Spirit's activity

---

[36] Johnson, *Scripture and Discernment*, p. 105.

is not a reason simply to dissolve or subsume reflection and debate about the Spirit into reflection and debate over scripture. Such a reduction will leave us merely paying lip-service to the hermeneutical significance of the Spirit. Instead, if Christians are to follow the examples found in Acts 10–15 and read scripture with the Spirit, that is, as the Spirit reads, then it will be essential to learn to read the Spirit, to discern what the Spirit is doing. In this section I would like to point out several practices, habits, and structures related to the specific contexts of Acts 10–15 which appear to be crucial for the characters' abilities to discern what the Spirit is doing and to act upon this discernment.

It is clear that in both Acts 11 and 15 Peter's testimony (among others') that Gentiles had received the Spirit upon hearing the Gospel is the primary component persuading those in favor of Gentile circumcision that this was not necessary.[37] It is perhaps not surprising to claim that both the practice of testifying or bearing witness and the practice of listening wisely to such testimony are essential to a community's ability to "read the Spirit."[38]

From law courts to shows such as Donohue and Oprah, we can find numerous types of utterances which might count as testimony. In fact, it may well be that our society and our churches are overrun with "testimony" of one sort or another. There are, however, several distinguishing features about the practice of testifying in Acts 10–15 that separate this type of speaking from both the adversarial nature of a law court and the self-promotional context of a television talk-show.

First, it is testimony about the Spirit by those who are already recognized as people of the Spirit. Peter stresses that God has poured out the same Spirit on the Gentiles as he and his fellow Jews had received. It is the Gentiles' reception of this same gift, apart from circumcision, that is ultimately decisive here. The basis for Peter's claim is his, and his fellow Jews', prior reception of the same Spirit. In the next chapter I will say more about the importance of the character of the one who claims to interpret the Spirit's work. For now, it is sufficient to note that Peter's status as one who already knows the Spirit lends weight to his testimony about the Spirit's work in the lives of others. It may well be the case, then, that giving testimony about the Spirit is not something that normally can be done well by just anybody. Testimony about

---

[37] As will become clear in the next chapter's discussion of Galatians, Peter seems to change his mind. My points about Peter in Acts are separable from Galatians and discussions about the historical Peter.

[38] Tannehill's comment (*The Narrative Unity of Luke–Acts*, vol. 2, p. 130) regarding 10:1–11:18 is applicable to the entirety of this section, "Study of the composition of the narrative also reveals another important factor in discernment of the will of God: the sharing of divine promptings with other persons."

the Spirit's work in others tends to be done best by those who have experienced the Spirit's work themselves.

While noting that those who are recognized as people of the Spirit are likely to be the best ones to testify about the Spirit's work, it is also crucial to note that Peter's testimony is in two crucial respects not *his* testimony. That is, there are two respects in which Peter is not the subject of his testimony. First, Peter's testimony is not so much about what he has done as what he has seen God doing. In the various accounts he offers, Peter makes it plain that the inclusion of the Gentiles is not his pet project; rather it is the work of God. This is made most clear in 15:8 when he claims that God has testified (ἐμαρτύρσεν) to the "cleansed hearts" of the Gentiles by "giving them the Holy Spirit." Here God not only becomes the subject of Peter's testimony, but the primary witness to it as well.[39]

The second respect in which Peter's testimony is not strictly his testimony concerns the fact that his account is not so much about what God has done to him (although that figures in passages such as 10:34) as about what God had done to others. Peter's testimony is not about himself and his experience of the Spirit. Rather the subject of Peter's testimony is the work of the Spirit in the lives of others. Moreover, in the case of the visit to Cornelius, Peter's testimony is attested to by "those of the circumcision" who went with him from Joppa to Caesarea.

To be able to read the Spirit well, Christians must not only become and learn from people of the Spirit, we must also become practiced at testifying about what the Spirit is doing in the lives of others. In our present age, which favors self-authentication above all else, we may find it hard to recognize this as a crucial element in testimony about the Spirit's work. One example of this might be found in the emphasis in so much work in contemporary pastoral care and group process on getting people to make "I statements." Presumably the intentions here are to keep people focused on what they know and, thus, to shield their comments from certain sorts of criticisms. Nevertheless, this emphasis seems to contribute to moving us further and further away from a situation in which we might be expected to render an account of what the Spirit is doing in the lives of others – let alone articulate the type of judgment James does, which then becomes the basis for communal consensus.

Both ecclesially and socially we can become so isolated from others that when we must make judgments about scripture, about our common life, or

---

[39] See also Peter's claim in 5:32, "And we are witnesses of these things, and so is the Holy Spirit whom God has given to those who obey him."

about others, we have little recourse but to rely on the self-authenticating testimony of virtual strangers or merely to repeat the practices, demands, and strictures we have used before. This is not to say that we should always innovate, ignoring or actively transgressing past convictions and commitments. At the Jerusalem Council past commitments and convictions are articulated and applied in what seems to be an obvious way – Gentiles joining this Jewish body must be circumcised and obey Torah. The burden of proof seems to lie with those who would innovate. In response, Peter (along with Paul and Barnabas) testifies to the work of the Spirit in the lives of Gentile converts, interpreting this work in such a way that indicates that God does not demand circumcision. James articulates a judgment that both accounts for the Spirit's creative movement and, by means of both his scriptural citation and reliance on the Torah-based practical "burdens" to be placed on the Gentiles, aims to retain both long-range continuity with God's work among the people of Israel and practical continuity exhibited in a unified table fellowship.

Of course, such continuities are always contestable matters of interpretation. There are no guarantees that our attempts to follow the Spirit will always result in belief, practice, and worship that faithfully continue the life of the people of God. Christians can hope in God's providential care. This, however, cannot be an excuse for inaction. Moreover, as I have already noted, simply repeating what has been done before will not insure fidelity. Changing historical circumstances will change the significance, meaning, and effects of traditional words and practices whether we like it or not. Christians have no choice but to struggle, argue, and debate with one another over how best to extend our faith, worship, and practice in the present and into the future while remaining true to our past. In this struggle, testimony about the Spirit's work in the lives of others must become as central to contemporary Christians as it was to the characters in Acts.

The only way to counter the privatizing tendencies of contemporary church life, which make it unlikely or impossible that Christians would be in a position to testify about the work of the Spirit in the lives of their sisters and brothers, is to enter into friendships with them. There are at least two respects in which the practice of testifying depends upon Christians' abilities both to overcome their tendencies towards isolation and to nurture and sustain certain types of friendships. First, no matter how acute our spiritual insight, we will not be able to detect the Spirit's work in the lives of others unless we know them in more than superficial ways. While the narrative of Acts 10–15 is quite compressed, we still get a hint of the importance of forming particular sorts of friendships through the brief but significant announcements of hospitality and welcome being extended. When they finally meet, Cornelius is not exactly a stranger to Peter. Those sent to Joppa to find Peter informed him (testified?) about Cornelius. They stayed with Peter and traveled from Joppa to Caesarea together. Cornelius, too, extends hospitality to Peter. Initially, we must assume that Peter would have called Cornelius "unclean." In the course of directly encountering him and speaking the good news to Cornelius in his home, Peter is able to recognize the Spirit being poured out on Cornelius and his household and to come to see the practical significance of this in regard to all Gentile converts. We do not know if Peter would have called Cornelius a friend. We do know that Peter did not consider him some alien element who can only be labeled "unclean." Further, when Paul, Barnabas, and the others from Antioch arrive in Jerusalem they are welcomed and experience the hospitality of Christians there (15:4). Moreover, the "burdens" placed on the Gentiles seem primarily directed towards allowing Jewish and Gentile followers of Jesus to sit at table together. Throughout this narrative the offering and receiving of hospitality always seems to be in the background supporting and enabling the sorts of friendships that allow Christians with differing convictions to listen together to the voice of the Spirit.

Secondly, the formation of friendships is crucial to Christians' abilities to be wise hearers of testimony. I will say more about this in the next chapter regarding Paul and the churches in Galatia. In the case of Acts, it seems likely that Peter's relationships with the various parties whom he confronts in Jerusalem affect the ways in which his testimony is received. We are more likely to respond wisely to the testimony of someone we know. Unlike the adversarial nature of a law court, where we look for jurors who do not have connections to either the defendant or witnesses, wise listening in the church is usually founded on friendships between witnesses and listeners.

Even within the context of specific friendships, which can sustain and act upon testimony about the Spirit's work, discerning the work of the Spirit takes time.[40] It is only on the third time of reflecting on the events surrounding his visit to Cornelius that Peter comes to the conclusion that the upshot of God pouring out the Spirit on Gentiles apart from their circumcision indicates that the church should not require that Gentile converts become Jews as well. Even for the most insightful testifiers, and for the wisest listeners, interpreting the Spirit so that one can interpret with the Spirit demands patience, or what Luke

---

[40] L. Gregory Jones has provided an important homiletical meditation on this point in "Taking Time for the Spirit," *The Christian Century* (April 29, 1992), p. 451.

Johnson calls "the asceticism of attentiveness."[41] More basically, simply forming the friendships needed to be able to detect, much less interpret, the Spirit's work in the life of another is time consuming. Rushing into judgments risks lapsing into the patterns of discrimination characterized in Acts by the use of διακρίνω as opposed to the κρίνω offered by James which "seems good to the Holy Spirit and to us." It is only within communities that both sustain and nurture certain types of friendship and exhibit patience in discernment that we will find the sort of consensus emerging that is narrated in Acts. I am not claiming that such consensus is always necessary. In fact, without the communal friendships and patience needed to testify to the work of the Spirit, Christians should not really expect such consensus to emerge. In such cases, however, the remedy is not further reflection on the processes needed to achieve consensus, but more fundamental revisions to a common life that is not yet adequate to consensus-forming. As an illustration of this I want to turn to a set of issues that currently occupy many American churches.

Thus far, I have argued that close study of Acts 10–15 provides crucial insights into the hermeneutical significance of the Spirit. This narrative (among other passages) indicates that if Christians are to interpret with the Spirit, they will also need to learn how to interpret the Spirit. Further, our prospects for interpreting the Spirit are closely linked to our proficiency at testifying to the Spirit's work, particularly the Spirit's work in the lives of others. Such testimony depends on the forming and sustaining of friendships in which our lives are opened to others in ways that display the Spirit's working. Welcoming strangers and the extension of hospitality become building blocks for such friendships. Finally, building such friendships, becoming people of the Spirit, and recognizing and interpreting the work of the Spirit all take time and demand patience from us. I would now like to turn to two recent attempts to read a contemporary ecclesial interpretive dispute – the role and status of homosexual Christians – through Acts 10–15. While these proposals open up promising options, they also point out how difficult it is to attempt to read with the Spirit in the absence of the ecclesial practices that enable us to read the Spirit.

Homosexual Christians and Gentile Inclusion

Over the past 15 years or so, all of the mainline churches have engaged in discussion and debate over the role and status of homosexual persons in the

---

[41] See "Debate and Discernment, Scripture and the Spirit," *Commonweal* (January 28, 1994), pp. 11–13. This is now part of *Scripture and Discernment*, p. 144.

church.[42] Despite the differences in these debates there are at least two elements that always seem to be evident. First, aside from the subject-matter, the public discussion and debate closely resembles the most bitter partisan political debates one might hear on the floor of Congress, though members of Congress tend to be a bit more charitable to their opponents. The debates are adversarial, divisive, and acrimonious; there is an absence of interpretive charity; posturing prevails over persuasion, lending credence to Alasdair MacIntyre's claim that politics in liberal democracies (such as most churches aim to be) is civil war carried out by other means.[43]

Secondly, there are always appeals to and/or discussions about scripture. This, of course, is as it should be. The focus of these discussions is almost always of the sort "What (if anything) does the Bible say about homosexuality?" Typically, texts such as Gen. 1–2, 19 (Sodom and Gomorrah); Lev. 18:22, 20:13; Rom. 1:26–7; 1 Cor. 6:9, and 1 Tim. 1:10 become the focus for debate. As those who have studied this issue will attest, there is an abundance of scholarly and popular literature on these passages and how they should be read. While there are several exegetical questions surrounding these passages, the real issues seem to focus on which, if any, of these texts are most apposite to our present situation.

Recently, two New Testament scholars have proposed that the most apposite text for discussing the role and status of homosexuals within the church is Acts 10–15. In what follows, I would like to examine this move further. My discussion here about the possible analogical extension of Acts 10–15 to address contemporary debates about homosexuality within the church should not be taken as a full-fledged argument about the subject. Even if one is persuaded about the relevance of Acts 10–15 to this issue, there are still a number of outstanding issues that would need to be addressed. For my purposes, I will focus on those who have recently argued that Acts 10–15 is particularly important for this debate.

In a brief article which first appeared in *Commonweal*, Luke Johnson has raised the possibility that just as experience of the Spirit in Acts convinced someone like Peter to argue for Gentile inclusion without circumcision, so

---

[42] In general I am not persuaded that there is a single issue called "homosexuality" about which Christians must have a position. (On this point see Stanley Hauerwas, "Gay Friendship: A Thought Experiment in Catholic Moral Theology," *Irish Theological Quarterly* [forthcoming].) My purposes here are primarily concerned with these issues as they involve scriptural interpretation.

[43] See *After Virtue*, 2nd edn (Notre Dame: University of Notre Dame Press, 1984), p. 253. I think, however, that Jeffrey Stout is right to note that civil war carried out by other means is still preferable to real civil war.

recognition of the Spirit's work in the lives of homosexual Christians might lead the church to re-consider the moral status of homosexuality.[44] In regard to Acts, Johnson notes,

> On the basis of this experience of God's work, the church made bold to reinterpret Torah, finding there unexpected legitimation for its fidelity to God in surprising ways (Acts 15:15–18) How was that work of God made known to the church? Through the narratives of faith related by Paul and Barnabas and Peter, their personal testimony of how "signs and wonders" had been worked among the Gentiles (Acts 15:4, 6–11, 12–13).[45]

Johnson concludes his essay by asking whether there are narratives of homosexual holiness, analogous to the narratives of Gentile holiness related by Peter, Paul, and Barnabas, to which the church ought to begin listening. Such testimonies might lead the church to raise the question, "Is homosexual covenantal love according to the 'mind of Christ', an authentic realization of that Christian identity authored by the Holy Spirit, and therefore 'authored' as well by the Scripture despite the 'authorities' speaking against it?"[46]

Johnson rightly emphasizes the role of testimony in the church's decision-making in Acts. Further, I agree that any analogous application of Acts 10–15 to issues of homosexual inclusion will need to be grounded in testimonies of "homosexual holiness." Johnson's comments, however, indicate that the burden of providing such testimony is on homosexual Christians. This is a departure from the testifying practices of Acts. It is crucial that Peter, Paul, and Barnabas were all circumcised Jews testifying about the work of the Spirit in the lives of uncircumcised Gentile believers. It is not the responsibility of the Gentiles to provide testimony to their own reception of the Spirit. It should not, then, be the responsibility of homosexual Christians to provide "narratives of homosexual holiness." Instead, the onus is on other Christians who may enter (or have already entered) into friendships with homosexual Christians out of which they might offer testimony of their friends' holiness. Alternatively, it may be the case that such friendships generate calls to repentance from one friend to another.[47] Several things need to be said in this regard. First, the point of such friendships is not simply to be able to make inquiries and judgments about the sexual practices of another

---

[44] Johnson, *Scripture and Discernment*, p. 145.

[45] Johnson, *Scripture and Discernment*, p. 147.

[46] Johnson, *Scripture and Discernment*, p. 148.

[47] I gather this might be the force of the story Richard Hays tells in his essay, "Awaiting the Redemption of Our Bodies," *Sojourners* 20 (July 1991), pp. 17–21.

person. Friendships are not to be a form of field work from which one can then make judgments about others. That is, like all friendships between Christians, these friendships are to be marked by the habits, practices, and dispositions that enable friends to deepen their communion with each other and with God. Through prayer, conversation, argument, tears, and laughter, these friendships are to be part of the transformations that God seeks to work in both friends' lives, conforming them ever more nearly into the image of Christ. Christian friends both assist in each others' struggles to live faithfully before God and exemplify for each other the shape of faithful living in particular contexts.[48] Of course, and perhaps most importantly, this cannot happen in the absence of habits of hospitality. That is, Christians have no reason to think they understand how the Holy Spirit weighs in on the issue of homosexuality until they welcome homosexuals into their homes and sit down to eat with them.

Jeffrey Siker, a New Testament scholar and Presbyterian minister, offers this sort of testimony in a recent essay.[49] Having surveyed various analogies used to situate homosexual Christians within the church, Siker argues, "I believe a more appropriate constructive analogy . . . is to view homosexual Christians today in the same way the earliest (that is, Jewish) Christians approached the issue of including Gentile Christians within the community."[50]

As Siker rightly notes, Acts initially indicates that for the earliest Jewish Christians (and all other Jews), Gentiles *qua* Gentiles could not be members of the people of Israel, even the eschatologically reconstituted Israel represented by the followers of Jesus. Gentiles were, by definition, unclean, as

---

[48] "By spending time together with people who are good, by sharing and delighting with them in our mutual love for the good we are more fully impressed with the good ourselves. Friendship is not just a relationship; it is a moral enterprise. People spend their lives together doing good because that is what they see their lives to be." Paul Wadell, C.P., *Friendship and the Moral Life* (Notre Dame: University of Notre Dame Press, 1989), p. 62. See also Hauerwas, "Gay Friendship," for a further account of the moral significance of friendship.

[49] "Homosexuals, The Bible and Gentile Inclusion," *Theology Today* 51 (July 1994), pp. 219–34.

[50] Siker, "Homosexuals, The Bible . . . ," p. 229. Christopher Seitz in a long footnote attacks Siker's article on several fronts. See "Human Sexuality Viewed from the Bible's Understanding of the Human Condition," *Theology Today* 52 (July 1995), p. 240 n.3. One of Seitz's points is that attempts to justify homosexual practice as simply a natural inclination that must be allowed in the loving community of Jesus' followers despite explicit prohibitions against it, both run counter to Jesus' own practice and leave one in the position of adopting a supersessionist approach to the Old Testament. Siker's position, however, need not entail the claim that Christians should always be free to follow their natural inclinations.

attested by Peter in Acts 10.[51] "And yet the experiences of Peter and Paul led them, and eventually many others, to the realization that even as a Gentile one could come to know God, worship God, and to receive and show the Spirit of God."[52] Siker recognizes that for the earliest Christians, the decisive argument for including the Gentiles as Gentiles is the recognition (through the testimony of Peter in particular) that God's Spirit had been poured out on the Gentiles. In this light, Siker goes on to "confess:"

> Before I came to know various Christians who are also homosexual in their sexual orientation, I was like the hard-nosed doctrinaire circumcised Jewish Christians who denied that Gentiles could receive the Spirit of Christ as Gentiles. But just as Peter's experience of Cornelius in Acts 10 led him to realize that even Gentiles were receiving God's Spirit, so my experience of various gay and lesbian Christians has led me to realize that these Christians have received God's Spirit as gays and lesbians, and the reception of the Spirit has nothing to do with sexual orientation.[53]

In a footnote to this quote, Siker relates that it was a particular friendship with a gay Christian which brought this home to him. In the light of my earlier comments on Acts 10–15, it strikes me that this note should have played a more central role in Siker's argument. It is the one point where he gives specific testimony to the presence of the Spirit in the life of a particular homosexual Christian.

There is much in Siker's argument I have not addressed here. Further, I am not sure the conclusions that follow from seeing issues surrounding homosexual Christians as analogous to issues surrounding Gentile inclusion in Acts are as clear and straightforward as Siker thinks. For example, there is a built-in ambiguity in the notion of including Gentiles as Gentiles that would need to

---

[51] Here it is important to note that although Siker's wording is ambiguous, a charitable account of his position would take his claims about the "earliest Christians'" views about Gentiles to be fairly straightforward inferences and deductions based on what Seitz would have to call a "plain sense" reading of Acts 1–11. Seitz, alternatively, reads Siker's claims about the "earliest Christians" to be an attempt to set up an original moment as a sort of straw figure which is then easily undermined from a modern perspective. As Seitz notes, this would be a mistake. This is not the only way to read Siker's claims, however.

[52] Siker, "Homosexuals, The Bible . . . ," p. 230.

[53] Siker, "Homosexuals, The Bible . . . ," p. 230. The final clause of the quote, "the reception of the Spirit has nothing to do with sexual orientation," deserves some comment. If all Siker means by this is that the reception of the Spirit is not dependent upon one's sexual orientation, then his point is clear and follows well from his previous argument. If he means reception of the Spirit has no bearing on one's sexual orientation and practice, then one would have to say that this is not a claim justified by the evidence he cites.

be clarified in any attempt to draw analogies between Acts 10–15 and the present. On the one hand, being a Gentile simply designates a non-Jew. In this sense, by accepting Gentiles as Gentiles, the first followers of Jesus did not require these non-Jews to become Jews. On the other hand, the designation "Gentile" could also implicate one in a host of unacceptable practices such as idolatry which needed to be abandoned upon entering the church (cf. Eph. 2). These practices seem to be in view in the "burdens" placed on Gentiles in Acts 15:19–21. In this respect, Gentiles were not straightforwardly accepted as Gentiles.[54] Leaving these issues aside for the moment, I do have to say that Siker has opened up a new avenue in this debate, drawing some promising analogies that might allow us beyond our present sterile, if not acrimonious debates.

The obvious question one must ask is how does one know that God's Spirit has been poured out on homosexual believers?[55] It is at this point that Siker's argument begins to wind down. Rather than focus on his own testimony of witnessing the work of the Spirit in the life of a homosexual friend, Siker begins to tackle this question by drawing an analogy to the way Paul in Gal. 3 addresses this same issue of whether Gentile believers need to be circumcised and obey Torah:

> Paul calls upon them, and us, to pay attention to their experience of the Spirit.
> Did they recognize the Spirit through a doctrinal orthodoxy and orthopraxy

[54] In his recent book, *The Moral Vision of the New Testament* (San Francisco: Harper San Francisco, 1996) Richard Hays briefly addresses Johnson's and Siker's arguments, calling them "richly suggestive" (p. 396), but ultimately rejecting them until such time as those advocating this view can (as Paul does with the issue of Gentile inclusion) offer readings of scripture to show that "this development can be understood as a fulfillment of God's design for human sexuality as previously revealed in Scripture" (p. 399). Hays is skeptical that such a reading can be offered. It may well be the case, however, that there is more scope here than Hays thinks. First, as Hays himself knows, Paul's readings of scripture were quite audacious and ran against what most would consider to be the preponderance of scriptural testimony. Secondly, Hays may have artificially prejudiced the matter by requiring such readings that fit into God's design for human sexuality. Christians need to remember that "human sexuality" is a modern notion that may include a variety of assumptions and presuppositions that fit badly with Christian convictions about God's design for humans and creation. If this is the case, then there may be ways of reading scripture that fit certain types of relationships and practices which we now cover under the term "homosexuality" within an account of God's economy in ways that do not fit under the description "human sexuality."

[55] Towards the end of the essay Siker raises these very questions very briefly. Unfortunately, he does not really tie these issues together with his own testimony about he role of the Spirit in his friend's life. Nor does he explore ways in which these questions are addressed in the narrative of Acts 10–15.

now being called for by troublemakers who insisted that the only good Gentile was a "Jewish Gentile"? Or did they recognize the Spirit through their faith? And so today we are called to ask an analogous question: Despite our experience, do we insist that homosexual Christians can only have the Spirit of God if they are "heterosexual homosexual" Christians? Or with Peter and Paul are we up to the challenge of recognizing, perhaps with surprise and with humility, that even gay and lesbian Christians, as gays and lesbians and not as sinners, have received the Spirit in faith?[56]

I will address the specifics of Galatians 3:1–5 in the next chapter. For now, I want to note that Siker's conclusion here is underdeveloped. Spirit experience, in both the New Testament and the present, is not self-interpreting. It is often quite difficult to read the Spirit.[57] As I have already indicated, as related in Acts, the very manner in which the Gentiles were included as full members of the people of God presupposes a whole set of ecclesiological practices which are largely absent from Christianity in the US. Most churches do not train and nurture people in forming the sorts of friendships out of which testimony about the Spirit's work might arise. Moreover, Christians are generally suspicious about claims concerning the Spirit; we are not generally a people who either testify well or listen wisely to the testimony of others. We largely favor self-authentication and despise common patterns of discernment. We abhor the notion that our lives ought to be disciplined by a concern for one another. In short, most Christian communities lack the skills and resources to debate what a life marked by the Spirit might look like in the present. In the absence of these ecclesial practices and structures one cannot be hopeful that most Christian churches will be able to follow Siker's proposal here without replicating the same sorts of indecisive, divisive, and acrimonious debates that have already marked discussion of this issue. In short, Siker's essay nicely illustrates that reading with the Spirit cannot be done apart from reading the Spirit's work. Further, it provides a sort of testimony to the work of God in the lives of homosexual Christians. What it falls short of recognizing, however, is that Christians cannot aspire to either of these apart from forming and nurturing certain types of common life.

[56] Siker, "Homosexuals, The Bible . . . ," p. 234.

[57] In response to comments I made to Siker on this essay, he added some comments recognizing the difficulties in recognizing Spirit reception both in Acts and in the present when the essay was reprinted in *Homosexuality in the Church: Both Sides of the Debate*, ed. J. Siker (Louisville: Westminster/John Knox Press 1994), pp. 178–94. These additional comments did not change the substance of his argument.

It should be clear that my reservations about Siker's argument are different from those raised by Christopher Seitz in his attack on Siker's position. The most important claim Seitz makes is that one cannot invoke the Spirit to override the "plain sense" of Old Testament texts without taking a supersessionist view of the Old Testament. Although he does not give a comprehensive list, on Seitz's view the texts whose "plain sense" is threatened by Siker's approach would be those texts forbidding sex outside of marriage and those prohibiting same-sex sexual contact. Seitz seems to miss the point of Acts 10–15. It seems quite clear that the initial presumptions of the characters in Acts are that the "plain sense" of texts such as Gen. 17:9–14 demands that Gentiles joining themselves to the people of Israel must be circumcised. It is recognition of the Spirit's work through the testimony of Peter, Paul, and Barnabas that leads James to invoke Amos 9:9–12 as part of a decision to include Gentiles without forcing them to be circumcised.[58] I will address more fully the question of whether or not this counts as a supersessionist approach to the Old Testament in the next chapter. For now let me simply say that I do not think it is supersessionist in any sense of that term that might lead Christians to opt for something like Marcion's approach to this issue. It does, however, raise again the sharp issue about how compatible a static notion of the "plain sense" of scripture, a plain sense located in the text rather than the believing community, is with Christian theological approaches to the Old Testament.[59]

Conclusion

Thus far, I have argued that Christians have every reason to expect the Spirit to play a role in scriptural interpretation. Based on a reading of John's

[58] Seitz's claim that in Acts 13:47 Paul uses Isa. 49:6 to justify going to the Gentiles *qua* Gentiles is simply inaccurate. Paul uses Isa. 49:6 to justify going to the Gentiles in the light of rejection by the Jews in Psidian Antioch. This passage is completely silent about whether these Gentiles should become Jews upon hearing the gospel. It is only the Spirit's work that resolves this question later.

[59] This is what I take to be the difference between Frei's and Tanner's notion of the "plain sense" (discussed in chapter 1) and the view Seitz lays out by implication. I think the fact that Seitz is a professional Old Testament scholar and the fact that Frei was and Tanner is a theologian accounts for much of this difference. This raises the further question of the extent to which one can simultaneously function as a professional scholar of the Old Testament and as a Christian theologian. See further Jon Levenson's *The Hebrew Bible, The Old Testament and Historical Criticism* (Louisville: Westminster/John Knox Press, 1993).

comments on the Spirit, it is clear that the role that the Spirit plays and the interpretation the Spirit enables will faithfully display the will of the triune God. Even in a case like John 12:16, it is evident that Spirit-inspired interpretation is going to involve innovative re-readings of scriptural texts in the light of the life, death, and resurrection of Jesus. The issue of the inclusion of the Gentiles in Acts 10–15 gives a more detailed account of Spirit-directed interpretation. This narrative makes it clear that if Christians are to read with the Spirit (as they agree they must) then they must also become adept at reading the Spirit's activity in their midst. The good working of this process depends on Christians' abilities both to testify to the work of the Spirit in the lives of others and to listen wisely to such testimony. These abilities are directly related to the forming and maintaining (through acts of hospitality) of certain types of friendships.

I then examined some attempts to bring the patterns of reasoning related in Acts 10–15 to bear on the contemporary issue of how and under what circumstances homosexuals are to be recognized and included in the church. These attempts will fail as long as the ecclesial practices of forming friendships through acts of hospitality which then enable Christians to testify about the work of the Spirit are in disrepair.

At this point there are still several questions about how Spirit experience and Spirit-inspired interpretation might be connected to each other. In this chapter I have focused on how reading the Spirit and reading with the Spirit are connected to specific structures in the common life of Christian communities. In addition to these, it is also clear that both reading the Spirit and reading with the Spirit involve individuals in acts of interpretive power. In the next chapter I want to explore the nature of this interpretive power and its close connection to the character of the interpreter.

Chapter Five

WHO CAN READ ABRAHAM'S STORY?

Introduction

In the previous chapter I sought to display the complex interactions between the ways in which the Spirit guides and directs Christian interpretation of scripture and the ways in which Christians come to interpret the work of the Spirit. Christians' abilities and successes in reading with the Spirit and reading the Spirit depend on their participation in a particular set of practices related to being able to offer and listen to testimony about the work of the Spirit. These practices are maintained by the friendships that Christians are able to form and sustain.

These matters were all presented against the backdrop of a dispute within the first Christian communities concerning how and under what circumstances Gentiles were to be included in the church, related in Acts 10–15. I also made some observations and suggestions about how the issues addressed in this passage might bear on discussions about the role and status of homosexuals within the church.

In this chapter I wish to build on the work of the previous chapter by further displaying the interactions between interpretations about the work of the Spirit and interpretation of scripture as seen in the particular disputes addressed in Galatians. There Paul offers both an incisive interpretation of the work of the Spirit in the Galatian congregations and a dramatic and unconventional interpretation of a variety of scriptural texts. Paul powerfully reads both the Galatians' experience of the Spirit and the story of Abraham to argue that Gentile Christians in Galatia need not be circumcised and take on the yoke of Torah. Ultimately, I want to argue that Paul justifies his powerful interpretive moves in Gal. 3–4 by means of an account of his character which he renders in Gal. 1–2. This will lead to a discussion of the importance of the character of the interpreter, an issue as vitally important for Christian interpretation of scripture as it is irrelevant for professional biblical scholars. The issue of the character of the interpreter will be particularly important in any consideration of whether and how contemporary Christians might interpret scripture like Paul does.

Prior to turning to Galatians, however, it will be important to address some other issues arising from the end of the previous chapter. These concern more general questions about Christians' relationship to the Old Testament, particularly in the light of my claims about the role of the Spirit in interpretation.

To Supersede or Not to Supersede?

Towards the end of the previous chapter I noted that Christopher Seitz charged Jeffrey Siker's account of Acts 10–15 with being supersessionist. In general, the vast variety of ways this term can be used renders it less than helpful as a description of any particular pattern of reading. Instead, both within the academy and most contemporary churches, to call an interpretive proposal "supersessionist" is to invoke a term of abuse.[1] It is not necessarily, however, to claim anything significant. In particular, as Seitz uses the term he seems to mean that Siker reduces "the plain sense of the Old Testament to an ancient teaching in need of repair by a new word from the spirit-filled community."[2] Without returning to the specifics of Acts 10–15, I should simply reiterate that it would appear that the "plain sense" of Old Testament texts regarding membership in the people of Israel indicates that circumcision (among other things) is mandatory.[3] The text of Acts makes it clear, however, that those involved in these matters struggled seriously with the issue of how Gentiles were to be included in the church. They did not treat their scripture as an "ancient teaching in need of repair by a new word from the spirit-filled community." Rather, they related scriptural texts with testimonies about the Spirit's work in complex ways to develop a position that "seemed good to the Holy Spirit and to us." If this counts as supersession, so be it. It is clearly not marcionite nor would it support any form of persecution of Jews.

---

[1] By implication one may (or may not) seek to connect the "supersessionist" to a pattern of interpretation and practice that would ultimately (if not intentionally) underwrite the persecution of Jews.

[2] C. Seitz, "Human Sexuality viewed from the Bible's Understanding of the Human Condition," *Theology Today* 52 (July 1995), p. 240 n.3.

[3] As will be clear shortly, this seems to be the view of Paul's opponents in Galatia.

Nevertheless, it may be useful at this point to clarify further how an emphasis on reading with the Spirit such as I have argued for here leads me to regard the Old Testament. Rather than discuss this issue in terms of supersession, I will try to lay out a variety of interpretive habits and presumptions that Christians must seek to avoid, along with some convictions they need to maintain.

Christians must avoid the presumption that the Old Testament is radically discontinuous with God's activity in Jesus and the church. As Paul rightly understood in Romans, the "righteousness of God" is at stake here. A god who could make promises to Abraham and the people of Israel, promises within which the gospel writers clearly situate Jesus, and who could then abandon those promises in favor of something new called the church, is not a god to be trusted. Nevertheless, as we shall soon see, the continuities constructed within the New Testament are often quite surprising, relying on what would have been very unconventional interpretations of certain texts. What was crucial for Paul, for example, and must remain crucial for Christians, is the commitment to struggle with the Old Testament rather than eliminate it from the canon.

Neither, however, does the significance of the Old Testament simply reside in its capacity to point to Christ. If this were the case, then upon Christ's arrival, there would be little further need for the "pointer." The character of the God whom Jesus calls "father" is rendered in the Old Testament and Christians will cut themselves off from that God should they treat the Old Testament as in any way superfluous. Further, the story of Israel with which the church must see itself in substantial continuity is laid out in the Old Testament. Christians would needlessly truncate their identity by failing to attend to this story. In short, the Old Testament both renders the character of the God of Abraham, Sarah, Moses, Zipporah, and Jesus and helps shape the identity of the church. Any approach to the Old Testament which abandons these considerations must be avoided.

Indeed, it was precisely this diligent concern with the Old Testament that created the dilemmas worked out in Acts 10–15. The earliest Christians showed no desire to abandon their convictions about their scripture, what is now the Old Testament. Just as clearly, however, they came to revise and reconceive those convictions in the light of what they saw the Spirit doing in the lives of Gentile converts.

In his response to Siker, Seitz claims that the Old Testament must retain "its own proper voice, not in simple historical, but in complex theological relationship with the witness of the New."[4] As I already indicated in chapter

---

[4] Seitz, "Human Sexuality," p. 240 n.3.

1, I have no objection in principle to this as a formal claim. I suspect, however, that Seitz and I might disagree about where the "proper voice" of the Old Testament is articulated. That is, given that the notion of texts having voices is a way of talking about the communities in which these texts are read, then Christians must hold some form of the view that the proper voice of the Old Testament is heard within those communities that read the scriptures under the guidance of the Spirit in the light of the life, death, and resurrection of Jesus. It is not the case that the guild of professional Old Testament scholars establishes something like the autonomous voice of the Old Testament, which is then related in a complex way to the autonomous voice of the New Testament (established by professional New Testament scholars). In the final chapter of this book I will say more about the positive uses which the church might make of professional biblical studies. This use, however, will always depend on the church keeping its own particular convictions about scripture paramount.[5]

The New Testament manifests a variety of interpretive approaches to the Old Testament, the scripture of the first Christians. Despite this variety, it is clear that the Old Testament is interpreted under the guidance of the Spirit and in the light of the life, death, and resurrection of Jesus. As one might expect, these convictions work to generate what must have been some very unconventional interpretations.

As a way of discussing further the relationships between the Spirit's work and Christian scriptural interpretation, I want to examine some of Paul's very unconventional readings of scripture found in Galatians. I want to argue that the type of counter-conventional interpretations Paul offers in Gal. 3–4 are closely connected to arguments about his character which he makes in Gal. 1–2. This discussion leads to the questions about how and in what ways Christians are encouraged and enabled to read as Paul does. Any answers to these questions will also be linked to issues about how to read the Spirit discussed in the previous chapter as well as issues concerning the character of the interpreter similar to those found in Galatians.

---

[5] I take it that Jews would hold to similar views. That is, the Old Testament is not really seen as an "autonomous" voice. Rather it is read in the light of its subsequent commentaries by those committed to living faithfully (as they see it) before the God of Israel. As Jon Levenson notes, discussions between Jews and Christians over the Bible that demand that both Jews and Christians abandon these particular commitments in favor of the commitments of professional biblical studies are not an exercise in ecumenism. Rather, they result in the distortion of both traditions. See *The Hebrew Bible, The Old Testament and Historical Criticism* (Louisville: Westminster/John Knox Press), ch. 4.

Paul's Ecclesiocentric Approach to Scripture

The figure of Abraham, as narrated in Genesis, figures prominently in the argument of Paul's epistle to the Galatians. Indeed, Gal. 3–4 is one of those places in Paul's epistles where he deals with scripture in a fairly sustained way. As such these chapters play a major role in Richard Hays' *Echoes of Scripture in the Letters of Paul*. Hays' examination of these chapters (among others) leads him to make two important claims about Paul's reading of scripture. First, Paul's interpretive strategies are ecclesiocentric rather than christocentric.[6] For Hays, this is not to deny that it is Paul's convictions about Christ that lead him to read scripture as he does. Rather, when Paul reads scripture it is not so much the person and work of the Messiah he sees therein as his vision of the church – the unified body of Jews and Gentiles that stands as the continuation of God's activity with Israel. A second central claim of Hays' account (particularly in Gal. 3–4) is that, on Paul's view, scripture is to be read in the light of his experience of the Spirit rather than the other way around. That is, when faced with the question of whether the Spirit illumines the text of scripture or whether scripture measures and constrains one's experience of the Spirit,

> Paul's unflinching answer, to the dismay of his more cautious kinsmen then and now, is to opt for the hermeneutical priority of Spirit-experience. This choice leads him, to be sure, not to a rejection of Scripture but to a charismatic rereading, whose persuasive power will rest precariously on his ability to demonstrate a congruence between the scriptural text and the community summoned and shaped by his proclamation.[7]

In the previous chapter I noted that while this view is a useful corrective to previous discussions, it operates with a set of false alternatives. It is, therefore, misleading to push this argument about the priority of Spirit

---

[6] Based on the way Hays describes this opposition, it seems clearer to say that Paul's use of scripture is ecclesiocentric rather than messiahcentric. That is, in contrast to the early chapters of Matthew and John, for example, Paul does not mine scripture for messianic proof texts to apply to Jesus. Hays further refines this notion in "On the Rebound: A Response to Critiques of *Echoes of Scripture in the Letters of Paul*," in *Paul and the Scriptures of Israel*, ed. J. Sanders and C. F. Evans (Sheffield: Sheffield Academic Press, 1993), pp. 77–8, where he introduces the term "ecclesiotelic" – God's activity pointing to the formation of a people.

[7] Hays, *Echoes of Scripture in the Letters of Paul* (New Haven: Yale University Press, 1989), p. 108.

experience too far, implying that Paul and others interpreted the work of the Spirit in ways that were not already shaped by scriptural interpretation. Given this caveat, however, I agree with Hays' claims; in the course of this chapter I want to push them a bit further by examining the ways Paul reads Abraham's story in Gal. 3–4. As I hope to show, Paul's reading here is counter-conventional in ways similar to those articulated by David Dawson in his account of allegory in *Allegorical Readers and Cultural Revision in Ancient Alexandria*. Thus, although Paul only uses the term ἀλληγορούμενα in regard to 4:21–31, the whole of Gal. 3–4 might be seen as allegorical. Rather than pushing a particular view of allegory, however, my aim is to use Dawson's account to show the continuity in Paul's manner of interpretation from 3:1 through 4:31. Hence, the use of ἀλληγορούμενα to account for what is going on with Hagar, Sarah, and their respective sons in 4:21–31 does not signify a radical departure from Paul's previous pattern of interpretation.[8] That is, Paul does not decisively shift from a "literal" reading in 3:1–4:20 to an "allegorical" reading in 4:21–31. Rather, throughout the entire passage Paul follows a counter-conventional pattern of interpretation.

Such counter-conventional, allegorical reading always involves an exercise of rhetorical and interpretive authority. Such authority is needed if one is to supplant conventional and accepted interpretations. This authority is presupposed in Paul's presumptions that there is something obscure, inadequate, or misleading about the conventional interpretation of Abraham's story operative in the Galatian congregations and that he can correct this.[9] Such authority, however, is not merely a function of Paul's words and the manner in which he uses them. Instead, his interpretive authority is related to his character, to his ability to give an account of the concrete circumstances of the Galatians and to the material effects he hopes to bring about in the Galatian congrega-

---

[8] This is opposed to G.W. Hansen, *Abraham in Galatians* (Sheffield: Sheffield Academic Press, 1989), p. 144, who argues that 3:1–4:11 and 4:21–31 represent two different types of exposition.

[9] In this sense I would agree with Herbert Marks that Paul's interpretation is an exercise of *exousia* (see H. Marks, "Pauline Typology and Revisionary Criticism," *Journal of the American Academy of Religion* 52 (1984), pp. 71–92, esp. p. 80). As will be clear, however, I fundamentally disagree that Paul's reading of scripture is an attempt to exercise personal autonomy as a way of overcoming the sort of 'anxiety of influence' elaborated by Harold Bloom. Paul is indeed a powerful reader of scripture; it is also clear, however, that the continuity both between the church and Israel, and between the scriptures of Israel and the life of the Spirit, is the end toward which Paul's reading aims. I particularly concur with Hays' criticism of Marks in *Echoes*, pp. 156–60.

tions (cf. 4:30). I will speak more about the nature of this authority in due course.

In the case of Galatians 3–4, Paul's most significant move is his insistence that the story of Abraham should be read in the context of the Galatians' experience of the Spirit. In doing this Paul aims to forge the argument in Galatians in such a way that it not only counters his opponents but also alters the Galatians' faith and practice. This aim will require Paul both to move the props on the Galatian stage on which competing accounts of Abraham are played out and to change the way the script is read. Further, I will argue that at least one of the functions of the autobiographical comments in chapters 1–2 is to support Paul's authority to interpret as he does in chapters 3–4. This support comes from Paul showing that he is a recognized faithful interpreter of the gospel, one who will exercise interpretive authority wisely.

With these arguments in place it will appear that Paul's reading of Abraham's story is not only ecclesiocentric in the sense Hays claims, but that the internal coherence of Paul's reading presupposes and requires that Abraham's story be read within the context of an ecclesia that has experienced the Spirit in the way the Galatians have. Moreover, while Paul insists on the hermeneutical priority of the Galatians' experience of the Spirit, it is an experience interpreted by Paul. The Galatians' Spirit experience is not self-interpreting. Because of this, it cannot serve as a point of presupposed common agreement between Paul and the Galatians on which Paul can build his account of Abraham. Rather, this experience itself must be interpreted by Paul in such a way that it creates a space in which he can read the story of Abraham in the way he does. Following this discussion, I will then move to address how and in what ways contemporary Christians are to read like Paul.

Allegory and Interpretive Conventions

To begin, however, I need to show that Paul's reading of Abraham's story is allegorical throughout Galatians 3–4. As one might expect, a large portion of this claim rests on a particular use of the term allegory. My usage largely relies on Dawson's *Allegorical Readers and Cultural Revision in Ancient Alexandria*. For Dawson, and for my own purposes, allegorical readings (and compositions) are interpretations that either explicitly or implicitly counter conventional views about a text, a character or an event.

> An "allegorical meaning" obtains its identity precisely by its contrast with this customary or expected meaning. Because of this contrast at its very origin,

allegory necessarily offers a challenge and possible alternative to that customary reading (p. 8).[10]

That is, allegory is not simply an unconventional way of interpreting; it is *counter*-conventional. Inherent in this view of allegory, then, is the notion of interpretive struggle. For any number of reasons, the allegorical interpretation is trying to supplement or supplant the conventional view by providing "the deeper," "the spiritual," or "the true" meaning of the subject-matter. This means that allegorical interpretations are to some extent parasitic in that they both presuppose a conventional interpretation and try to undermine it. On this account, then, the line separating the conventional and the allegorical is not stable. Over time, counter-conventional readings can be so successful that they become the conventional interpretation. At this point they would no longer be allegorical according to Dawson's account.[11]

Further, while an allegory may rely on metaphor, etymology, or personification in order to generate its counter-conventional account, such substitutions are not in themselves an allegory (or an allegorical interpretation) until they are extended into a narrative account. For example, consider the metaphor "War is a chess game." Such a comparison, left unelaborated, would not be an allegory. If, however, that metaphor is extended into a novel about a chess match between American and Soviet chess champions with the aim of telling a story about the end of the Cold War and the demise of communism in Eastern Europe, then the metaphor has become an allegory.[12]

As Dawson admits, this is a hybrid notion of allegory, drawing on both classical and modern accounts. Further, Dawson's is a somewhat looser notion of allegory than, for example, the common view that allegory treats words, phrases, or stories as ciphers for something else. On this more common view of allegory, the surface text is simply a code that can be broken once one has the interpretive key.

Dawson's view, although more wide-ranging, has several merits. First, it clearly distinguishes allegory from metaphor, etymology, personification, and

[10] Dawson, *Allegorical Readers and Cultural Revision in Ancient Alexandria* (Berkeley: University of California Press, 1992), p. 8.

[11] It could be the case, however, that patristic and medieval commentators might well use terms like "literal" and "allegorical" to describe readings that were conventional. There can, of course, be more than one conventional reading at any given time. It needs to be kept in mind, therefore, that Dawson is not attempting to describe the ways that patristic and medieval authors used terms like *allegoria*.

[12] This example is given by Dawson in *Allegorical Readers*, pp. 5–6.

other types of figurative interpretation.[13] Further, and most importantly for Dawson, it accounts both well and charitably for the reading strategies of Philo, Valentinus, Clement, and, I would argue, Paul in some cases. At the same time, it renders allegory as a serviceable rhetorical strategy in the present, sophisticated enough to capture the attention of literary critics such as Harold Bloom and Paul de Man.

Alternatively, "allegory as code," which seems to arise out of a Romantic distinction between symbol and allegory,[14] does not account well or charitably for the reading strategies of Philo, Valentinus, or Clement. It makes them appear simplistic and naive. Further, it cannot account for why clearly sophisticated modern critics would be interested in allegory as a rhetorical strategy. In addition, this view of allegory renders the so-called literal meaning of the text superfluous once the code is broken and the allegorical meaning of the text clarified.

It must be said, however, that I am not committed to fighting to the death

---

[13] One might well ask what difference there is between allegory and typology on this view. First, Dawson notes that the sharpness of this distinction arises during the Reformation. Since the reformers saw allegory as a particularly Roman Catholic interpretive approach, typology became a way in which one displayed the continuity between the Old and New Testaments. As Dawson notes, "However, the decision to divorce typology from allegory has obscured the underlying formal similarity of the two procedures by focusing on material theological considerations. If the literal sense is the product of an act of reading, allegorical (nonliteral) and nonallegorical (literal) readings can be understood as formally oppositional and mutually defining before they are defined as materially different. Consequently, in this book, typology is understood to be simply one species of allegory; the historical practice of giving texts other meanings (allegory) includes a certain subpractice of giving texts other meanings according to certain 'rules' (typology). On this view, typology is simply a certain kind of allegorical reading promoted as nonallegorical for specific theological and rhetorical reasons" (Dawson, *Allegorical Readers*, p. 16).

More recent New Testament scholarship has sought to formulate the distinction between typology and allegory in terms of typology's emphasis on history. See, for example, Hays' view, which stands in the tradition of L. Goppelt's *Typos*, that typology is a 'species of allegory distinguished by its propensity for representing the latent sense of a text as temporally posterior to its manifest sense" (*Echoes*, p. 215 n.87). Given this distinction, New Testament scholars typically contrast Paul's use of typology with Philo's use of allegory. If Dawson's reading of Philo is correct, however, then one must recognize that Philo's allegorical interpretations draw all of their force from the temporal relationships between Moses and the moral and philosophical achievements of Hellenistic culture (see, for example, Dawson, *Allegorical Readers*, pp. 112–13). If this is the case, then this way of distinguishing between typology and allegory begins to blur.

[14] See Dawson, *Allegorical Readers*, pp. 14–15.

for Dawson's account of allegory; and nor, I gather, is Dawson. What ultimately is important are the accounts of particular characters' interpretive strategies. If one is persuaded by these, but is still unwilling to describe them as allegorical, then I, for one, would gladly abandon the term in favor of a different one.

For the time being, however, Dawson's view of allegory adequately accounts for Paul's interpretation of the Abraham story in Galatians. It allows me to note the continuity of interpretive practice throughout 3:1–4:31. In these verses, Paul employs a number of figurative interpretive moves to produce a counter-conventional interpretation of certain crucial aspects of the Genesis account of Abraham in order to oppose the seemingly ascendant interpretation held by at least some in Galatia.[15] The story of Abraham becomes the field of battle on which Paul struggles to re-orient the faith and practice of the Galatian Christians.

Abraham in Galatians

Given the context of the epistle it is clear why the ability to give a persuasive account of the relevance of Abraham to the Galatians' faith and practice would be such an important issue to Paul and his opponents. This is because at its root the controversy is about how the Galatian Christians are to live in continuity with those who look to the God of Abraham, Sarah, Isaac, Jacob, and Jesus as their God. It has been noted before, but it bears remembering, that this is not primarily a dispute between Paul and Judaism as such. Paul and his opponents seem to share a great number of views about Jesus, about the followers of Jesus being the continuation of Israel, and about the inclusion of the Gentiles in this renewed people of God.[16] That is, the issue is

---

[15] I have no great desire to manufacture a full picture of Paul's opponents in Galatia. There are numerous problems and pitfalls in such an enterprise. See, for example, John Barclay's essay, "Mirror-Reading a Polemical Letter: Galatians as a Test Case," *Journal for the Study of the New Testament* 31 (1987), pp. 73–93. On the other hand, the story of Abraham seems to run so counter to Paul's argument that the best way of accounting for its presence in the epistle is that it was a text on which his opponents relied. One of several scholars who make this point is C. K. Barrett, "The Allegory of Abraham, Sarah and Hagar in the Argument of Galatians," in *Essays on Paul* (Philadelphia: Westminster Press, 1982), p. 159.

[16] J. Louis Martyn has rightly reminded us of the fact that Paul does not see the history of God's salvation as one uninterrupted road from Abraham to Christ. Rather the Law (at some unspecified point) introduces a rupture or road-block that God's intervention in Christ overcomes. See "Events in Galatia: Modified Covenantal Nomism versus God's

not whether Gentiles can be children of Abraham, but how.[17]

For Paul's opponents, the conventional reading of the story of Abraham indicates that Gentile believers must be circumcised (cf. Gen. 17:9–14),[18] observe a range of Jewish rituals, and take on a general attitude of obedience and service to Torah. Paul counters this with his own reading of crucial aspects of the Abraham story beginning in 3:1.

The first five verses of Gal. 3 lay out the hermeneutical standard which the Galatians should employ in relation to Paul's account of Abraham. This standard is their experience of the Spirit. Hays is right to claim that here the Galatians' experience of the Spirit guides the interpretation of scripture and not the other way around.[19] What also needs to be said, however, is that this strategy seems not to have been immediately self-evident to the Galatians themselves. Whether they were "ignorant," "bewitched," or simply forgetful is beside the point here. What is important is that Paul is the one who both establishes the hermeneutical priority of the Galatians' experience of the Spirit and interprets this experience as a sign of participation in the blessing promised

---

Invasion of the Cosmos in the Singular Gospel: A Response to J. D. G. Dunn and B. R. Gaventa," in *Pauline Theology*, vol. 1, ed. J. Bassler (Minneapolis: Augsburg Fortress, 1991), esp. pp. 166–74. It seems to me that one can both grant Martyn's point and still assert the theological importance for Paul of some sense of continuity in God's activity in Abraham and God's activity in Christ.

[17] Many scholars misstate the issue when they characterize it in terms such as: "The whole question at issue between Paul and his opponents is clearly: to whom do the promises really belong? Who are the children of Abraham?" (See N. T. Wright, *The Climax of the Covenant: Christ and the Law in Pauline Theology* (Minneapolis: Fortress Press, 1992), p. 144. Wright is simply the most recent scholar to state the matter this way.) This way of stating things indicates that the dispute is over whether Gentile believers can be children of Abraham rather than how they are to do so, which seems to be the real point at issue in Galatians. E. P. Sanders in *Paul, the Law and the Jewish People* (Philadelphia: Fortress Press, 1983) is more accurate when he says that the subject of Galatians "is the condition on which Gentiles enter the people of God" (p. 18, see also p. 20). Also see H. Hübner, *Das Gesetz bei Paulus* (Göttingen: Vandenhoeck and Ruprecht, 1978), pp. 16–17.

[18] Without phrasing the matter quite this way, Hübner seems to recognize the fact that the conventional reading of Abraham runs counter to Paul's when he notes, "so hatten die Gegner in der Tat ein leichtes Spiel: Sie brauchen nur auf Gen 17 zu verveisen und zu sagen: 'So steht's geschrieben in der Schrift, die auch Paulus zitiert'" (*Das Gesetz bei Paulus*, p. 17).

[19] This is against Hansen (*Abraham in Galatians*, pp. 99ff.) who argues that Paul uses the Abraham story to authenticate the validity and authority of the revelation given to him. I am claiming that Paul's argument is that because of the revelation given to him (and recognized by others), Paul is able to read the Abraham story rightly and the Galatians ought to recognize this.

to Abraham. If the Galatians already had seen their experience of the Spirit in this light, then they would never have been in the danger Paul imputes to them.[20] This is the first, and perhaps most important, act of interpretive power in Paul's reading of the Abraham story. By setting the Galatians' previous experience of the Spirit as the key to understanding their relationship to Abraham, Paul has created a space in which he can propose his own counter-reading of the Abraham story.

This counter-reading begins at 3:6 with a citation from Gen. 15:6: "Abraham believed God and it was reckoned to him as righteousness." Paul then forges a link between Abraham, who believed God and was reckoned righteous, and those who are ἐκ πίστεως. This claim is justified in 3:8–9 by a reading of the blessing promised to Abraham in Gen. 12:3; 18:18; 22:18; and 26:4.[21] Here Paul invokes an independent voice, noting that scripture itself preached the good news to Abraham that God would justify the Gentiles ἐκ πίστεως. That is, the blessing promised to Abraham is that all who live ἐκ πίστεως are Abraham's children.[22]

> Thus, the gospel sneak preview granted to Abraham is ecclesial rather than christological in content: it concerns the inclusive scope of the promise rather than the means whereby the promise is to be fulfilled. The message preproclaimed to Abraham is a gospel about God's people rather than about a Messiah.[23]

Although Abraham is still in view, Paul turns to other texts in 3:10–12. In these verses he uses a series of scriptural quotations from Deut. 27:26; Hab. 2:4 and Lev. 18:5 to undermine the position of those who claim continuity with Abraham εξ ἔργων νόμου. Instead of being children of Abraham, they are accursed.[24] Paul's argument in 3:10–12 is that the law cannot put you in

---

[20] As David Lull suggests, Paul and his opponents disagree about how to interpret the Galatians' experience of the Spirit. See *The Spirit in Galatia* (Atlanta: Scholars Press, 1980), pp. 103–4.

[21] Paul's citation in 3:8 seems to be a conflation of these texts.

[22] See Hays' discussion, *Echoes*, pp. 105–11. Hays attributes this move to Paul's chutzpah. I would prefer to call it interpretive power. By shifting the claim that the promise to Abraham is fulfilled in the church away from himself and onto the independent voice of scripture, Paul casts himself as scripture's willing instrument rather than its powerful interpreter. For more on this see below.

[23] Hays, *Echoes*, p. 106. Again, even if the constructive point here is clear, the contrast between the ecclesial and the christological is unfortunate.

[24] Hays (*Echoes*, p. 109) notes that the blessing/curse combination of Gen. 12:3 may be reflected here in the curse/blessing dichotomy presented in 3:10–14.

continuity with Abraham because it was never intended to do that. Alternatively, by quoting from Hab. 2:4 in v. 11 Paul reminds the Galatians that God has always aimed to justify people by faith, as was the case with Abraham in 3:6.[25] This leads Paul to introduce Christ in v. 13. Christ takes on the curse of the law to redeem Jews[26] from the curse of the law and in order to enable the Gentiles to receive the blessing promised to Abraham, which, as their reception of the Spirit indicates, they have already tangibly received by faith.[27] In

[25] The curse mentioned in 3:10 has inspired a wide variety of accounts about Paul's conception of the law and the ability of individuals to fulfill the law, particularly in the light of comments Paul makes in Phil. 3:6. Adjudicating the variety of positions would take me beyond the scope of this chapter. This variety is well represented, however, by J. D. G. Dunn, *Jesus, Paul and the Law: Studies in Mark and Galatians* (Louisville: Westminster/ John Knox Press, 1990), pp. 215–41; Hübner, *Das Gesetz*, pp. 19–20; H. Räisänen, *Paul and the Law* (Philadelphia: Fortress Press, 1983), pp. 94–6; and Sanders, *Paul, the Law . . .*, pp. 20–5. To my mind one of the most promising suggestions in regard to these issues is presented by N. T. Wright in *The Climax of the Covenant*, chs 7 and 8. Wright argues that the context of Paul's quotation from Deuteronomy would indicate that the curse is that curse which falls on the nation of Israel in Deut. 27–30 for failure to keep the covenants rather than the result of individual sins as Räisänen, Hübner, and others argue. Wright continues, "But, if Paul really is invoking the train of thought of the last chapters of Deuteronomy, his point is not that individual Jews have all in fact sinned, but that Israel as a whole has failed to keep the perfect Torah (see Romans 3:1ff.), and as a result, that Torah cannot therefore be the means through which she either retains her membership in the covenant of blessing *or* becomes – and this is the point of vv. 10– 14– the means of blessing the world in accordance with the promises to Abraham" (p. 146). For a reading of this passage similar to Wright's, see Frank Thielman's *From Plight to Solution* (Leiden: Brill, 1989), pp. 68–9, 72. The great advantage of these readings over those of Dunn, Hübner, Räisänen, and Sanders in particular is that they allow Paul to hold premises which are not radically opposed to those which some of his Jewish contemporaries might hold, while at the same time presenting a more or less internally coherent argument about the role of Jesus in removing the curse over Israel for failing to keep the law. The issue that a position like Wright's raises, but cannot answer, is whether the Galatians would have picked up the larger context alluded to by Paul's quotation of a single verse.

[26] This interpretation requires one to read ἡμᾶς in v. 13 as "we Jews." It seems that no matter how one takes the curse spoken of in 3:10–12, there is no way that it could apply to Gentiles except to the extent that they had become Jews.

[27] In his book *Paul the Convert* (New Haven: Yale University Press, 1990), Alan Segal makes the following claim about this passage: "Paul argues that Scripture shows the Gentiles to be included in God's plan for salvation. He describes the relevant social groupings on the basis of Scripture, but his conclusion comes from his conversion experience, not from Scripture" (p. 118). Segal is right to note that Paul's reading of Scripture is driven by something prior to scripture. As 3:1–5 indicates, however, it is Paul's vision of the Galatians'

3:15–18 Paul makes it clear that the promises made to Abraham precede the Mosaic covenants. This, of course, is a matter of common knowledge. Presumably the point at issue here is whether adherence to the Mosaic covenants is the way in which one establishes continuity with the promises to Abraham. That is, the issue here is how one becomes allied with the "seed" of Abraham. For Paul, it is clear that because the promises are to Abraham's seed (Gen. 13:15; 17:8; 24:7), a singular noun, this seed must be the singular person Christ.[28] Hence, to be in Christ, to have put on Christ in baptism (3:27), which the Galatians have already done, means that they are now allied with the seed of Abraham. They are now children of Abraham (3:29). There is nothing more they need to do to establish this continuity with Abraham.[29]

In Galatians 3 Paul has given a reading of the Abraham story which fits well with the notion of allegory proposed earlier. He has made several key figurative interpretive moves such as connecting the belief which justifies Abraham with those who are ἐκ πίστεως (vv. 6–7) and identifying Christ as the σπέρμα of Abraham. He both exploits the temporal distance between Abraham and the law and telescopes the temporal distance between Abraham and the gospel through the use of the voice of scripture. On their own, however, these interpretive moves do not lead me to claim that Galatians 3

---

experience of the Spirit rather than his conversion that provides the key to understanding scripture. Clearly, Paul's conversion and his pneumatology are not opposed to each other. Indeed, this chapter will argue that Paul's account of his conversion is used to justify his reading of Scripture, but not quite in the way Segal proposes.

[28] See Wright's comment: "ὅς ἐστιν Χριστός could then perhaps be not so much an exegetical note, an attempt by Paul to read "the Messiah" out of "your seed" in Gen. 13:15 etc., but rather an *explanatory* note, informing his readers that the 'one family' spoken of in the promises is in fact (as he will prove) the family created in Christ" (*Climax*, p. 166). While this is true, one cannot escape the fact that Paul reads σπέρμα in Gen. 13:15 in a counter-conventional (if not counter-intuitive) way. Indeed if one operates with the "allegory as code" view, then this is clearly a case of allegory like 1 Cor. 10:4 (this is true despite Paul's use of τυπικῶς in 1 Cor. 10:11).

[29] Indeed, if Wright's reading of 3:19–20 is correct, then the Mosaic law again threatens to undermine God's plan to make one unified family of Abraham from Jews and Gentiles. This is because the law establishes two distinct families rather than the unified body of Jews and Greeks, slaves and free, men and women established by Christ, the σπέρμα of Abraham. While I agree with Wright's account of these very difficult verses, I do think he underplays the interpretive power Paul displays in claiming that the σπέρμα of Abraham is Christ.

is as much a part of Paul's allegorical reading of Abraham as 4:21–31. Rather, it is the fact that these interpretive devices are employed in a reading of the story of Abraham designed to counter the more conventional account rendered by Paul's opponents that leads me to see them as allegorical in much the same way that 4:21–31 is. In addition, Paul begins Gal. 3 by laying out the terms in which his reading should be judged. That is, the Galatians' experience of the Spirit should be the standard used to confirm Paul's interpretation.

As Gal. 4 begins, Paul continues to address the matter of how one becomes a child of Abraham.[30] Here we find the contrast between being a son and being a slave which will figure later in the discussion of Hagar and Sarah. In this section the law is characterized as a power under which "we" were enslaved (4:3–5). Through the work of Christ those "under the law" have now become sons (4:5–6). This connection of the law with slavery is a crucial presumption which fuels Paul's account of Hagar and Sarah. Hence, it is rhetorically important that he establish this prior to 4:21–31.

While Paul does not cite scripture in this section, his reasoning is similar to that employed in 3:1–29. He begins from the Galatian communities' experience of the Spirit (4:6–7).[31] He works retrospectively to elaborate the condition of people under the law. If the Galatians' present experience of the Spirit in Christ and apart from the law confirms that they are indeed children of God, then the law must represent that alternative status of being a slave. Given this, it is no surprise that Paul would express wonder at the Galatians' willingness to enter into servitude under the law.

Paul again makes the Galatians' experience of the Spirit the basis for his argument against their desire to take on the law. On the other hand, if the connection between reception of the Spirit and sonship were already clear to them, they would not be in the kind of danger that leads Paul to fear for them. Hence, while Paul is not interpreting scripture in this section, he is laying the groundwork for his account of Abraham's two sons.

When Paul comes to account for Abraham's two sons in 4:21–31 he has already laid out the opposition between sonship and slavery and established that the Galatians are sons by virtue of their reception of the Spirit apart from the law.[32] These earlier interpretive moves at least make the interpretive ingenuity

---

[30] Hays in *The Faith of Jesus Christ* (Chico, CA: Scholars Press, 1983), p. 229, argues that the narrative structure of 3:23–9 parallels that of 4:3–7.

[31] See Lull's discussion of these verses, *The Spirit in Galatia*, pp. 105–9.

[32] C. K. Barrett suggests that Paul's opponents may have used Gen. 21:1–10 to argue for circumcision in a manner analogous to Jub. 16:17–18. See "The Allegory of Abraham, Sarah and Hagar," pp. 161–2.

of 4:21–31 seem continuous with Paul's argument, if not less audacious.[33]

Paul begins by fitting Abraham's two sons into his already established categories of slave and son by linking one to the slave woman and one to the free woman.

> Though the summary looks concise and neutral, Paul has already framed the categories within which his counterreading will proceed. The two sons are marked not by their circumcised or uncircumcised status, but by the slave/free polarity which distinguishes their mothers.[34]

To be more precise, the son of the slave woman, Hagar, is κατὰ σάρκα. Paul has already connected the flesh with the Galatians' willingness to take on the law and opposed this fleshly path to the way of the Spirit in 3:3. The son of the free woman is through the promise. Again, Paul's earlier reading of Abraham in 3:15–18 has established that the promise to Abraham both precedes the law and is enabled through Christ, the seed of Abraham. Baptism into Christ has already established the Galatians as true children of Abraham apart from circumcision.

Given all of this prior interpretive work, it is not altogether surprising that Paul goes on to assert that the story about Hagar and Sarah is really a story of two covenants. On the one hand, we find Hagar, who is Sinai,[35] slavery, and the earthly Jerusalem. On the other hand, the free woman is freedom in the Jerusalem above, the eschatological center to which all the nations will come (cf. Isa. 2; 54:10–14; 60–2; Ezek. 10–14; Zech. 12–14; Rev. 21:12).[36] Hays, however, is right to caution us when he notes,

> The "two covenants" of Gal. 4:24 are not the old covenant at Sinai and the new covenant in Christ. Rather, the contrast is drawn between the old covenant at Sinai and the older covenant with Abraham, which turns out in Paul's reading to find its true meaning in Christ.[37]

---

[33] If one is to trace out the inner logic of 4:21–31 so that it seems less out of place, one has to show how it develops out of the interpretive moves Paul has made earlier in chs 3 and 4 rather than begin by focusing on the various elements of 4:22–30 as C. Cosgrove does in "The Law Has Given Sarah No Children," *Novum Testamentum* 29 (1987), pp. 219–35.

[34] Hays, *Echoes*, p. 113.

[35] For a summary of textual issues involved in reading Ἁγάρ in v. 25 as well as various attempts to rationalize the connection between Hagar, Sinai, and Arabia, see H. D. Betz, *Galatians*, (Philadelphia: Fortress Press, 1979), p. 245, or Cosgrove, "The Law," pp. 221–7.

[36] For a fuller account of the background to the notion of the heavenly Jerusalem, see A.T. Lincoln, *Paradise Now and Not Yet* (Cambridge: Cambridge University Press, 1981), pp. 18–22.

[37] Hays, *Echoes*, p. 114. This is against Lincoln, *Paradise*, p. 16, and Betz, *Galatians*, p. 243, who read the two covenants here in the light of 2 Cor. 3:6.

Further, by identifying the Galatians with the eschatological heavenly Jerusalem, Paul connects these Gentile believers with Isaiah's promise in 54:1 of numerous children to her who was called barren.[38]

In 4:28 Paul goes on to make what at this point is the obvious claim that the Galatians are already children of the promise like Isaac. He then notes the parallel between Ishmael's 'persecution' of Isaac and the agitators' 'persecution' of the Galatians. Given this parallel, Paul can invoke the sanction of Gen. 21:10[39] to justify casting out these troublemakers from the Galatians' midst (4:30).[40]

Here, as in Gal. 3, Paul's allegorical reading of Abraham rests on a whole range of interpretive moves. He re-asserts the hermeneutical priority of the Spirit, which allows him to make his initial and crucial distinction between law and slavery on the one hand and sonship and the Spirit on the other. We also find a whole range of figurative interpretations which identify various characters of the Abraham story with some rather unconventional elements. All of these together are used to produce a counter-reading of this part of the Abraham story. This counter-reading both resists the claims of those wanting the Galatians to adopt the law and sanctions the expulsion of these "agitators" from the Galatians' midst.

Throughout, Paul's allegorical reading of Abraham has been an act of resistance to another, more conventional reading. The success of this (and similar) acts of resistance will in large measure always rely on the authority of the interpreter. This is because the fact that allegory provides an interpretation which counters a more conventional reading presupposes that there is some obscurity or problem surrounding the text in question which renders the conventional reading inadequate. Since texts rarely identify, much less interpret, their own obscurities, it requires a powerful reader both to identify the obscurity and to clarify it.

Such obscurity may be imputed to the text that is under consideration, or it can be part of the manner and context in which the text should be read, or some combination of both. In this case it is Paul's initial insistence that Abraham's story be read from within the context of the ecclesia of Jews and Gentiles who have experienced the Spirit apart from the law that allows him

---

[38] Hays (*Echoes*, p. 119) finds this text echoing all the way back to Isa. 51. Thielman (*From Plight to Solution*, p. 85) also notes the similarities between Sarah and the judgment of Zion, "mother of us all," in 4 Ezra 10:6-9, 25-7.

[39] Paul adjusts the LXX text slightly here to fit his slave/free distinction.

[40] Lincoln (*Paradise*, p. 28) calls 4:30 the "punchline of Paul's polemical midrash." Cosgrove ("The Law," p. 233) sees this injunction as a secondary warning.

then to plumb the depths of this narrative. Both the insistence on this context for reading Abraham's story and the figurative way in which it is read are exercises in interpretive authority. This is manifested in the act of forging a reading which opens new possibilities for reading and acting upon a text, and which is achieved against the tide established by a more conventional reading.

Clearly, the Galatians themselves would not have read Abraham's story both from the perspective Paul establishes and in the way Paul does without Paul's direction. Because there is little if anything in the conventional way of reading Abraham's story that would have led the Galatians to adopt Paul's views, and because it seems to be the case that the Galatians had not already adopted the perspective Paul takes in reading Abraham, it took a powerful intrusion on Paul's part to make his point.

How might such a counter-conventional reading convince an audience? Certainly, Paul's connection of Abraham to the Galatians' experience of the Spirit smoothes the road over which his reading must run. While this is true, it simply pushes the question one step further back. Why should the Galatians make the sorts of connections between their experience of the Spirit and Abraham's story that Paul demands? Clearly, in their interaction with the "agitators" urging them to take on the law, this was not a connection they had previously made.

Paul could, of course, try to coerce the Galatians to see things his way. It seems doubtful, however, that the churches in Galatia had enough institutional cohesion to allow a single individual, let alone someone who was not even on the scene, forcibly to impose his interpretation on them as a group against their will. Instead, Paul lays the groundwork for his powerful reading of Abraham by focusing on his own character. Since he cannot rely on the conventional interpretation of Abraham to justify his position, he must focus on those characteristics which seem to have endowed him with the authority he exercises in his reading of Abraham's story. I will now turn to discuss Paul's claims about himself and the way they work to authorize the interpretive power he exercises in Gal. 3–4.

Paul's Account of Himself

When it comes to justifying both his interpretations and his qualities as an interpreter, Paul does not claim that he is a better scholar than his opponents, that he is more learned than they. Rather, he focuses on his status as an apostle, on a revelation which he claims to have received and which others, who would not be expected to agree with him, have recognized.

He alludes to his personal integrity and the recognition – even among those who would not be expected to agree with him – that God has worked in his life.[41]

Of course, these are all elements that are part of the autobiographical section of the epistle which runs from 1:10–2:21, including the account of Paul's confrontation with Peter in Antioch in 2:11–14. This section leads directly into Paul's allegorical reading of Abraham's story in Gal. 3 and 4.[42] While it is Paul who is giving the account of his own life in 1:10–2:21, he also goes to some lengths to position himself as an agent who is acted upon by a higher power. In 2:20 he goes so far as to say that he no longer lives, rather Christ lives in him. This, however, comes as no surprise when it is remembered that from conception God has set apart Paul, like the servant of the Lord (Isa. 49:1) and Jeremiah (Jer. 1:5), for a special task (1:15). In addition, 2:8 indicates that God is working in and directing Paul (and Peter). These conditions allow Paul to refer to his message and mission as a gift which has been given him (2:9). Further, when the Judean churches hear of Paul's turnabout from persecutor to preacher, they glorify God for what has been done in Paul's life (1:23–4). The powerful, authoritative Paul of Gal. 3 and 4 is cast as a willing instrument in 1:10–2:21.[43] In fact, it is the case that, according to the rhetoric of the epistle, the interpretive power Paul exercises is directly related to the claim that it is not really Paul's power, but the power of God working through Paul.[44] This notion is reiterated in 4:12–14 where Paul reflects on his oneness with the Galatians and their reception of him as an angel or messenger of God despite

---

[41] "The whole labored argument essentially rests not on the scriptural passages cited nor on the logical acceptance of Paul's premises by his opponents . . . but on the Galatians' acceptance of his authority in making these proclamations and their experience of Paul's teachings." G. A. Kennedy, *The New Testament through Rhetorical Criticism* (Chapel Hill: University of North Carolina Press, 1984), p. 149.

[42] I am in sympathy with Beverly Gaventa's attempt to integrate Gal. 1–2 with the more theological discussion in chs 3–4 and the paraenetic claims of chs 5–6. See "Galatians 1 and 2: Autobiography as Paradigm," *Novum Testamentum* 28 (1986), pp. 309–26. It would seem that chs 1 and 2 can play numerous complementary roles in any particular analysis of Galatians. I do not want to deny the constructive points Gaventa makes. Rather, I simply want to illustrate another role that these chapters may play in the rhetoric of the epistle.

[43] See the comment of John Schütz: "because he is in Christ and of Christ the apostle is himself the vessel of God's work through Christ," in *Paul and the Anatomy of Apostolic Authority* (Cambridge: Cambridge University Press, 1975), p. 232.

[44] Where Gaventa ("Galatians 1 and 2," p. 326) claims, "Paul sees in his experience an example of the Gospel's power and employs that example for the exhortation of others," I would add that Paul sees in his experience an example of the gospel's power and exercises that power in his theological exhortations to the Galatians.

his physical infirmities. By assenting to and living by Paul's interpretation, the Galatians are merely conforming themselves to the will of God. The appropriateness of this assent is then confirmed by the presence of the Spirit in their congregations.

The claim that Paul is a faithful instrument of God is not simply a claim he makes about himself. It is a judgment which others have recognized, most notably Cephas, James, John, and the other Jerusalem apostles. Although Paul seems to have a rather ambivalent relationship to the Jerusalem apostles, being able to cite their recognition of his message and mission certainly supports his exposition of the gospel.[45] Presumably, Paul's opponents would have considered James, Peter, and John to be pillars even if Paul is, at the same time, eager to stress his indifference to their status. While there seems to be a shift here from a discussion of Paul's personal credibility in 1:11–23 to the credibility of Paul's gospel in 2:2–10, it would be a mistake to overstress this distinction. "In a sense all that the apostle does is a reflection of what the gospel does; all that he is, is a reflection of what the gospel is."[46] Indeed, noting that the "pillars" of the Jerusalem church recognized and validated Paul's gospel would probably do more to buttress his credibility as an interpreter of the gospel than the account of his own transforming experience of the gospel.

Following this account of Paul's reception in Jerusalem, there is an account of Paul's confrontation with Peter in Antioch. This passage has been well mined for the information it might yield about such things as the nature of table fellowship in early Christian congregations, the relationship between this incident in Antioch and the Jerusalem conference related in Acts 15, the reason for the split between Paul and Barnabas and Paul's relationship to the church at Antioch, the development of Paul's view of the law, and many other things.[47] While these may be in fact the most interesting questions to address to this passage, they go beyond the scope of this present chapter. Rather, I wish to look at how this passage continues the strategy of underwriting the interpretive authority Paul will exercise in Galatians 3–4.

Coming immediately after Paul has recounted the reception of his gospel

---

[45] See Bengt Holmberg's comment in *Paul and Power* (Philadelphia: Fortress Press, 1978) that Paul "is careful to point out to his opponents and detractors the incontrovertible fact that he was officially and irreversibly acknowledged by the Jerusalem 'pillars' as Apostle to the Gentiles, with a competence and 'gospel of his own'" (p. 16).

[46] Schütz, *Anatomy*, p. 232. See also Gaventa, "Galatians 1 and 2," p. 317.

[47] For a rich discussion of many of these issues, see J. D. G. Dunn, "The Incident at Antioch," in *Jesus, Paul and the Law*, pp. 129–83; also Schütz, *Anatomy*, pp. 150–7. Again, it is important to remember that issues regarding the historical Paul and Peter are separable from the accounts of Acts and Galatians rendered here in this book.

by the Jerusalem apostles, this passage further emphasizes Paul's integrity and constancy as an interpreter of the gospel in contrast to Peter (and Barnabas). The divergent views about the law expressed in vv.15–21 allow Paul to lay some of the groundwork for his discussions in Gal. 3 and 4, but the primary accusation against Peter is not bad theology, but hypocrisy (2:13).[48] Peter and the others are "not walking along the straight path of the truth of the gospel" (2:14). As Schütz notes, by phrasing the issue in this way the conflict is not between two conflicting apostles, but about whether or not Peter will submit to the independent authority of the gospel as Paul has done.[49]

Put in this light, neither man's apostleship is put on the line. It is not Peter's power versus Paul's; rather, we again see Paul presenting himself (and Peter) as instruments of the higher authority found in the "truth of the gospel." Such rhetoric furthers Paul's claims to be a faithful interpreter of the gospel while at the same time making the exercise of interpretive power involved here less a matter of Paul's personal whims.[50]

This account serves to validate Paul as someone who is fit to exercise the sort of interpretive authority we find in Gal. 3 and 4. The aim of such rhetoric is to persuade the Galatians that in a dispute over how to understand Abraham's story, Paul is the kind of person who can render a faithful and decisive, albeit allegorical, account – an account, which, if followed, will keep the Galatian congregations as faithful heirs of the promises made to Abraham and fulfilled in Jesus.

Apart from Paul's comments here in Gal. 1–2, there are other occasions in the epistle where Paul substantiates his claims to be an authoritative interpreter. These occasions are usually found in Paul's allusions to his sufferings as an apostle (see particularly 4:11; 6:14). The upshot of these allusions is that Paul has remained constant in his message, even when it has meant persecution. Indeed, Paul's claim in 6:17 to bear the marks of Christ on his body serves (quite literally) to underwrite his claims to exercise interpretive power.

In the light of my subsequent comments about the character of the interpreter, there are two elements in Paul's account of his character which seem most important. First, the claim that Paul is a trustworthy interpreter of the gospel is supported by others who would not normally be expected to

---

[48] "What vexes Paul is the inconsistency of Peter's response and its potentially deleterious effects should others decide to take Peter himself as an authority" (Schütz, *Anatomy*, p. 154).
[49] "The charge of hypocrisy leveled at Peter accuses him of acting inconsistently, out of accord with an authority he himself means to recognize" (Schütz, *Anatomy*, p. 152). See also Holmberg, *Paul and Power*, p. 32.
[50] Such an independent voice is, as Hays notes, even applied to Abraham in 3:8. See Hays' discussion of the voice of scripture in *Echoes*, pp. 105–7.

agree with him. There is a sort of public recognizability to his life and teaching that elicits the assent of other trustworthy characters. Secondly, Paul is able to render an account of his life that fits his story into the larger story of God's activity in Christ. Paul's account of himself has a christological density that enables him to say such things as "I have been crucified with Christ. It is no longer I who live, but Christ who lives in me" (2:20). It is not that Paul's self has been obliterated in favor of Christ. Rather, just as he initially learned to narrate his life as a story of zealous devotion to Judaism (1:13–14), he subsequently learned to narrate his life within a larger story marked by the death and resurrection of Jesus.

So far, I have argued that when it comes to reading Abraham's story, Paul's strategy is ecclesiocentric in the sense Hays talks about. It is also ecclesiocentric, however, in that Paul's reading depends on and presupposes the existence of communities of believers who will recognize him as one who by virtue of his character can exercise interpretive authority. It is also the case that Paul's counter-conventional reading of Abraham is based on and judged by the Galatians' experience of the Spirit. That experience, however, is not self-interpreting. Paul must initially render an account of the Galatians' experience (3:1–5) and render that account in such a way that it can become the basis for reading Abraham's story. In many respects Paul's interpretive practice in Galatians parallels that found in Acts. Interpretation of scriptural texts under the Spirit's guidance is related in complex ways to interpretation of the Spirit's work in the lives of believers. In Acts and Galatians the mere fact of Spirit-experience is not self-interpreting. The central characters need to read the Spirit as much as they need to read with the Spirit – and one cannot be done without the other. In Galatians, however, we find that there seems to be a conventional set of interpretations about how to read Abraham's story. Further, it seems that the Galatians ought to fit themselves into the narrative of Abraham's story in the light of their convictions about Christ and their experience of the Spirit. In response, Paul offers a counter-conventional reading of Abraham's story and how the Galatians fit into that story. The upshot of his account is that by virtue of their experience of the Spirit, the Galatians know that they are children of Abraham, firmly situated within the narrative of election and promise that begins in Genesis, reaches its climactic moment in the death and resurrection of Jesus, and carries on in the power of the Spirit in the presence of the Galatian (and other) congregations. They need not do anything more to secure a place in this ongoing story, particularly in regard to circumcision and taking on the other obligations of Torah. As Hays rightly notes, it is Paul's account of the Galatians' reception of the Spirit in 3:1– 5 which becomes the basis for his subsequent reading of Abraham's story.

What must also be recognized, however, is that Paul establishes his authority to offer such counter-conventional interpretations by giving an account of himself in Gal. 1–2. This account situates Paul's life story (or at least crucial aspects of that story) within a larger narrative of Christ and the church. This account works to underwrite Paul's interpretive practice by showing that he is recognized as a wise and faithful interpreter of the gospel. It now becomes important to ask if it is possible to make more general claims about Christian interpretation of scripture in the light of this account of Galatians.

How Pauline Can We Be?

At the ends of their respective books on the ways in which Paul read scripture, both Richard Longenecker and Richard Hays address the issues of whether and how contemporary Christians can interpret like Paul.[51] Both Longenecker and Hays rightly recognize that this is a theological question that cannot directly be answered in terms consonant with the concerns of professional biblical studies.

Both Hays and Longenecker recognize the theological necessity of maintaining Paul's (and the other New Testament writers') interpretations of scripture.[52] This is not to say that there will always be agreement about the interpretation of any particular text. For Christians, however, these texts are part of their scripture. They must be engaged and embodied for Christians to worship and live faithfully before the triune God. These texts are as crucial as the Old Testament is both for rendering the identity of the God of Jesus Christ and for forming Christian identity. On this point, virtually all theologians agree: the specific interpretations of the Old Testament found in the New Testament are materially normative for Christians.

The issue that is far more difficult concerns whether and how contemporary Christians can read like Paul. On this point, Longenecker and Hays diverge. Longenecker seeks to limit severely the extent to which Christians are authorized to interpret the way Paul does. According to Longenecker, there are two bases for these limitations. The first concerns the difference between Jesus and the apostles, on the one hand, and all subsequent Christians, on the other hand.[53] The second limitation is based on a

---

[51] See Richard Longenecker, *Biblical Exegesis in the Apostolic Period* (Grand Rapids: Eerdmans, 1975), pp. 214–20. Hays addresses these issues in the final chapter of *Echoes*.

[52] Hays, *Echoes,* pp. 183ff. Longenecker notes that Christians must be committed to "the reproduction of the apostolic faith and doctrine" (*Biblical Exegesis*, p. 219).

[53] See Longenecker, *Biblical Exegesis*, p. 218.

distinction between the culturally specific interpretive methods and contexts of the New Testament writers and the "transcultural and eternal gospel" they proclaimed.[54]

For Longenecker, it is important to note not just a temporal, but a qualitative distinction between Jesus and the New Testament writers and all subsequent Christians. "While we legitimately seek continuity with our Lord and his apostles in maters of faith and doctrine . . . we must also recognize the uniqueness of Jesus as the true interpreter of the Old Testament and the distinctive place he gave to the apostles in the explication of the prophetic word."[55] Without blurring the uniqueness of Jesus, the gospel texts make it quite clear that Jesus grants his followers a certain interpretive authority and obliges them to carry on his teaching (Matt. 28:20; Luke 24:44–50; John 13–17). Paul in particular, seeing the ecclesia as a form of the eschatological fulfillment of Jer.31:31, argues that "we all" are empowered to read as he does to the extent that we are being transformed by the Spirit into the likeness of the Lord (see 2 Cor. 3:1–4:6).[56] Moreover, Paul calls believers to imitate him (1 Cor. 4:6; 11:1; Phil. 3:17) While there are numerous respects in which we might imitate Paul, "Surely to imitate him faithfully we must learn from him the art of reading and proclaiming Scripture."[57] While there will, no doubt, be differences between believers regarding their proficiency in this matter, Paul himself does not recognize a difference in kind between himself, as apostle, and other believers when it comes to the practice of interpreting scripture.[58]

Further, Longenecker posits a difference between the culturally contingent methods of interpretation found in the New Testament and the eternal, transcultural gospel those methods proclaimed. This allows him to note that while Christians are committed to "the reproduction of the apostolic faith and doctrine," they are not obliged to reproduce their interpretive practices except where "historico-grammatical exegesis" can reproduce the conclusions the New Testament writers arrived at by very different means.[59]

---

[54] Longenecker, *Biblical Exegesis*, p. 218.

[55] Longenecker, *Biblical Exegesis*, p. 218. A further way to extend this limitation which the Protestant Longenecker does not explore is by limiting it to those who are ordained to exercise a specific apostolic office. My response to Longenecker also covers those who would impose this sort of limitation as well.

[56] See Hays' powerful reading of this difficult text in *Echoes*, ch. 4.

[57] Hays, *Echoes*, p. 183.

[58] Paul does at times seem to claim that his apostolic status might render his particular interpretation better than his opponents'.

[59] Longenecker, *Biblical Exegesis*, pp. 219–20.

Whether or not Longenecker intends to bring back a form of "Lessing's ditch" and all of its attendant problems is unclear. What is clear is that it is difficult if not impossible to separate elements of "apostolic faith and doctrine" such as the Trinity and orthodox christology from the ways in which the biblical writers read the Old Testament. There simply is no way to separate apostolic faith from the patterns of apostolic exegesis without distorting that faith.

Moreover, as Hays notes, Longenecker's position commits believers to a "peculiar intellectual schizophrenia in which we arbitrarily grant privileged status to past interpretations that we deem to be unjustifiable with regard to normal, sober hermeneutical canons . . . . Longenecker has circumscribed [Paul's hermeneutical freedom] for Paul's followers by granting hermeneutical veto power to a modern critical method of which Paul himself was entirely innocent."[60]

For Hays, it is clear that Christians must both find Paul's (and presumably the other New Testament writers') interpretations of scripture materially normative *and* find Paul's interpretive methods formally exemplary.[61] For Hays, the difficult issues concern the appropriate constraints to be put on this interpretive freedom. As a way of addressing these concerns, Hays first lists the characteristic interpretive habits of those who "learned from Paul how to read Scripture." I will touch on those I take to be most significant.

To learn to read scripture like Paul means learning to read ecclesiocentrically. "Scripture discloses its sense only as the text is brought into correlation with living communities where the Holy Spirit is at work."[62] Scripture simply cannot be understood apart from a community's ongoing struggle to embody its interpretation in the aid of faithful, obedient living. Hays also rightly notes that those who learn to read as Paul does "would read as participants in the eschatological drama of redemption.[63] Like Paul, Christians must learn to situate their present temporal location within God's ongoing dramatic engagement with the world. Paul's sense that the decisive turn in this drama had occurred in the death and resurrection of Jesus and in the subsequent pouring out of the Spirit on an ecclesia of Jews and Gentiles provided him with the perspective from which he could propose his often counter-conventional interpretations. "If we are unable to share Paul's sense of participating in the community of the endtime, then his reading strategies will appear arbitrary and grandiose; we would do better to adopt hermeneutical practices that more

---

[60] Hays, *Echoes*, p. 181.
[61] Hays, *Echoes*, p. 180.
[62] Hays, *Echoes*, p. 184.
[63] Hays, *Echoes*, p. 185.

adequately correspond to our own modest sense of temporal location and historical relativity."[64]

These habits leave Hays open to the same criticism I addressed in chapter 3; namely, how can Christians interpret scripture in ways that respond adequately to the dangers of self-deception and caprice in interpretation? He notes three types of constraint that seemed to operate for Paul and that Christian communities can, and should, invoke as well in response to these well-documented dangers. First, no reading can be true if it "denies the faithfulness of Israel's God to his covenant promises." Secondly, "No reading of Scripture can be legitimate if it fails to acknowledge the death and resurrection of Jesus as the climactic manifestation of God's righteousness." Finally, and most importantly, "No reading of Scripture can be legitimate, then, if it fails to shape the readers into a community that embodies the love of God as shown forth in Christ."[65] I have no disagreement with these. Indeed, it would not be difficult to find parallel and analogous concerns firmly embedded in the history of Christian doctrine.[66] What must also be said, however (and what has been the focus of several chapters of this book) is that these constraints cannot really be expected to have any direct effect on the ways Christians read scripture apart from Christians' abilities to form and sustain certain communal habits and practices. In the case of Paul's reading of Abraham's story, it is clear that it fits the first two criteria and clearly seeks to achieve the third. To meet these criteria Paul has had to offer a boldly counter-conventional reading of specific texts. Further, he has had both to interpret the significance of the Galatians' experience of the Spirit and to show how it is to be the standard against which Abraham's story must be read.

To establish his authority to make these interpretive moves Paul has offered an account of himself which shows him to be a known and faithful interpreter of the one Gospel.[67] Paul's character is one of the decisive components in his interpretation. In fact, it may be the one thing that keeps his counter-

---

[64] Hays, *Echoes*, p. 185.

[65] Hays, *Echoes*, p. 191.

[66] The first two of Hays' constraints are formally similar, and certainly compatible with, the "Rule of Faith" as found in Irenaeus' *Against Heresies* (esp. 2.27.1–2.28.1). The final constraint fits with Augustine's strictures about scriptural interpretation in *On Christian Doctrine*. Further, the closing paragraph of Athanasius' *On the Incarnation* closely links abilities to understand scripture with issues of character in ways similar to Hays'.

[67] 1:6–9 stresses the importance of the singularity of the gospel. See further, B. R. Gaventa, "The Singularity of the Gospel," in *Pauline Theology*, vol. 1, ed. J. Bassler, pp. 147–59.

conventional interpretation from simply being arbitrary assertion. If Christians are to learn to read like Paul (among others), both reading the Spirit and reading with the Spirit, then the character of the interpreter will also become a factor in the offering, hearing, and enacting of their interpretations. I want to conclude this chapter by saying more about what this means.

Character and Interpretation

First, it is important to note that Christians are not always called to offer counter-conventional interpretations. The interpretations which Paul offered the Galatians were initially counter-conventional. These same readings must now be conventional for Christians. Nevertheless, from time to time Christians may have to offer and act upon counter-conventional interpretations of scripture in order to fulfill their proper ends.

This may be due to sinful habits and practices so distorting the common life of Christian communities that sinful, oppressive interpretation becomes conventional for them. An obvious example of this would be the rise to conventionality of readings of Gen. 9:18–27 which slave-holding Christians in the US offered to justify the kidnapping and enslavement of the "sons of Ham." In response to this, some African-American Christians developed the "Hamitic Hypothesis." The "Hamitic Hypothesis" was a boldly counter-conventional reading of Gen. 9:23–7 which interpreted the passage intratextually in the light of Ps. 68:31 to render this "curse" as a portent of divine blessing.[68] In other cases, changing circumstances may demand counter-conventional interpretations so that the community can keep in step with the movements of the Spirit. James' interpretation of Amos 9:9–12 in Acts 15 and Paul's reading of the Abraham story in Gal. 3–4 would be good examples of this. There may well be other types of situation which would call Christians to read counter-conventionally. My point is not to list them all. Rather, I simply wish to note that there may well be occasions (such as the recognized work of the Spirit in the lives of homosexual Christians?) that will require Christian communities to offer, hear, and enact counter-conventional interpretations in order to fulfill their proper ends.

As with the Galatian congregations, contemporary Christians can expect these interpretations to be contested. Indeed, the "burden of proof" will

---

[68] For a fuller analysis of the "Hamitic Hypothesis" see M. G. Cartwright, "Ideology and the Interpretation of the Bible in the African-American Christian Tradition," *Modern Theology* 9 (1993), pp. 141–58.

always fall on those advocating counter-conventional interpretations. In such cases (as well as others) Christians may find that the character of those offering counter-conventional interpretations becomes as decisive for them as it was for the Galatians.[69] In this case, I would argue that just as Paul's account of his visits to Jerusalem was able to show that he and his gospel were acceptable to those Christians outside his own circle, so contemporary interpreters also need to be relatively widely recognized as trustworthy. If this is to be the case, then Christians will need to develop the sort of common life in which their lives are both appropriately visible and appropriately known. These requirements set some of the points made in the previous chapter in a wider context. There I noted that, for heterosexual Christians, forming friendships (through hospitality) with homosexual Christians was the most important task in being able to offer testimony about the work of the Spirit in their lives. In the light of issues about character and interpretation raised by Paul's reading of the Abraham story in Galatians, it becomes clear that the formation of friendships in Christ is one of the most significant practices of any Christian community that desires to read scripture in order to worship and live faithfully before the triune God. The authority which generates and underwrites the counter-conventional interpretation on which Christians will need to rely arises out of friendships.[70] These friendships can only be formed and maintained if Christians open their lives to each other in very particular ways.

I do not mean to say that Christians are to display fully everything about their lives. There is still a place for a distinction between what is public and what is private. As we will see more fully in the next chapter, however, Christians will need to construct this distinction very differently from what is commonly accepted in the wider culture of the US in the late twentieth century. Further, it should also be clear that this distinction will be constructed very differently from the distinction between the professional and the personal that operates in the guild of biblical scholars. Indeed, the distinction between professional and personal works to render issues relating to the character of the interpreter irrelevant for professional biblical scholarship. The aim of such scholarship is to

[69] In saying this, I don't intend to rule out the possibility of edifying insight and even faithful counter-conventional interpretations coming from outsiders or from completely unexpected members of the community. Christians must always be open to such possibilities, but they will not be the norm.

[70] In "A Story Formed Community" in *A Community of Character* (Notre Dame: University of Notre Dame Press, 1981) Stanley Hauerwas insightfully reads *Watership Down* to display the relationships between an authority that arises out of friendships and authority based on a coercive use of power. Further, if the church is to maintain its peaceable identity then it will have to base its authority on such friendships (see pp. 22–36).

produce readings that can be offered, understood, and evaluated by anyone with the requisite background knowledge. What a scholar does outside of those things directly related to her acts of interpretation is irrelevant for the understanding and evaluation of her interpretation. Thus, a very clear boundary is established and maintained between the personal and the professional.[71] Indeed, it may be the case that this is as it should be if the profession is to fulfill its aims. This cannot, however, be the case for Christian interpretation of scripture. In order for Christian communities to fulfill their ends – faithful life and worship – they will need to avoid this particular distinction between the personal and the professional. Nevertheless, they will want to construct distinctions between public and private. In a discussion of Dietrich Bonhoeffer's *Letters and Papers from Prison*, Rowan Williams shows how Bonhoeffer recognized that there is a theological need to conceal certain elements of our lives from public view. "Since the Fall, concealment is necessary and good in the sense that there is plenty in human thought, feeling, and experience that *should not* be part of shared discourse. We are alienated, divided, and corrupted; but to bring this into speech (and to assume we thereby tell a better or fuller truth) is to collude with sin."[72] Hence, the lives of Christians have to be appropriately (as opposed to fully) visible to one another.

It would be impossible to specific abstractly and in advance of a specific case exactly what Christians need to reveal to each other. Presumably there is much about his life that Paul did not make known to the Galatians. Alternatively, he also assumes that what they do know about him and his life in Christ is sufficient for the Galatians to assent to Paul's counter-conventional interpretation. The account Paul renders in Gal. 1–2 stresses a life of fidelity in word and deed to the Gospel over time. Moreover, it clearly situates God as the true subject of the narrative of Paul's life. Paul's voice and God's voice converge. These would be elements that friends in Christ should be able to know about each other if they are to grant each other interpretive authority.

Most Christians are wary of granting authority of any sort to others. Moreover, there is a great suspicion of anyone who might seek to have us view their voice as converging with God's voice. Recent history in particular is full of accounts of ways in which Christians (and clergy in particular) abuse those entrusted to their care. The media report a steady stream of stories, ranging from the comic to the catastrophic, in which individuals have convinced

---

[71] It must be granted, however, that some non-western biblical scholars and some types of feminist and liberationist scholars might seek to blur this distinction.

[72] See R. Williams, "The Suspicion of Suspicion: Wittgenstein and Bonhoeffer," in *The Grammar of the Heart*, ed. R. Bell (San Francisco: Harper and Row, 1988), p. 44.

others that they speak with the voice of God only to prove later to have been charlatans. Alternatively, Christians believe that God's providential care often operates through human agents.[73] There is no question that in this matter Christians need to exercise great wisdom and even suspicion. Nevertheless, if Christians are required at times to offer, hear, and enact counter-conventional interpretations of scripture, they may well find themselves in the position of having to grant to one another interpretive authority.

There is no risk-free way of doing this. The only real way for Christians to proceed in this regard is to begin the process of forming and maintaining friendships with each other so that they will know each other sufficiently well to be able to grant one another a measure of authority to interpret in counter-conventional ways on occasions.[74] The alternatives to this would leave Christians either credulously handing themselves over to anyone claiming to speak with the voice of God or reducing interpretive authority to a form of coercion exercised by powerful individuals or groups. Another, all too common, alternative is for scriptural interpretation to become the activity of more or less isolated individuals, mingling their interpretations with those of strangers. Such Christians would not have a common life sufficient to generate conventional interpretations, much less counter-conventional ones.[75]

In the course of making judgments about character, Christians should expect that just as Paul was able to provide a christologically dense account of his life, such christological density would also be characteristic of the lives of those offering trustworthy counter-conventional interpretations. That is, such Christians ought to be able to fit their accounts into that larger story of Christ's life, death, and resurrection and the continuation of that story in Christ's body, the church.[76]

This claim presumes two things about Paul's character and the rendering of character more generally. First, on the account I have offered, characterizing oneself or another is a narrative achievement. That is, it requires one to fit that character into a narrative sequence of actions.[77] This is not to say that

---

[73] As Eugene Rogers notes, Aquinas considered providence as the prudence (practical wisdom) of God (see "How The Virtues of the Interpreter Presuppose and Perfect Hermeneutics," *Journal of Religion* 76 (1996), p. 78).

[74] In addition, all these risks must be undertaken in the light of practices of forgiveness, repentance, and reconciliation as discussed in chapter 3.

[75] Christians in such situations who are serious about scriptural interpretation tend to adopt the interpretive conventions of professional biblical scholars.

[76] I say more about this in chapter 7.

[77] This point is not original to me. Alasdair MacIntyre, Charles Taylor, and Stanley Hauerwas have all made similar claims. For my remarks here I will rely on MacIntyre's

it is impossible to characterize someone by means of a non-narrative remark. Think, for example, of the characterization "Paul is an apostle." This remark, while not a narrative in itself, presupposes a narratable sequence of events which both display what an apostle is and which can be attributed to Paul in ways that result in the non-narrative judgment that Paul is an apostle. Failure to provide such a narrative when required (as in the case of the Corinthian correspondence, for example) would lead one to consider this characterization of Paul unintelligible, incorrect, or the result of devious motives. (Of course, all of these judgments would require narrative display as well.)

In addition, the claim that offering an account of one's character presupposes the ability to narrate is not to say that the narrative always stays the same. Clearly, Paul's account of himself in Gal. 1–2 is an excellent example of someone who revises the narrative he tells about himself.[78] Both Paul's account of himself and the larger story into which he fits his story change in the course of moving from being Christ's antagonist to being Christ's apostle. No matter how revisable or unstable the narrative, an intelligible character can only adequately result from narration.[79] To recognize that characterization is a narrative achievement is also to recognize that characterization is always a contestable practice. To order events in a particular way, to endow them with specific significance, to begin at a certain place and end in another, to embed the life of a character within a larger story, all reflect decisions which could be made otherwise.[80]

Secondly, in following Paul's example, contemporary Christians will end up with notions of human selfhood that are very different from those which have dominated modern discussions of selfhood. The modern self is characterized by presumptions of autonomy, individualism, unencumbered rationality, essential stability, and an absence of historical and social contingency. To the extent that individual Christians view themselves in this way they will never be able to offer accounts of anyone's character that will have the

---

account in *After Virtue*, 2nd edn (Notre Dame: University of Notre Dame Press, 1984). For a more detailed account of this practice in Paul's life and its theological consequences see my essay, "Learning to Narrate Our Lives in Christ," in *Theological Exegesis: Experiments in Canonical Criticism*, ed. C. R. Seitz and K. Greene-McCreight (Grand Rapids: Eerdmans, 1998).

[78] This would also be clear from comparing Gal. 1–2 with Phil. 3.

[79] See *After Virtue*, pp. 216ff.

[80] This is a point MacIntyre makes in *After Virtue*, pp. 212–13. In this section MacIntyre is attacking historians like Louis Mink who seek to deny the epistemological importance of narrative for historiography. See, for example, Mink's "History and Fiction as Modes of Comprehension," *New Literary History* 1 (1970), pp. 541–58.

christological density of Paul's account.[81] Paul's self is completely enmeshed in historical and cultural contingencies. Through his encounter with the crucified and risen Christ, Paul's standards of rationality are radically undermined and gradually reconstituted in a cruciform manner (see Gal. 2:20 and Phil. 3:2–16). Of course, for Paul, as well as for virtually all other pre-modern people, the radically autonomous self of modernity would have been an odd, if not dangerous, notion. Even for the pre-Christ Paul, one was never autonomous. The important questions were not about how to achieve autonomy, but about how to serve the one true God as opposed to being in bondage to false gods. By claiming that it is no longer he who lives, but Christ who lives in him, Paul has not obliterated a previously autonomous self. Rather, he has re-situated his life in a different story, the story of Christ. Paul's account of his character testifies to the power of God's grace to reconstitute a self under the lordship of Christ. Unless Christians can offer this sort of christological density to their judgments about the character of any particular interpreter, they will have good reason to be suspicious of that interpreter's counter-conventional interpretations.

Thus far I have tried to display the workings of Paul's counter-conventional reading of Abraham's story in Gal. 3–4, where Paul both reads with the Spirit and reads the Spirit. Further, I have argued that Paul's interpretive practice is largely authorized by the account of his character offered in Gal. 1–2. Moreover, I have, along with Richard Hays, claimed that contemporary Christians must seek to read like Paul. In the final chapter of this book I will further discuss the ways Christians need to be formed to read like Paul. Further, to read as Paul did means that from time to time Christians will need to offer, hear, and enact counter-conventional interpretations of scripture. In addition, for Christians to read as Paul did they will need to form and sustain friendships that will enable them to know each other well enough that they can grant to one another the interpretive authority necessary to sustain counter-conventional interpretations. The formation and maintenance of such friendships depends both on Christians opening their lives to each other in appropriate ways and in being able to render christologically dense accounts of themselves. I have also indicated here that while Christians will need to maintain certain boundaries between what is public and what is private, they

---

[81] The contrast with Paul's example nicely shows the profoundly anti-theological implications of modern notions of selfhood. For an explicit demonstration of this see Seyla Benhabib, *Situating the Self* (Cambridge: Polity Press, 1992), ch. 1 and esp. pp. 42–3. Benhabib is seeking to revise an account of the modern self in the light of Habermas' discourse ethics.

will need to construct these boundaries along lines very different from those found in the culture at large. In the following chapter I wish to extend this discussion further by looking at the relationships between Christians' abilities to speak the truth to each other and issues about the ways they acquire and hold wealth.

Chapter Six

MAKING STEALING POSSIBLE:
CRIMINAL THOUGHTS ON BUILDING AN ECCLESIAL COMMON LIFE

Introduction

Throughout this book I have presented the view that Christian interpretation of scripture is not primarily an exercise in deploying theories of meaning to solve textual puzzles. Rather, Christian interpretation of scripture is primarily an activity of Christian communities in which they seek to generate and embody their interpretations of scripture so that they may fulfill their ends of worshipping and living faithfully before the triune God. Moreover, in engaging scripture in this way Christians participate in an ongoing activity which brings them into a historically and geographically extended debate about how best to interpret scripture in specific contexts. In a sense, then, each interpretive effort is an attempt to extend faithfully Christian faith, life, and worship in the present in ways that are sometimes surprising, contestable, and even counter-conventional, yet continuous with those faithful interpretations which have gone on before.

Interpretation as the reduction of puzzlement is measured in a punctilious way, in terms of problems encountered and solved. Interpretation ceases when there are no more puzzles. Alternatively, Christian interpretation of scripture is to be a more or less continuous activity. It often involves the taking up of previous debates, discussions, and decisions and carrying them on in specific contexts. In this light, it is to be expected that such interpretation will generate and result in further debate, discussion, and disagreement. In this respect, my arguments about scriptural interpretation parallel many of the positions

Alasdair MacIntyre has staked out regarding traditions in general.[1] If a tradition is to live and carry on into the future, it must be able to sustain a certain amount of debate, argument, and disagreement about how to carry on the tradition in the present in ways continuous with the past. In this light, it is important to note that issues are not all of equal importance. Certain issues allow for substantial levels of disagreement without threatening the continuation of the tradition. In other cases disagreement can actually work to place one outside a tradition. Further, even widespread agreement can still undermine a tradition if it turns out that the agreement, rather than being a continuation of the tradition, actually disrupted one tradition and started something new, similar yet different. It is very difficult, however, to make judgments in this regard apart from considering a specific debate. Moreover, in this chapter I am concerned with what I take to be a prior set of considerations regarding debate and discussion within a tradition.

In this chapter I am primarily concerned with noting that a tradition that cannot sustain debate, discussion, and disagreement has long since ceased to have a viable future. Of course, too much disagreement and debate would be equally disastrous. Without some minimal level of agreement, there would be no basis for a disagreement. Members of a tradition would simply be talking and disagreeing about different things. This, of course, would raise serious questions about the coherence of such a tradition. It is impossible, however, to know in advance how much disagreement is too much. What can be done, and what I have tried to do in several chapters here, is to talk about the ways in which Christians might bring some of their specific convictions and practices to bear on these interpretive debates, discussions, and disagreements in ways that will enhance their prospects of worshipping and living faithfully before the triune God. That is, rather than eliminate interpretive debate, I have tried to point out ways in which Christians' convictions and practices regarding such things as forgiveness, repentance, and reconciliation along with their views about the Holy Spirit should shape and be shaped by their debates about scriptural interpretation. Moreover, it is primarily within communities that can nurture and sustain certain sorts of friendships that these convictions and practices will best work to inform and be informed by scriptural interpretation.

I want to continue this line of argument here by looking at how this ongoing debate and discussion about how to interpret scripture requires a host of largely verbal or rhetorical practices such as truth-telling, as well as habits

---

[1] See *After Virtue*, 2nd edn (Notre Dame: University of Notre Dame Press, 1984) esp. ch. 15.

of gracious and edifying speech, if these discussions and debates are to help Christian communities fulfill their proper ends. This much is not very surprising. In some respects, then, this chapter furthers the discussion of interpretive charity found in chapter 3. I will, however, argue that success in manifesting these verbal skills will be connected to very material issues about how, for example, Christians get and hold wealth.

Christian Philology

As I have noted, debate and discussion about scriptural interpretation is a constituent part of the Christian life. To engage in these debates in ways that enhance rather than frustrate Christian life and worship requires Christians to exercise what Nicholas Lash has called philology or word-care.[2] Lash argues that Christians' concern with word-care is rooted in their doctrine of God, the Word. Christians are made ministers of God's one Word, a Word that creates and orders all things, a word that is God's self. "In the last resort he [God] utters only one thing, which is himself as eternal salvation in the Spirit of the incarnate Logos."[3] The singularity of God's Word does not obviate either God's tri-unity or the diversity of things in the world. Rather, it indicates that all things are capable of being viewed and spoken of in relation to the Word. Moreover, "To *think* as a Christian is to try to understand the stellar spaces, the arrangements of micro-organisms and DNA molecules, the history of Tibet, the operation of economic markets, toothache, King Lear, the CIA and grandma's cooking – or, as Aquinas put it 'all things' – in relation to that uttering, utterance and enactment of God which they express to represent."[4] Lash continues,

> The story of the world, as Christianly told under the aspect of Word or logos, is the story of God's utterance of a world as a place for his indwelling. This is the story of the world as told in relation to God the promiser, God the promise, and God the achievement of the promise. To tell the story of the world in this way, and to try to act in conformity with this narrative and its implications, is to set a very high value indeed on the proper use of words.[5]

---

[2] See "Ministry of the Word or Comedy and Philology," *New Blackfriars* 68 (1987), pp. 472–83.

[3] Lash, "Ministry of the Word," p. 476, quoting Karl Rahner, "The Word and the Eucharist," *Theological Investigations IV*, trans. K Smyth (London: Darton, Longman and Todd, 1966), p. 255.

[4] Lash, "Ministry of the Word," p. 476.

[5] Lash, "Ministry of the Word," p. 476.

Thus, Lash takes the claim of Pére Chenu that the theologian is first of all a "philologist" to extend to all Christians:

> Commissioned as ministers of God's redemptive Word, we are required, in politics and in private life, in work and play, in commerce and scholarship, to practise and foster that philology, that word-caring, that meticulous and conscientious concern for the quality of conversation and truthfulness of memory, which is the first casualty of sin. The Church, accordingly, is or should be a school of philology, an academy of word-care.[6]

Lash goes on to point out how such word-care should characterize the church's engagement with "Mrs. Thatcher's Britain." This is not my particular concern here. His argument, however, is readily applicable to the issues with which I am concerned. Given that Christians are called to interpret and embody scripture in the various contexts in which they find themselves, such a calling requires Christians to engage each other in ongoing discussion and debate about how best to do this. These debates and discussions demand a specific form of word-care. This word-care is a central component in ensuring that the debate and discussion constitutive of Christian interpretation of scripture aids rather than frustrates Christian communities in fulfilling their ends. Word-care works to keep the arguments constitutive of Christian interpretation of scripture from becoming destructive of the life of the very community such arguments are designed to further. As Lash has already indicated, this word-care is ultimately rooted in the character of God, the Word. Further, this word-care must be fostered within the common life of Christian communities. What Lash's essay does not develop is the point that fostering and maintaining a care for words, which must be a crucial matter for scriptural interpretation, is related to a variety of other issues that on the face of it are not at all related to word use. These are issues that most contemporary Christians have relegated to the realm of the private and personal. Relegating such matters to the private sphere puts them beyond the bounds of public, communal scrutiny and criticism.

As a way of illustrating this point I would like to go on to show that any Christian community's success in fostering and manifesting a care for words is closely tied to how its members hold their possessions. In particular, I will show how these issues are connected in the epistle to the Ephesians. Specifically, Ephesians shows how such verbal practices as truth-telling and edification are linked to the Ephesian's abilities to address stealing in their

[6] Lash, "Ministry of the Word," p. 477.

midst. Further, Paul's commands to the Ephesians concerning how to deal with those among them who are stealing presumes that the Ephesians hold their wealth in such a way that it is evident that some people in the congregation are stealing – perhaps even from other members of the congregation. Unlike our contemporary situation, the getting and holding of possessions is not a private matter. Making it a private matter will ultimately undermine Christians' abilities, for example, to speak truthfully. When this happens it becomes impossible to exercise the sort of word-care needed to debate and discuss how best to interpret and embody scripture. On the basis of this specific illustration, I will then make some more general comments about the relationships between word-care and practices which Christians in the US largely consider to be matters of individual choice, private matters.

Stealing in Ephesus

In the light of Lash's call for churches to be academies of word-care, consider the following passage from Ephesians:

> So then, putting away falsehood, let each of us speak the truth with our neighbor, for we are all members of one another. Be angry yet do not sin; do not let the sun go down on your anger and do not make room for the devil. Those who steal must stop stealing. Rather, let them do honest work with their own hands, so as to have something to share with those in need. Let no evil talk come out of your mouths, but only what is good for building up as fits the occasion, that it may impart grace to those who hear. Do not grieve the Holy Spirit of God in whom you were sealed for the day of redemption. Put away from you all bitterness and wrath and anger and wrangling and slander together with all malice, and be kind to one another, tenderhearted, forgiving one another, as God in Christ forgave you. Therefore, be imitators of God, as beloved children and walk in love as Christ loved us and gave himself for us, a fragrant offering and sacrifice to God. (Eph. 4:25–5:2)

This passage offers a series of sharp injunctions about the way Christians ought to use words. Paul (or whoever wrote the letter)[7] admonishes the Ephesians to put away falsehood and to speak truthfully with one another. He warns of the dangers of letting one's anger fester, thus giving the devil opportunity to

---

[7] I have no particular stake in the debates over the pauline authorship of Ephesians. I will use "Paul" throughout this chapter as a way of identifying the author of the epistle without either implying or denying that it was written by the apostle Paul.

lead the Ephesians into sin.[8] These injunctions about word-use lead to a further series of injunctions proscribing a whole range of attitudes. Each of these attitudes is generally, but not exclusively, manifested in certain types of speech. All of these injunctions lead to the final demand of this passage, that the Ephesians "walk in love as Christ loved us. . . ." Paul's instructions in this paragraph seem concerned precisely with how and what Christians ought to speak, which attitudes and emotions they ought to cultivate and which they should avoid in order to build up one another.

It comes as a surprise, then, to read in 4:28 that Paul says that those who steal must stop and take up honest work so that they may have something to share with those in need. Why in the midst of a discussion about "word-care" does Paul raise the issue of stealing? Indeed, this verse seems so out of place that if it were removed from chapter 4 I don't think anyone would notice.[9] Why was such an earthy, material, physical action as stealing brought into this discussion about words and attitudes?[10] Was there a particularly large number of practicing cat burglars in the Ephesian church? Was there some sort of deviant teaching running through the congregation advocating that Christians ought to steal from the rich to give to the poor? If this were the case, such a teaching would seem to merit more than the almost off-hand attention it receives here.

Moreover, the text is phrased in such a way that, false teaching or not, it seems clear that there were those in the congregation who were stealing.[11] Without mitigating this disturbing fact, it is probably important to recognize

---

[8] The quotation, "Be angry yet do not sin" comes from Ps. 4:5 (LXX) but the notion of festering anger providing opportunity for the devil seems to be a direct allusion to Gen. 4:7, where God warns Cain that sin desires to take hold of him. Of course, Cain then uses deceptive speech to lure Abel to his death.

[9] Heinrich Schlier, *Der Brief an die Epheser* (Düsseldorf: Patmos Verlag, 1962), is one of the few who remarks on this, "Ohne Übergang und inneren Anschluss folgt v. 28 . . . " (p. 225).

[10] It is possible to claim that in this passage Paul is simply stringing together a diverse series of moral exhortations. The use of moral *sententiae* is a fairly common rhetorical device among Hellenistic philosophers (see, for example, the comments of A.T. Lincoln, *Ephesians* (Waco: Word, 1990), p. 295). Nevertheless, this manner of moral exhortation does not seem either random or arbitrary. What is more important here, particularly from a theological point of view, is to try to understand why these particular *sententiae* were brought together in this specific context.

[11] See Marcus Barth, *Ephesians*, 2 vols, Anchor Bible (Garden City: Doubleday, 1974), vol. 2, p. 515 and Schlier, *Epheser*, p. 225. There is no reason for taking Paul's injunction in 4:28 as a reference to those who previously were thieves. That is, the reference is not to "those who stole." There is a long list of those who read the text this way running at least from Chrysostom (Homily 14 on Ephesians) to Sondra Wheeler (*Wealth as Peril and Obligation* (Grand Rapids: Eerdmans, 1995), p.129).

that Paul does not use the Greek word for "thief" here (contra the NRSV). Rather he uses a participle, which is better rendered into English as "those who steal," as opposed to those who have made stealing their vocation. In this light, the types of things which might be considered stealing in this passage include the numerous small-scale ways in which slaves might pilfer their masters' goods (see Philem. 18). Those in the market place who use unfair scales or engage in price fixing, and petty con artists might also fit the bill. Calvin seems to have grasped this point quite well. In his 31st sermon on Ephesians (preached sometime between 1558 and 1559) he says,

> Now when St. Paul speaks here of thefts, he does not refer to such thieves as men punish with whipping or with hanging, but to all kinds of sly and crafty dealing that are used to get other men's goods by evil practices such as extortion, deeds of violence and all other similar things . . . . Although a merchant may be accounted a man of good skill, yet he will still have a store of tricks and wiles, and they will be like nets laid for the simple and such as are without experience, who do not perceive them. The case is the same with those who follow the mechanical arts, for they have the skill to counterfeit their works in such a way that men shall be deceived by them. Again, with regard to prices, there is no trusting the sellers . . . . In short, there is no class of men in which there are not infinite faults and extortions to be seen for every man wishes to get the upper hand and make himself stronger than the rest.[12]

We may get a further picture of the type of situation Paul is addressing when we recognize that this whole passage, with its repeated use of phrases like "one another" (vv. 25, 32) and its emphases on building up the body of Christ, is directed at the common life of the Ephesian church. It may well be the case that those who were stealing were stealing from other members of the congregation. This, of course, is not a foreign notion to the New Testament. The story of the "neglect" of the widows of the "Hellenists" in Acts 6 might serve as an appropriate example of the type of stealing Paul proscribes in 4:28. Alternatively, Paul might be talking about a scenario in which some members of the congregation, who either through idleness or misplaced views about the *parousia*, were living as parasites off the charity of the church like those addressed in 2 Thess. 3. It would not be unreasonable to characterize similar activities in the Ephesian church as stealing. Although it does not appear to have been a problem, the status divisions within the Corinthian church might well have spawned an atmosphere in which stealing might have occurred.

[12] John Calvin, *Sermons on Ephesians*, revision of 1557 translation of A. Golding (London: Banner of Truth Trust, 1973), pp. 451–2.

While all these examples show that disputes over possessions are not unknown to the New Testament, we must admit that we do not know exactly what types of behavior Paul was addressing when he told certain Ephesians to stop stealing: whether from those inside the church or those outside it. Presumably, those who first read the epistle had a pretty good idea of what Paul was talking about.

I have already noted that this entire passage is directed towards maintaining the common life of the church. These are not demands addressed to isolated individuals to make of what they will. Rather, they are admonitions to a community about how they must talk and live with each other in order to maintain their unity and faithfulness under Christ. In this light, it is not hard to see that lying (v. 25), allowing one's anger to lead one into temptation (vv. 26–7), stealing (v. 28), destructive speech (v. 29), grieving the Spirit (v. 30), along with bitterness, rage, wrath, quarreling, blaspheming and the like (v. 31) and the inability to forgive one another (v. 32) are all potentially mortal wounds to the common life of the church. Such practices stand in sharp opposition to the life of agape commended by Paul and exemplified by Christ (5:1–2). Given that Paul's aim in this passage is maintaining the common life of the church as a faithful testimony to the work of God, it is no more odd for him to address the issue of Christians stealing (particularly from each other) than it is for him to emphasize truth-telling.

Further, it is not difficult to imagine that the fact that certain Ephesians were stealing would be quite destructive of the trust and honesty needed to speak truthfully, and to engage in all of the other verbal activities which contribute to the building up of the church.[13] What the combination of all of these injunctions in 4:25–5:2 makes clear is that some Ephesians were engaged in stealing (perhaps from other members of the congregation) and that such activity was a distinct threat to the common life of the church. In particular, stealing posed a distinct threat to the Ephesians' abilities to speak the truth, to be angry without sinning, to put away bitterness, rage, and so forth. This much seems relatively straightforward.

There are two further points I wish to develop from this. The first concerns the specific issue of stealing and its deleterious effects on a community's abilities to exercise the word-care Paul enjoins in this passage. The second

---

[13] Indeed, a quick look at the episode of Ananias and Sapphira in Acts 5 shows how closely linked issues of stealing and lying are. Ananias and Sapphira are not judged for stealing from the community. Peter asserts that both their property and the proceeds from its sale belonged to the couple. It was their conspiracy to lie to God which brings such an extraordinary judgment.

point examines the presumptions about the common life of the Ephesian church lying behind this passage and the relevance of this sort of common life to contemporary Christian communities. First, if stealing frustrates word-care in the ways Paul implies, it may be fruitful to explore the relationship between word-care and the alternative to stealing.

Stealing, Generosity, and the Character of God

In his *Treatise on Good Works* (1520) Martin Luther addresses the commandment against stealing. Like Calvin, he takes the prohibition against stealing to extend well beyond matters of simple theft. It covers "every kind of sharp practice which men perpetrate against each other in matters of worldly goods. For instance, greed, usury, overcharging, counterfeit goods, short measure, short weight and who could give an account of all the smart, novel and sharp-witted tricks which daily increase in every trade."[14] The cause of these practices is a fundamental anxiety that there will not be enough for oneself. This stems, as John Milbank points out, from a lack of faith: "In fearing that there will not be world enough or time, we insist on our identity, our truth, our space, denying that of others – thereby rendering their coyness always a crime. This, according to Luther, is why *stealing* is a temptation; *not at all* because there is a limited supply and we should allow others their share, as legalism presumes, but on the contrary because we fear there will not be enough for us."[15] Anxiety over scarcity not only drives stealing, it eliminates the conditions under which speech might be truthful.

The alternative to the anxiety that founds stealing and frustrates truthfulness is generosity. "A man is generous because he trusts God and never doubts but that he will always have enough."[16] The commandment against stealing can, therefore, be positively stated as "be generous." As Milbank notes, "Generosity or true not stealing acts out of the assumption of plenitude, our confidence in God's power."[17] Milbank's point here is not to deny the obvious fact that there are those with abundant faith, yet few material goods. Neither does he reject the fact that death is the fundamental manifestation of scarcity.

---

[14] From the translation of James Atkinson, vol. 44 of *Luther's Works* (Philadelphia: Fortress Press, 1968), p. 107.

[15] John Milbank, "Can Morality be Christian?," in *The Word Made Strange* (Oxford: Blackwell, 1997), p. 225.

[16] Luther, *Treatise on Good Works*, p. 109.

[17] Milbank, "Can Morality be Christian?," p. 225.

Further, he notes that in our present broken, damaged state, self-sacrifice may be called for at times. Nevertheless, his point is that

> Under the original will of God, no sacrifice of self is required, and while it is true that under the dispensation of death, this *will* (when the occasion arrives) be necessary, we should never fall into the trap of an absolute celebration of self-sacrifice, especially our own. Luther's view of why stealing is wrong seems almost closer to the idea that stealing is not truly in our self-interest than many more moralizing accounts.[18]

Therefore, a life of generosity based on the assumption of plenitude is not a willful denial of contingent manifestations of scarcity and the anxiety and covetous struggle generated thereby. Rather, it signifies a rejection of the logic which presumes such an agonistic situation is natural. Of course, stealing is not the only manifestation of this agonistic situation. All human intercourse, including speech, gets caught up this cycle of struggle, thus frustrating attempts at the word-care enjoined in Eph. 4.[19] The assumption of plenitude "is grounded in a refusal of the contrast between my interest and that of the other. I exist in receiving; because I receive I joyfully give."[20] The great temptation to stealing, as Luther recognizes, lies in the initial presumption that scarcity is natural and that therefore creation is to be seen as the struggle to secure one's own possessions, time, and selfhood over against the desires and incursions of others. "Despite scarcity, despite our submission to the law which it imposes, we must act as *if* there were plenitude, and no death, since to believe is to believe that this is what really pertains despite the fall. It is, of course, quite simply impossible to be a Christian and to suppose that death and suffering belong to God's original plan, or that the struggle of natural selection (which one doubts is even proven as a full account of evolution) is how creation *as creation* rather than thwarted creation genuinely comes about."[21]

The notion of plenitude which undermines stealing and thereby helps to enable proper care for words among Christians is - like the very notion of word-care itself - rooted in a doctrine of the triune God's inner life and

---

[18] Milbank, "Can Morality be Christian?," p. 228.

[19] For a discussion of how the generosity characteristic of the triune God founds and enables the speech needed to articulate and construct selfhood in a non-competitive relationship with other selves see Rowan Williams' "Interiority and Epiphany: A Reading of New Testament Ethics," *Modern Theology* 13 (1997), pp. 29–51. Interestingly, Williams also discusses Ephesians, but not the passage under consideration here.

[20] Milbank, "Can Morality be Christian?," p. 228.

[21] Milbank, "Can Morality be Christian?," p. 229.

creative activity. A Christian doctrine of creation assumes that creation is characterized by plenitude rather than scarcity. Further, this plenitude is the gift of the triune God who creates out of a superabundance of love rather than out of necessity. The plenitude characteristic of creation allows abundant diversity to exist peaceably and harmoniously because it obviates the need for struggle due to scarcity. Indeed, the very character of the Trinity lies in God's eternal self gift, simultaneously receiving and responding.[22] Although the fall brings death and scarcity, the church is to testify to that "already commenced and yet to come restoration of Creation as Creation."[23] The church does this as it assumes that plenitude is God's intention for the world. Within this framework, the notion of a Christian stealing points not so much to moral flaw as to an incoherent act. It represents a failure to understand the nature of the community into which one has been baptized.

It is here that I wish to develop my second point in relation to Paul's discussion of stealing in Ephesians. That is, Paul's discussion presumes, but does not really articulate, a particular vision of the life of the Ephesian community. If contemporary Christians are to recognize the connections between stealing and word-care, they must also understand that this connection presupposes the existence of a particular sort of community.

The Possibility of Stealing

Once one recognizes that this passage is not directed to isolated individuals but to a community of believers, it also becomes evident that this passage presumes a certain level of intensity in the common life of the Ephesians, an intensity largely absent from most churches in the US. The verbal activities of this passage, both those encouraged and those discouraged, are all public sorts of activities. That is, to be performed at all they have to be performed in the presence of others. As I already noted, Paul addresses the issue of stealing in 4:28 as if his audience would understand what he meant without saying much more. This means that the Ephesians had enough knowledge

---

[22] According to Milbank's "trinitarianism without reserve," this dynamic activity is not primarily marked by the "fontal plenitude" of the Father. Rather, "Because the divine *actus* is *infinite*, and therefore, 'interminably terminated' it comprises a non-temporal dynamic or mutual 'play' between an infinite 'conclusion' of expression in the Son, and an endless 're-opening' of the conclusion by the desire of the Spirit which re-inspires the paternal *arche*." See "The Second Difference," in *The Word Made Strange*, p. 187.

[23] Milbank, "Can Morality be Christian?," p. 229.

about each others' lives to know that some among them were stealing. For the reality of stealing to be as great a danger to the fabric of the common life of the Ephesians as lying or slandering one another, the lives and indeed the possessions of the members of the community had to be relatively accessible to other members of the community. This text presupposes that the common life of the Ephesian church was such that they had some access to each others' possessions.

While it is doubtful that the Ephesian Christians held all things in common after the manner of Acts 4:32ff., it is also the case that they had not taken excessive precautions to secure their possessions from the intrusions of one another.[24] Neither could they have made the issue of possessions an entirely private matter separate from the ongoing life of the community. The line constructed between public and private seems to have located possessions squarely in the public realm. It is a profound testimony to the poverty of the common life of most contemporary churches that Christians have so secured their possessions from each other that they can barely imagine what it might be to acknowledge openly, in the manner of Eph. 4, that Christians might steal (even from each other).

This, of course, is not because of the excessive virtue of contemporary Christians. It would not be surprising that on any given Sunday, in almost any church, embezzlers sit next to those who cheat on their taxes or steal from their employers or customers. Any astonishment one registers would result from finding out about such stealing. Nevertheless, the manner in which Paul addresses this issue in Eph. 4 makes it painfully clear that the fact that such stealing was going on in the Ephesian church was no secret. Alternatively, should I or anyone else in the church I attend be caught stealing, particularly stealing from others in the congregation or the congregation as a whole, the general response would be that such news should be buried under a thousand layers of silence.[25] To the extent that such stealing became known it would only be through gossip and innuendo. Whether it remains covered up or exposed only in limited hidden ways, this stealing is irrelevant for a contemporary community's abilities to speak truthfully with each other. This is because the community's very ability to speak truthfully has already been shown to be wanting by the way it has addressed the matter of stealing.

One can in a small way understand the importance and interconnectedness

---

[24] For an extensive account of Acts 4:32ff. see Brian Capper, "The Palestinian Cultural Context of Earliest Christian Community of Goods," in *The Book of Acts in its Palestinian Setting*, ed. R. Bauckham (Grand Rapids: Eerdmans, 1995), pp. 323–56.

[25] The obvious exceptions to this are the highly publicized escapades of some televangelists.

of these issues of stealing and the verbal practices of the Ephesians if one has ever lived or worked in a situation where several people share a refrigerator. This small manifestation of common life can quickly threaten the harmony of a social group when one goes to get a can of soda only to find that the Coke put there yesterday to get cold for today is no longer there. Further, it does not take much imagination to see that in this situation the boundary between stealing and borrowing becomes very fluid. Our assumptions about what is appropriate to share will bang up against the assumptions of others. Under such conditions, disputes and arguments are bound to arise. If disputes about the use of goods in the refrigerator are not to tear the house or office apart, one will have to enter into the sorts of communal practices where issues of truth-telling, forgiveness, and the other practices mentioned in Eph. 4 will play major roles.

In the course of writing a version of this chapter I was told about a church where the staff shared a refrigerator. Stealing became such a divisive issue that the church secretary spent the best part of a week dividing up the refrigerator into individual bins assigned to each staff member. Each individual's bin is sacrosanct. One is not to interfere in any way with the bin of one's neighbor. It appears that Christians can either have the sort of community in which possessions are made accessible to one another and stealing and/or knowledge of stealing is a real possibility, or they can privatize their possessions as best they can, thus securing their goods at the expense of their common life. It is ostensibly the case that stealing led to the division of the refrigerator into individual cubicles. This, however, is only a surface problem. When the stealing began, these Christians also suffered from an inability to put away falsehood and to speak the truth with each other. Their anger got the best of them; they failed to engage in the practices of confession and forgiveness and repentance. For any particular group of Christians, privatization of property, that is, making possessions merely a personal matter, is both the easiest and least threatening way to deal with the impoverishment of their common life. To do anything else not only raises the specter of stealing, it will demand that they be truthful, able to deal with conflict without lapsing into sin and capable of asking for and receiving forgiveness from each other. Yet it is precisely these practices which must be cultivated if Christians are to participate in that ongoing discussion about how to interpret and embody scripture in the various contexts in which they find themselves.

Paul's discussion of stealing in Eph. 4:28 stands as a profound challenge to the common life of any Christian community. The challenge is to counter the tendencies in modern American life to individualize and privatize large sections of our lives, including our wealth.[26] There are some rare exceptions to this. For example, all United Methodist clergy are required to publish their salaries in the journal of their Annual Conference and I gather this often provides a basis for some stimulating conversation. Any attempt to make this a requirement for all baptized Methodists, however, would provoke widespread rebellion. Without a common life, however, in which the ways in which Christians get and hold wealth are much more accessible to each other, Christians will also find it much more difficult to engage in the other practices Paul prescribes in this passage: truthfulness rather than triviality, anger that leads to forgiveness rather than bitterness, gracious words which build up as opposed to vacuous compliments which support one another's self-deceptions. Without such a common life, Christians will have almost no verbal resources when they try to engage scripture in the ways that they must if they are to fulfill their ends in the world.

Thus far I have argued that in order for Christians to engage in the debates and discussion needed to interpret scripture as part of their struggle to worship and live faithfully before God, they will have to foster and maintain a certain sort of word-care as part of their common life. The particular sorts of practices that are involved in this word care are nicely laid out in Eph. 4:25–5:2. What this passage also indicates, however, is that Christians' abilities to speak truthfully with each other, to offer edifying and gracious words, to be angry without sinning, and so forth, are directly connected to issues about how they acquire and hold wealth. Further, the intimate connection of issues of word-care and issues of wealth (in this case stealing) presupposes a certain level of intensity in the common life of the Ephesian church. If contemporary Christians are to manifest the sort of word-care that is essential for their interpretation and embodiment of scripture, then they, too, will have to manifest the sort of common life that intimately connects issues of speaking with issues of wealth. I realize that this argument spills out on to a variety of issues that each in its own right might be the subject of volumes. I can here address none of these as fully as one might. I will,

---

[26] As Sondra Wheeler states, "The idea that moral reflection and moral reformation about the status of possessions must take place in communities of discernment and mutual accountability entails a number of things about the nature of the groups that might find the New Testament's moral instruction useable. One is that it presupposes a high level of commitment to the shared life of the group . . . . More deeply, commitment is required because any serious consideration of the spiritual perils of wealth will involve a degree of honesty and self-disclosure that can be sustained only in an atmosphere of genuine care and trust" (*Wealth as Peril and Obligation*, p. 145).

however, try to make some general comments which are analogous extensions of the arguments I have made about word-care and wealth. This will lead me back to a more concrete discussion of stealing as a way of furthering the argument I have already started.

Word-care and Christian Communities

I have focused my arguments about the interconnections between such things as truth-telling and stealing in relation to the common life of Christian communities because this happened to be the issue addressed in Ephesians. However, I think it possible to extend the basic points of the argument more generally. That is, the sorts of very public verbal and rhetorical practices that one rightly associates with issues of scriptural interpretation are inextricably bound up with much more material, often privatized, practices (e.g. the getting and holding of wealth). These practices are so closely bound up with each other that failure in regard to these material issues (e.g. stealing) will frustrate Christians' attempts to engage in the verbal practices so crucial for scriptural interpretation. Christians' prospects for avoiding failure in regard to the material practices are related to their refusal to allow these practices to become simply matters of individual concern and private choice. This can only happen as they form, nurture, and maintain the sort of common life that allows these material concerns to become issues for the community as a whole.[27] For this to be the case, members of a community will also need to be exercising sufficient word-care in their conversations that once-privatized issues can be brought into the public life of the community in ways that are not ultimately destructive.

In this light, the issue is not simply the relationship of wealth to word-care. Questions about raising children, what one eats, how one participates in material culture, and a host of other topics can all be seen as connected to a community's success in fostering and maintaining the sort of word-care necessary for truth-telling, edification, and so forth, practices which are themselves crucial for the interpretation of scripture. To the extent that

---

[27] When the argument is put this generally, it becomes clear that Christians from the base communities of Latin America and Africa have been saying much the same thing for some time. For discussions of how such material concerns touch on the interpretation of scripture in these contexts see Carlos Mesters, *Defenseless Flower*, trans. Francis McDonagh (Maryknoll: Orbis, 1989) and the work of Gerald West and others associated with the Institute for the Contextual Study of the Bible at the University of Natal.

questions about raising children and so forth are normally considered to be private matters of individual choice, they will need to become "public," that is, part of the fabric of the common life of a community, if their proper connection to word-care is to be maintained. As I indicated in the previous chapter, this is not a call for Christians to be absolutely and unreservedly self-revealing, nor is it a call to demand such self-revelation of others. Rather, the point here is to recognize that the line between public and private is not natural. It is constructed socially within communities. Christian communities will need self-consciously to construct this line in ways that recognize that they cannot engage in the verbal practices enjoined in passages like Eph. 4:25–5:2, and which are crucial for interpretation of scripture, if they are not willing to consider how their abilities to put aside falsehood and speak truthfully and graciously with each other are related to ways they get and hold wealth, raise children, celebrate holidays, care for elderly parents, and a host of other practices.

To the extent that Christian communities (at least in the US) adopt the public/private distinctions operative in the larger culture, they will find it difficult and frustrating to cultivate the care for words that is essential for the debates and discussions which are crucial for interpreting scripture in ways that foster faithful life and worship. In this light, it is not surprising to find that such debates and discussions as there are within churches more closely reflect the acrimonious and divisive discourse that is characteristic of contested issues within society as a whole.

Alternatively, as Christian communities begin to reconstruct lines between public and private that are more appropriate both to the type of community they are called to be and to the character of the God they worship, they will find that issues such as the care of elderly parents, patterns of consumption, use of contraception, and so forth all become matters of common concern. These matters would all need to be addressed from the same trinitarian theological perspective as Milbank brought to the issue of stealing. In addition, in the course of exploring these matters Christians will naturally turn to scripture. This will, of course, bring them into patterns of debate and argument about how to interpret and embody scripture in ways that will issue forth in faithful life and worship. This will of course re-emphasize the importance of word-care.

This turn to scripture raises an issue which has played a role in much of the discussion in this book, but which has yet to be addressed directly. As Christians turn to scripture in the course of debating and discussing these issues, the work of professional biblical scholars will, no doubt, come into play. Throughout this book I have both made recourse to the work of professional biblical scholars and distanced the concerns of Christian interpretation and embodiment of scripture from the concerns of the scholarly guild. In the next and final chapter I will try to articulate the convictions that lead to both of these attitudes. This will then lead me to spell out some of the future tasks facing Christian communities when it comes to forming and nurturing wise readers of scripture.

Chapter Seven

CONCLUSION:
PRACTICAL WISDOM,
CHRISTIAN FORMATION, AND
ECCLESIAL AUTHORITY

Introduction

My overriding concern in this book has been with Christian interpretation of scripture. In the course of making my various arguments I have tried to be clear that these arguments are primarily applicable to Christians and to Christian communities as they interpret and embody scripture as part of their ongoing struggle to worship and live faithfully before the triune God.[1] Because of Christians' particular relationship to scripture and because of the specific concerns, interests, and aims they bring to scriptural interpretation, they also need to bring certain convictions to bear on their interpretation. In addition, a variety of practices must be in good working order if Christians are to interpret scripture well. Further, Christian communities must form and nurture a certain common life if these practices and doctrines are successfully to shape and be shaped by scriptural interpretation.

At various points in this book I have noted that these particular concerns are very different from, if not starkly opposed to, the concerns of professional biblical scholars. At the same time, I have made ready and constructive use of the work of professional biblical scholars in making my arguments. One might well ask if I am trying both to have my cake and eat it, too. In short, can I make use of professional biblical scholarship without at the same time invoking practices and convictions that would put me at odds with, if not

---

[1] This is not to imply that my arguments are in principle inaccessible to non-Christians and incapable of being criticized and evaluated by them.

separate me from, those convictions and practices crucial to Christian interpretation of scripture? In response to this type of accusation I want to begin this chapter by laying out my views about how Christian interpretation of scripture might be related to the guild of professional scholars and its work. Christians may well make *ad hoc* use of the work of professional biblical scholars, but such scholarship is not necessary for Christians to interpret scripture in the ways they are called to do. Nevertheless, as a matter of contingent fact, Christians could usefully learn from the profession of biblical studies about the importance of forming people to read in particular ways. Indeed, I will argue that one of the chief tasks facing Christian communities concerns the formation of their members into being wise readers of scripture with at least as much success as the profession of biblical scholarship has shown in forming its members to be particular sorts of readers. This will lead to a discussion of the type of readers the church should endeavor to form. From this discussion it will become clear that one of the thorniest problems remaining for an account such as the one I have rendered in this book concerns matters of ecclesial authority. I will conclude by simply pointing out some of the most crucial issues in this regard as a sort of promissory note for a further work.

Plundering the Egyptians

I want to begin by addressing the charge that there is a sort of inconsistency in both distancing the interests of Christian interpretation of scripture from the interests of professional scholars and accepting and making use of the work of professional scholars. To use the work of others for my own purposes is simply to recognize that in making a specific argument, one must avail oneself of the best resources one can. Indeed, the interpretive charity I advocated earlier probably requires Christians to avail themselves of the work of those who do not otherwise read scripture with the same interests as Christians do. Such use, however, will always be on an *ad hoc* basis. In regard to Christians using the work of professional biblical scholarship in their interpretation of scripture this means that certain works, viewpoints, and ideas may prove helpful in one instance, but not in another. It is simply not the case that all professional biblical scholarship will be equally useful (if at all) all of the time. Therefore, it is not necessary for Christians to adopt a systematic view about any particular aspect of biblical studies.

Without question, works of professional scholars may raise issues which impinge directly on Christian interpretation of scripture and which Christians must address. I think, however, it will turn out to be the case that there are far fewer of these instances than one might expect. Of course, if scholarship could demonstrate that Jesus had never lived or that Jesus was never crucified by the Romans or if archaeologists were to uncover the bones of Jesus, these findings would pose a substantial challenge to Christianity. When and if such scholarship comes to the surface, Christians will have to address it.[2] Alternatively, the over-heated claims of the Jesus Seminar simply need to be cooled down and demystified.[3] The fact that some biblical scholars assume that professional scholarship raises a host of extraordinary difficulties for Christian biblical interpretation probably reflects the extent to which those scholars have adopted the interests of professional scholars and imposed them on Christian communities. An example of this might be Robert Carroll's book, *The Bible as a Problem for Christianity*. Alternatively, it is equally likely that large numbers of Christians have not properly understood the interpretive practices and convictions most crucial to their identity as Christians. For example, a Christian who feels that the well-established scholarly views that Moses did not write the Penteteuch and that Paul did not write the Pastorals undermines the authority of scripture, has not properly understood that, for Christians, the text of scripture is canonical, not the authors of particular biblical books.

In fact, the work of professional biblical scholars is usually quite complex, and diverse. Its conclusions are often quite limited and equivocal. Moreover, as the example of the Jesus Seminar makes clear, biblical scholars are quite capable of sensationalizing their claims in order to get the attention of the wider public. Even in less notable cases, the pressures on academics to publish in order to reap professional rewards can significantly shape what does and does not become a focus for scholarly interest. These are all caveats that need to be considered when Christians approach the work of professional biblical scholars. All of this is to say that to be able to evaluate and adjudicate the claims of professional biblical scholarship even with the aim of making *ad hoc* use of them, one has to be deeply acquainted with biblical scholarship's practices and habits as well as its results. Indeed, those who know it best will be able to make the best use of it on an *ad hoc* basis. They are the ones most likely to make use

---

[2] For a philosophically subtle account of the issues involved here see William A. Christian Sr, *The Doctrines of Religious Communities* (New Haven: Yale University Press, 1987), ch. 7.

[3] See the criticisms of the Jesus Seminar in Luke Johnson's *The Real Jesus* (San Francisco: Harper San Francisco, 1995); and Richard Hays' "The Corrected Jesus," *First Things* (May 1994), pp. 43–8.

of the works of others without at the same time undermining the very particular sets of interests, concerns, and practices Christians bring to the interpretation of scripture.

This attitude towards the intellectual achievements of those outside the church has a long theological pedigree. The actual practice of employing the works of pagans for Christian theological purposes begins in the very earliest Christian communities. As one might expect, there was no single view about how to engage pagan knowledge. One way of doing this, however, was to approach the works of pagan philosophers through the Exodus story, most specifically through the account of the "plundering of the Egyptians" in Ex. 12:35–6. In a letter (ca. 230) to the as yet unbaptized Gregory Thaumaturgos, Origen encourages Gregory to "extract from the philosophy of the Greeks what may serve as a course of study of a preparation for Christianity, and from geometry what will serve to explain the sacred scriptures, in order that all that the sons of the philosophers are wont to say about geometry and music, grammar, rhetoric and astronomy as fellow-helpers to philosophy, we may say about philosophy itself, in relation to Christianity."[4] Origen then goes on to claim that this very practice is foreshadowed in Ex. 12 when God commands Moses to tell the Israelites to ask the Egyptians for a variety of valuables prior to leaving Egypt, thus despoiling them. Origen goes on to note "how useful to the children of Israel were the things brought forth from Egypt, which the Egyptians had not put to proper use, but which the Hebrews, guided by the wisdom of God, used for God's service."[5]

About 160 years later Gregory of Nyssa would give a similar account in his *Life of Moses*. In the early part of the *theoria*, Nyssa's contemplative interpretation of Moses' life, Nyssa clearly indicates that an education in pagan philosophy (such as Moses would have received in Pharaoh's household) was, in itself, barren.[6] Moses, like all souls aspiring to virtue, had to leave his Egyptian mother and return to his natural mother, who, in fact, had also been his wet nurse. "This teaches, it seems to me, that if we should be involved with profane teachings during our education, we should not separate ourselves

---

[4] "Letter to Gregory," para.1 in *PG* 11.88–9. The translation quoted here is found in *The Ante-Nicene Fathers*, ed. A. Roberts and J. Donaldson (1885; rpt. Peabody: Hendrickson, 1994), p. 393.

[5] "Letter to Gregory," para. 2.

[6] *Life of Moses*, book 2, paras 10–12. A Greek text can be found in the *Sources Chrétiennes*. My quotations here are from the translation of A. Malherbe and E. Ferguson in the Classics of Western Spirituality series (New York: Paulist, 1978).

from the nourishment of the Church's milk, which would be her laws and customs."[7] In this early section, Nyssa is quite clear that pagan philosophy and Christian virtue are antagonists.[8]

Later, however, when he comes to account for Ex. 12:35–6, Nyssa comes to a view very similar to Origen's. Having ruled out any interpretation of these verses that would indicate that Moses was the leader of a band of thieves,[9] Nyssa goes on to give a "loftier" interpretation of this episode.

> It commands those participating through virtue in the free life also to equip themselves with the wealth of pagan learning by which foreigners to the faith beautify themselves. Our guide in virtue commands someone who "borrows" from wealthy Egyptians to receive such things as moral and natural philosophy, geometry, astronomy, dialectic, and whatever else is sought by those outside the Church, since these things will be useful when in time the divine sanctuary of mystery must be beautified with the riches of reason.[10]

As both Origen and Nyssa recognize, the image of plundering the Egyptians nicely points to the tensions involved in engaging pagan philosophy. They recognize that those who know it well can use it to benefit the church. At the same time they know that the aims and interests of pagan philosophers are at odds with those of the church. Further, they recognize that a knowledge of pagan philosophy, even when put to the service of God, is useful, but not necessary, for a holy life.

Having said this, there are some very real differences between the situations Origen and Nyssa address and the relationships between the church and the guild of biblical scholars. For Origen and Nyssa, the differences, oppositions, and boundaries between pagan philosophy and Christian theology were quite distinct. This is what gives force to the metaphor of plundering; they are dealing with something that is essentially antagonistic to their point of view. The lines between the church and the guild of biblical scholars, however, are not quite so clear cut. Many, if not most, biblical scholars would identify themselves as Christians. Often they will be employed by institutions affiliated with particular churches. Yet *as biblical scholars* they identify, in varying degrees, with the aims and concerns of the profession. Obviously, it is in

---

[7] *Life of Moses*, book 2, para. 12.

[8] *Life of Moses,* book 2, para. 13.

[9] It is this concern which seems to lead Nyssa to abandon the use of various forms of σκύλλω (despoil) found in the LXX and Origen in favor of λαβόντα which Malherbe and Ferguson translate as "borrow" in scare quotes.

[10] *Life of Moses*, book 2, para. 115.

principle possible both to participate fully in the church with its particular interpretive habits and aims and to be a full member of the guild of biblical scholars. While some in the profession would wish to rule out what they call "confessional" interpretation,[11] it would be impossible for the profession, in its current state, to articulate its aims and interests so exclusively. This is not to say that at some point in the future, things might not be different. Various institutional and ideological pressures may at some point so shape the concerns and interests of the profession that it would be difficult if not impossible to be both a biblical scholar and a Christian.[12] Currently, however, the fragmented plurality of interests characteristic of the profession works to keep the profession relatively open to those whose primary interpretive allegiance may lie elsewhere. Hence from one perspective, the profession lacks sufficient coherence to offer the sort of opposition to the church that would really suit the metaphor of plundering in a systematic way.

Nevertheless, what this metaphor ought to do is to remind Christians that their particular interests and concerns with scripture, as well as their specific interpretive convictions and habits, are not the same as, if not directly opposed to, those of the profession of biblical studies. There may not be outright enmity, but there is not much fruitful cooperation either.[13] Moreover, the ends towards which the church interprets and embodies scripture are simply not those of the profession. As a result, the work of professional biblical scholars must always be appropriated in an *ad hoc* way, on a case-by-case basis.[14]

This position stands in sharp contrast to those who argue that scholarly study of the Bible (usually meaning various forms of historical-criticism) is necessary

[11] For a recent, but badly flawed, argument advocating this policy, see P.R. Davies, *Whose Bible Is It Anyway?* (Sheffield: Sheffield Academic Press, 1995).

[12] This holds true for almost any occupation. From the very beginning of the Christian movement, Christians have recognized that at certain times and in certain circumstances specific occupations were incompatible with one's Christianity.

[13] As Jon Levenson has noted, the myth of cooperation is almost always perpetrated by those who have already seriously, albeit unconsciously, compromised their specific Jewish or Christian convictions. See "Theological Consensus or Historicist Evasion: Jews and Christians in Biblical Studies," in *The Hebrew Bible, The Old Testament and Historical Criticism* (Louisville: Westminster/John Knox Press, 1993).

[14] In making this claim, I am not, unlike Origen and Gregory, making a comprehensive proposal about the relationships Christians ought to have to pagan learning. That issue is both too large and too complex to admit of a single policy even if it is a policy of *ad hoc* engagements. The diversity of types of *ad hoc* engagements needed to offer such a proposal would move well beyond the confines of this book.

for the church in its interpretation of scripture.[15] The nature of this necessity, however, is less than clear. In some cases, the necessity of historical-critical concerns for Christian interpretation of scripture is grounded in the fear that eliminating historical-critical practices would lead to the Bible being read in an ahistorical and therefore anarchic way.[16] Since this is a situation Christians would wish to avoid, they must necessarily maintain the concerns and practices of historical-criticism. On the one hand, given the propensity among those in the US to view reality as an eternal present, there may be some merit in this concern. On the other hand, both professional biblical scholars and Christians need to recognize that the notion of an ahistorical reading is oxymoronic. We cannot avoid giving historical interpretations. All interpretation is always wrapped up in a whole range of historical concerns. As Jon Levenson has noted, "As soon as you have treated the discolorations on the page as language, you have made a historical judgment."[17]

What is interesting about the argument against ahistorical readings, however, is not so much the chimera it attacks (i.e. ahistoricality), but what it implicitly assumes: When historical critics argue against ahistorical readings they seem to assume that the only alternative is to be a historical critic. The sorts of historical investigations most biblical scholars are concerned with are limited, however, to a very narrow range of historical issues surrounding the various stages of production of the forms of the biblical texts that we now have. Those scholars particularly engaged in reconstructive tasks tend to be uninterested in the biblical text once it reaches its final form. By the time one gets to exploring issues regarding how subsequent generations read those

---

[15] A surprising place where just this sentiment is found is the report of the Pontifical Biblical Commission, "The Interpretation of the Bible in the Church," 1993 (English 1994).

[16] While this argument is often lodged against the movement known as "structuralism," the charge of ahistorical instability is also applied to most types of literary criticism of the Bible. Structuralism has long since ceased to be a vital movement within literary criticism and never really took hold in biblical studies. For a presentation of the claim that literary approaches to the Bible are inherently unstable see John Barton, *Reading the Old Testament* (Philadelphia: Westminster Press, 1984). The best map in regard to current debates over historical-criticism and literary critical alternatives is Stephen Moore's *Literary Criticism and the Gospels: The Theoretical Challenge* (New Haven: Yale University Press, 1989). Jon Levenson, however, makes the telling counter-point that an emphasis on reading scripture in terms of various reconstructed original contexts will result in a certain sort of theological anarchy. See his chapter, "The Eighth Principle of Judaism and the Literary Simultaneity of Scripture," in *The Hebrew Bible, The Old Testament and Historical Criticism.*

[17] Levenson, *The Hebrew Bible, The Old Testament and Historical Criticism*, p. 110.

texts, historical critics have largely fallen by the wayside.[18] Christians, however, need to be particularly attentive to how previous generations of faithful Christians have interpreted and embodied scripture.

Another way of arguing for the necessity of historical-criticism (if not biblical scholarship in general) is by claiming that only historical-criticism can provide the meaning of the biblical text which is essential to Christian application of scripture. "Meaning" in this case must refer to something like what the original author intended or what the original audience would have understood – what the text meant. These things can only be elucidated by the practices of historical-criticism. Once the historical critic has provided this raw material, it is up to Christians to "apply" the text in the present –what the text means. Clearly, if Christians had a systematic commitment to this particular construction of "meaning," there would, then, be a case for the necessity of the practices which delivered this "meaning." Christians may or may not be interested in authorial intentions or the original audiences of the biblical texts. Of course, a lot hangs here on notions of intention, of what an author is, and of a current community's relationship to any prior readers of a text. As I argued in chapter 2, however, ways of addressing these notions that seek to isolate a single, stable, unchanging meaning will at the same time frustrate the sorts of interests and concerns Christians need to bring to bear on their interpretation of scripture.[19]

In addition, some scholars have even lodged a theological argument for the necessity of historical-criticism, arguing that it is needed to repulse docetic interpretive tendencies.[20] A. K. M. Adam has recently offered a comprehen-

---

[18] Historical critics are, of course, interested in what previous generations of modern historical critics have said. This, however, is an extremely narrow slice of the history of a text's interpretation.

[19] In a recent article B. S. Childs also notes the importance for Christians of maintaining a "multi-level" reading of scripture, particularly of the Old Testament (see "Toward Recovering Theological Exegesis," *Pro Ecclesia* 6 (1997), pp. 7–26). Childs bases this approach, however, on the primacy of a version of the "literal sense" of scripture which is underwritten by a whole series of problematic metaphors about textual agency and textual properties. For example, the Old Testament text is repeatedly presented as having a "voice" or as "exerting theological pressure" (see pp. 21, 22, 24) that seems to operate independently of any interpretive community. Only in this way can Childs argue for theological exegesis as if it were a practice that can persist outside of specific Christian communities. See also my earlier comments on this essay in chapter 1.

[20] The first person to make this argument seems to have been Ernst Käsemann, "Vom theologischen Recht historisch-kritischer Exegese," *Zeitschrift für Theologie* 64 (1967), pp. 253–81.

sive refutation of this notion.[21] First, he notes we know very little about those identified as docetists. Nevertheless, what seems to be behind claims that historical-criticism combats docetism is the view that by establishing details about the life of the historical Jesus, historical critics thereby establish (or help to establish) Jesus' full humanity. The issues at stake in these christological controversies, however, are about the nature of Christ's humanity and divinity, not historical details about the life of Jesus. Historical-criticism may in some cases provide the latter; it cannot adjudicate the former.[22]

> In the end, though, historical interpretation lacks the distinctive capacity to detect and root out docetism which alone could warrant enshrining historical exegesis as the primary criterion of the church's interpretation of Scripture. Classical docetism does indeed pose a threat to theologically sound readings, but we avoid these dangers by Chalcedonian interpretation, not by a historical rigor that is constrained in principle to examine only Christ's humanity.[23]

Thus far, I have tried to give a theoretical account to support my *ad hoc* use of biblical scholarship in the course of this book. Christians can and should make use of biblical scholarship when and as they need to. Further, they may need to respond to particular issues raised by biblical scholars when and as they are relevant to Christian interpretive practices. Moreover, because of the complexity and diversity of claims made by professional scholars, it would seem to be the case that those most deeply acquainted with such scholarship will be able to make the best use of it in particular circumstances.

It still may seem, however, that having advocated an *ad hoc* approach to the work of professional biblical scholarship, I have slipped into the view that, at the very least, all Christians ought to become as familiar as they can with professional biblical scholarship. Moreover, given the obvious complexity and diversity of biblical scholarship, one might even say that my position moves much closer to the claim that all Christians ought to become professional biblical scholars so as to be able to make the best use of professional scholarship. This is neither possible nor desirable. Clearly, some Christians will become professional biblical scholars.[24] For them, the crucial issues will

---

[21] "Docetism, Käsemann and Christology: Why Historical Criticism Can't Protect Christological Orthodoxy," *Scottish Journal of Theology* 49 (1996), pp. 391–410.

[22] Adam, "Docetism, Käsemann and Christology," pp. 392–7.

[23] Adam, "Docetism, Käsemann and Christology," p. 399.

[24] Further, to the extent that churches do not provide the support necessary for scholarly theological work to be undertaken in the light of the particular ends that Christians bring

revolve around keeping the two sets of commitments, habits, and practices characteristic of both the profession and the church in some sort of appropriate order, recognizing overlaps, distinctions, and incommensurabilities. On the one hand, there is no fixed or predetermined way in which these relationships must be ordered in the lives of particular scholars seeking to live faithfully before God. On the other hand, one should avoid a sort of schizophrenia, common in many Christians, in which one's professional life is hermetically sealed off from one's confessional commitments.

For the vast majority of Christians and Christian communities, however, there are more important tasks. Rather than seeking to become well-versed in the skills, habits, convictions, and practices of professional biblical scholarship so that they can make useful *ad hoc* judgments about this work, Christians need to become much more well-versed in the skills, habits, convictions, and practices attendant upon Christian interpretation of scripture. Surprisingly, in this regard the profession of biblical scholarship may have more to teach Christian communities than it does in regard to questions concerning any particular biblical text. Let me explain.

One need only browse through any of a number of journals in biblical studies, or briefly visit a session of a scholarly conference on the Bible, to recognize two things. First, the material under discussion is both exceedingly diverse and complex. This is true of both the primary and the secondary literature. Secondly, those who are fully participating in the discussions and debates are able to deal with that complexity and diversity relatively well. This is not to say that they can speak authoritatively on any issue at the drop of a hat. Rather, they are able to figure out where the critical issues lie; they can evaluate the material, both primary and secondary; they can make judgments about the weight and relevance of particular points; they can, then, come to a decision which they can then defend, revise, re-formulate, or abandon in the face of new evidence or superior arguments. In short, they have been more or less well formed to interpret in particular ways. In some respects this might have been easier to see when the profession was more united about its ends, interests, and methods.[25] Of course, in other respects, a more monolithic

---

to scriptural and other types of theological study, then Christians should avail themselves of the resources provided by the profession as long as this is compatible with their overall theological ends.

[25] It should also be noted, however, that this more monolithic pattern of formation also worked to produce a profession that was almost exclusively white, male, Protestant, and located in Western Europe and America. This, however, is a contingent result of the type of formation, not of the general practice of forming readers.

profession could give the impression that professional formation is simply a matter of technical mastery of a stable, self-interpreting body of information. Nevertheless, even in its current fragmented state, with relatively isolated groups of scholars pursuing irreconcilably diverse interests, there is still a great deal of commonality in the formation that they all undergo.

One cannot simply enter into professional discussions and debates without prior formation and expect to participate with as much success and proficiency as one who has been trained to do so.[26] This is not simply because there is a great deal of technical information to learn. Rather, it is because this information is not self-interpreting. Technical information on its own cannot identify and articulate interpretive problems. Neither does it naturally or automatically order itself in ways that straightforwardly identify and address interpretive problems. Professional proficiency presumes technical proficiency. What marks it off as something different from technical proficiency, however, is the professional's ability to use her technical expertise to engage in interpretive debates and discussions and to re-formulate the issues as needed; to marshal evidence, both arguing for its relevance to the particular issue at hand and showing how the evidence should lead one to adopt a particular view about an issue; to defend, refine, re-formulate views in the light of counter-claims and thereby advance a particular interpretive debate or discussion.

Although it is rarely stated in this way, the key virtue that such training seeks to form in professional biblical scholars is a type of practical reasoning or *phronesis*.[27] That is, professional training, at its best, seeks to form scholars who not only have technical competence, but who have the practical wisdom to know how to deploy specific elements of their technical knowledge in ways that contribute to the advancement, re-formulation, or reopening of particular interpretive disputes and discussions. This practical wisdom works by being able to perceive similarities between a general rule, or norm, or scholarly standard and some particular interpretive problem, and then to move by

---

[26] Of course, this same point could be made about plumbing and, as Stanley Hauerwas has argued, bricklaying. See *After Christendom* (Nashville: Abingdon, 1991), ch. 5.

[27] The person who has in modern times made the most of the importance of *phronesis* to interpretive work is H.-G. Gadamer. See *Truth and Method* (New York: Seabury, 1975), esp. pp. 278ff. More recently, and with deep debts to Gadamer, Joseph Dunne has explored the role of *phronesis* and *techne* in both their Aristotelian contexts and in the work of several modern philosophers. See *Back to the Rough Ground* (Notre Dame: University of Notre Dame Press, 1993), especially chs 4 and 5 on Gadamer. In addition, see Alasdair MacIntyre, *Whose Justice? Which Rationality?* (Notre Dame: University of Notre Dame Press, 1988).

analogy to address the problem fruitfully. The well-formed, practically wise, scholar perceives the relevant similarities and dissimilarities between complex problems and already agreed standards and then moves by analogy to use already proven standards to elucidate the unknown. Having said this, it should be less surprising to claim that contemporary Christians might learn from the academy about the importance of forming practically wise readers.

As I have characterized it in this book, Christian interpretation of scripture is marked by specific debates, discussions, and disputes about how to interpret and embody scripture so as to worship and live faithfully before God. If these debates, discussions, and disputes are to enable rather than frustrate Christian living, Christians must manifest a variety of convictions, habits, and practices as well as a particular sort of common life. To this end, then, Christians can learn from professional biblical studies about the importance of forming people to be particular types of readers. This is not to say that Christians ought to undergo the same type of formation as professional biblical scholars. The formation of Christian interpreters of scripture is different both in its aims and in its scope from that of biblical scholars. Nevertheless, there are several important formal similarities which I want to note. Moreover, my point is that, at present, the profession, with all of its attendant flaws and incoherent elements, still does a much better job of forming its members to read in particular ways than the church currently seems to do.

There are several essential differences between the academy and the church which may always ensure that the academy is more uniformly successful in forming readers. First, professional biblical studies aims to form a relatively select group of readers. The body of people seeking to be formed in this way is very small. Being a professional biblical scholar is not, and need not be, for everybody. In addition, for better and worse, the profession excludes those who fail to be formed in the requisite ways. Christian communities, however, want to make universal claims about the importance of being a Christian. Moreover, the task of being formed to read scripture in particular ways is not the special task of a select few. Rather, it is incumbent upon all Christians. Of course, Christians have always recognized that in this life some will advance more than others in this regard. Moreover, success here cannot strictly be correlated to intellectual gifts. Whether the academy will always be more successful than the church in forming its members to be particular sorts of readers is ultimately a subsidiary matter. Of primary importance is the requirement that the church form its members to read scripture in ways that will enhance rather than frustrate faithful life and worship – the ends towards which Christians debate and discuss scriptural interpretation.

Having said this, I want to begin, at least, to unpack what might be involved in forming Christians to read scripture. First, it is now quite common for Christian scholars to lament the level of ignorance of biblical content in congregations across all denominational lines. Moreover, things are much worse when the subject-matter is basic Christian doctrine or church history. Without question, it is important for Christians to learn these things as well as they can. Further, failure to have some measure of knowledge of scripture tends to disable interpretive discussion at the outset. There needs to be some base of biblical knowledge to get an interpretive discussion off the ground. Nevertheless, questions about how one learns these things and in what context and for what purpose are equally important. For example, mastery of several Northwest semitic languages may be crucial for becoming a professional scholar of the Hebrew Bible. Such knowledge, however, would not ensure scholarly success apart from the practical reasoning that enables one to use those languages to perform certain interpretive tasks better. In the same way, knowing more "memory verses" does not ensure either Spirit-directed interpretation or faithful Christian living. As I have tried to show throughout this book, the relationships between scriptural interpretation, Christian convictions and practices, and the common life of Christian communities is both complex and theoretically underdetermined. For example, one could not specify in advance and in much detail when and how the character of an interpreter should influence interpretive decisions. Further, apart from concrete instances, it is difficult to determine whether the Spirit is working in the lives of others, directing the community to read and act in new and counter-conventional ways, or whether communal habits of self-deception have become so ingrained that a call to repentance is in order. Because of these complexities Christian communities need to train their members to manifest a particular sort of practical wisdom. The character of this wisdom and the way one acquires it, however, will be very different for Christians. To help articulate the character of Christian practical wisdom I want to turn to a brief discussion of Philippians. Here in a variety of ways Paul demonstrates, encourages, and enjoins the Philippians to manifest a particular sort of *phronesis*.

Phronesis in **Philippians**

In regard to Philippians, Wayne Meeks has argued that "this letter's most comprehensive purpose is the shaping of a Christian *phronesis*, a practical moral reasoning that is 'conformed to [Christ's] death' in hope of his resurrection."[28] That is, Paul is trying to form in the Philippians the intellectual and moral abilities to be able to deploy, by means of analogy, their knowledge of the gospel in the concrete situations in which they find themselves so that they will be able to live faithfully (or "walk in a manner worthy of the gospel" 1:27). Within this scheme, the story of Christ narrated in 2:6–11 functions as an *exemplar*, a concrete expression of a shared norm or rule from which Paul and the Philippians can make analogical judgments about how they should live.[29] By looking at the epistle as a whole one can see how some of these analogical judgments work.

The epistle makes it clear both that Paul is imprisoned and that the Philippian community seems to have been facing both hostility from without and some level of divisiveness within. It is not clear, however, to what extent the Philippians were being actively persecuted. They have opponents (1:28); Paul speaks of them being granted the privilege of suffering for the sake of Christ and being engaged in a struggle similar to Paul's (1:29–30). Within these bounds, however, Paul's comments about how the Philippians are to live in the light of this situation could apply to a wide variety of situations of persecution.

He begins the epistle by assuring the Philippians that God is indeed at work in them and will continue this work until the day of Christ (1:6, repeated in 2:13). If Paul's imprisonment and the suffering of the Philippians raised questions about the coherence or continuation of God's activity, Paul's comments in 1:3–18 would work to allay those concerns. Paul offers assurances about himself and reassures the Philippians by offering them assurances about God and God's desires and actions on their behalf (and on Paul's behalf as well).

Paul's confidence about these matters is not simply wishful thinking.[30] While he has yet to make specific reference to any particular account of God's

---

[28] See Wayne Meeks, "The Man from Heaven in Paul's Letter to the Philippians," in *The Future of Early Christianity: Essays in Honor of Helmut Koester* (Minneapolis: Augsburg Fortress, 1991), p. 333. Meeks' essay makes the same sort of arguments about Paul's moral reasoning as I made in *The Story of Christ in the Ethics of Paul* (Sheffield: Sheffield Academic Press, 1991), which appeared at the same time. Note also that the verb φρονεῖν occurs 10 times in Philippians.

[29] For a fuller accounting of this pattern in Paul's moral reasoning, see *The Story of Christ in the Ethics of Paul*, pp. 92–6, 198–207.

[30] Neither can it really be accounted for by the current scholarly consensus that Philippians ought to be seen as an instance of the "family letter" genre. See, for example, L. Alexander, "Hellenistic Letter Forms and the Structure of Philippians," *Journal for the Study of the New Testament* 37 (1989), pp. 87–101.

activity in Christ, it is fair to say that Paul's convictions about the coherence and continuation of God's activity are grounded in his convictions about God's activity in Christ and God's prior activity in Paul's own life and in the life of the Philippian church. As God redeemed and exalted the obedient, humiliated Christ (as narrated in 2:6–11), so God will redeem the obedient, though suffering, Paul and the obedient, though suffering, Philippians if they remain faithful, "standing in one spirit, striving together with one accord for the sake of the gospel" (1:27). What underwrites Paul's confidence in the first chapter of the epistle is not simply a cheerfulness which convention demands. Rather, it is a manner of practical reasoning (note the use of φρονεῖν in 1:7) which begins from convictions about what God has done in Christ. Those convictions, in turn, help provide Paul with a particular point of view, from which Paul can consider his own situation and that of the Philippians as not merely hopeful, but an example of God's "good work."

Paul moves on in 1:19–26 to reflect more systematically on his own situation. There is a close conceptual parallel between Paul's assurances in 1:12 that his circumstances have actually worked to advance the gospel, and Paul's conviction in 1:19 that "through the Philippians' prayers and the help of the Spirit of Jesus Christ," his situation will result in his "salvation/deliverance."[31]

In addition to its connections to what precedes, this passage also begins to articulate a position Paul will develop more fully in chapter 2. Here in 1:19–26 Paul notes his own preference to die and to be with Christ (1:21, 23). He also notes, however, that it is "more necessary" for the Philippians that he "remain and continue" in the flesh (1:24). He even goes so far as to claim that he has some sort of choice in the matter. "In 1.22, Paul writes, 'which I shall choose I cannot tell'. In 1.21 and 23, he seems to show a clear preference for death. However, because it is 'more necessary' to remain alive on account of the Philippians (1.24), Paul then resolves the tension created in 1.22 and announces that he will 'remain and continue with you all'."[32]

There are a variety of interesting questions arising from this passage. What sort of choice did Paul really have about his future? Did he contemplate suicide

---

[31] Both here and in that parallel Paul draws between his situation and the Philippians' in 1:28 he uses the term σωτηρία in ways that point both to deliverance from present distress and to eternal salvation.

[32] See C. Wansink, *Chained in Christ* (Sheffield: Sheffield Academic Press, 1996), p. 115. Wansink points to Cicero who, while in prison, wrote to his brother, Quintus, that he remained alive – presumably, not taking his own life – out of consideration for Quintus, as a clear parallel to this sort of reasoning. See Cicero, *Ad Quintum Fratrem* 1.3 and the discussion in Wansink, pp. 107–11.

or a more passive form of voluntary death? Was it really in his hands to choose to remain in the flesh? All of these questions have been the subject of scholarly discussion over the past few years.[33] What is most important for my purposes is how Paul's claims here are connected to the demands he makes of the Philippians in 1:27–2:4. In these verses, Paul urges the Philippians to unite in the face of opposition.[34] They must stand firm in one spirit and in one mind, striving together for the faith of the gospel (1:27). In chapter 2 Paul demands specific types of behavior to insure that steadfast unity will prevail. In 2:2 he commands the Philippians to be of the same mind (again, using φρονεῖν). In addition, the Philippians are to have the same love, bound together in one spirit. Repeating φρονεῖν, they are to have a common orientation or pattern of thought. Paul continues in vv. 3–4 to note that nothing would be more destructive of the unity which Paul sees as essential for the salvation of the community than for the Philippians to maintain a spirit of partisanship and empty conceit. In contrast to these vices, Paul urges the Philippians to adopt the virtue of humility, considering the needs of others rather than their own needs.

In Paul's discussion of his own disposition towards imprisonment, the Philippians find a specific manifestation of looking after the needs and concerns of others rather than one's own. Paul makes it clear that, given the options of whether "to depart and be with Christ" or to remain in the flesh in service to the gospel (and the Philippians), he prefers to depart. In 1:22 he claims that it is unclear which of these two options he will choose. By 1:24–5, however, he has resolved the matter in favor of looking after what is necessary for the Philippians rather than himself:

> Philippians 1.18b–29 has not often been linked to Paul's admonition to unity in 1.27–2.11. When it is assumed that Paul was unsure of whether he *preferred* to live or die, the apostle is robbed of personal initiative and is seen only as a passive figure. Paul, however, does not use verbs like βούλομαι or θέλω; he uses the verb αἱρήσομαι and, by doing so, presents himself as an example for his fractious sisters and brothers thereby initiating the pattern of 'life for others' which subsequently runs throughout the epistle.[35]

---

[33] See A. Droge, "Mori Lucrum: Paul and Ancient Theories of Suicide," *Novum Testamentum* 30 (1988), pp. 263–86; also A. Droge and J. D. Tabor, *A Noble Death: Suicide and Martyrdom Among Christians and Jews in Antiquity* (San Francisco: Harper and Row, 1992). Wansink (*Chained in Christ*, ch. 2) gives a fuller discussion of this passage in its wider epistolary context.

[34] See my *The Story of Christ in the Ethics of Paul* for a detailed exegetical discussion of these verses.

[35] Wansink, *Chained in Christ*, p. 118.

Paul uses reflections about his own life and death as a particular manifestation of the types of actions and dispositions he wants the Philippians to manifest in 1:27–2:4. Both Paul's reflections and the subsequent demands of 1:27–2:4, however, find their paradigmatic expression in the story of Christ rendered in 2:6–11.[36] Here we find a story about Christ who is in the form of God. In contrast to what one might expect, however, he refused treat his equality with God as something to use for his own advantage.[37] "The emphasis of v. 7 shows that the refusal described by this phrase was a refusal to use for his own advantage the glory which he had from the beginning . . . nothing described by either ἐν μορφῇ θεοῦ ὑπάρχων or by τὸ εἶναι ἴσα θεῷ is given up; rather, it is reinterpreted, understood in a manner in striking contrast to what one might have expected."[38] Thus, Christ's activity decisively characterizes the practice of not seeking after one's own concerns but those of others.

Given this starting point, in v. 6 the rest of the basic humiliation and exaltation story of vv. 7–11 takes on a very particular texture. The self-emptying described in v. 7 is not an account of Christ's stripping-off of divine attributes. It becomes an elaboration of the view that Christ's equality with God was not something to be used for his own advantage. It claims that the vocation commensurate with this exalted position is demonstrated through incarnation and steadfast obedience leading to crucifixion.[39] The exaltation related in vv. 9–11 then becomes God's vindication of Christ's obedience. The exaltation serves as God's affirmation that Christ's dispositions and actions related in vv. 6–8 are the actions and dispositions appropriate to one who is equal with God.

The force of the grammatically difficult 2:5 is to encourage the Philippians to let the picture of Christ presented in 2:6–11 guide their common life by means

---

[36] Many will already know that this passage has generated an enormous amount of critical scholarship. I am summarizing views I have argued for in more detail in *The Story of Christ in the Ethics of Paul* and in "Christology and Ethics in Phil. 2:5–11," in *Where Christology Began*, ed. B. Dodd and R. Martin (Louisville: Westminster/John Knox Press, 1998).

[37] I argued for this particular reading of ἁρπαγμός in 2:6 in *The Story of Christ in the Ethics of Paul*, based on R.W. Hoover's essay "The Harpagmos Enigma: A Philological Solution," *Harvard Theological Review* 64 (1971), pp. 95–119. N. T. Wright has developed Hoover's view and given it more depth so that the notion that ἁρπαγμός as "something to take advantage of" must now be considered the definitive position on 2:6. See N. T. Wright, *The Climax of the Covenant: Christ and the Law in Pauline Theology* (Minneapolis: Fortress Press, 1992), ch. 4.

[38] Wright, *The Climax of the Covenant*, p. 83.

[39] As Wright notes, "The real humiliation of the incarnation and the cross is that one who was himself God, and who never during the whole process stopped being God, could embrace such a vocation" (*The Climax of the Covenant*, p. 84).

of drawing analogies between this story of Christ and the situations the Philippians face. To put the analogy crudely: If the Philippians will devote themselves to concern for one another in steadfast adherence to the gospel (which will entail the practice of the virtues of 2:2–4), even in the face of opposition, then God will save them in the same way God saved the obedient, humiliated, and suffering Christ in 2:6–11. Paul's admonition in v. 5 is a call to recognize this, a call to apply analogically to their common life the precedent that is theirs by virtue of the fact that they are in Christ. To do this requires practical reasoning. As Wayne Meeks notes, 2:5 with its use of φρονεῖν might well be translated, "Base your practical reasoning on what you see in Christ Jesus."[40]

Paul's analogical extension of the story of Christ in 2:6–11 to the common life of the Philippian church is extended further in 2:12–18 by means of further admonitions to forsake factionalism (2:14) and encouragements to stand firm in the midst of hostile surroundings (2:15–16). Here we also get further assurances that God is at work in the lives of the Philippians (2:13). Again, the point here is not simply to calm the Philippians but to make strong assertions about the character of God, assertions that are underwritten by the story of what God has done in Christ. Paul seems to recognize that his own imprisonment and the opposition faced by the Philippians raises some questions about the coherence and even the presence of God's work in the world. Paul's point in 2:14–18 is that it is not suffering and opposition that threaten to render God's world incoherent as much as the Philippians' possible failure to remain faithful.

Further, within this context, Paul's "news" about Timothy and Epaphroditus in 2:19–30 is not meant simply to reassure the Philippians, but to offer them further models of those who do not seek after their own interests but the interests of others.[41] In fact, and I presume in the light of 2:6–11, there has been a subtle shift in phrasing regarding the attitude Paul is advocating here. Prior to 2:6–11, Paul advocated concern for the things of others rather than one's own concerns. Now the contrast is between looking after one's own concerns and the "things of Christ" (2:21). I take it, however, that Paul is describing one and the same practice. Paul's analogical reasoning, based on 2:6–11, can provide him, and the Philippians, with a rationale for commending the actions of Timothy and Epaphroditus and for admonishing Euodia and Syntyche in 4:2 to employ a common Christ-focused practical reasoning (again, φρονεῖν).

Paul offers, in a much more systematic way than in 1:19–26, an account of his own life in 3:2–16. This, too, can be read as a manifestation of a form of practical reasoning based on the story of Christ in 2:6–11. As his account

---

[40] See Meeks, "The Man From Heaven in Paul's Letter to the Philippians," p. 332.
[41] See Meeks, "The Man From Heaven in Paul's Letter to the Philippians," p. 334.

shows, one of the primary tasks of practical reasoning is learning how to view things in the right way. Once one does this, then one can draw the appropriate types of analogies and act in the appropriate ways. Throughout 3:2–16 Paul is seeking to combat those (presumably members of the Philippian church) whose *phronesis* is set on earthly things (3:19). The contrast Paul draws here is not between judgments which rely on *phronesis* and those that do not. Rather, the contrast is between the *phronesis* appropriate to those whose commonwealth is in heaven and those whose *phronesis* is directed by earthly concerns. Paul's account of his life in 3:2–16 is really an account of how his perspective or point of view was transformed through his encounter with Christ. This transformation enables Christ-focused practical reasoning which works to form a life that "knows the power of [Christ's] resurrection," and is capable of "sharing in his sufferings and becoming like him in his death" (3:10) since, as 2:6–11 make clear, this is the manner of life which God vindicates.

In this light, the call to become fellow imitators of Paul, his associates, and those who live in a similar way (3:17) is primarily a call to understand what God has done in Christ in the way that Paul has understood, embodied, and articulated it. From this, one can then walk as someone who is not an enemy of the cross of Christ (3:19). The imitation called for here is really a call to adopt Paul's manner of practical reasoning, a practical reasoning based on what the Philippians see in Christ Jesus (2:6–11). This is not a wooden sort of identical repetition, but a "non-identical repetition"[42] based on analogy, examples of which are seen in 1:19–26; 1:27–2:4; 2:12–18; 2:19–30; and 3:2–16. Given this account of Philippians, I will now make some more general comments about the character of Christian practical reasoning and then move to make some comments about how it might be formed in people.

The Character of Christian Practical Reasoning

Philippians makes it particularly clear that, for Christians, practical reasoning is Christ-focused. The account of God's activity in Christ rendered in 2:6–11

---

[42] I take this phrase from a variety of different works by John Milbank – most notably, "Can a Gift be Given? Prolegomena to a Future Trinitarian Metaphysic," in *Rethinking Metaphysics,* ed. L. G. Jones and S. E. Fowl (Oxford: Blackwell, 1995), pp. 119–61. This notion of non-identical repetition provides the basis for a theological response to Elizabeth Castelli's arguments in *Imitating Paul: A Discourse of Power* (Louisville: Westminster/John Knox Press, 1991). For a fuller account of this argument, see Fowl, "Christology and Ethics in Phil. 2:5–11."

is the norm or rule from which Paul then moves analogically to account for his own situation, for the situation of those known to the Philippians, and for how the Philippians ought to live in the light of their present struggles. What is significant here is not whether 2:6–11 simply takes over pre-existing material. Rather, what is significant is that Paul presents this account of Christ assuming its widespread acceptability. There is no "christological" dispute here. Unlike in the Corinthian epistles, Paul is not having to readjust the Corinthians' understanding of the cross and resurrection. Unlike in Galatians, Paul is not having to address "another gospel." He does not need to engage in counter-conventional readings of scriptural texts to show that Christ is the "seed" of Abraham. Rather, he appears to narrate the account found in 2:6–11 on the assumption that it would be understood and accepted by his audience.

This is not to say that Phil. 2:6–11 represents the only proper christological formulation on which to base Christian practical reasoning. Rather, it points to the fact that Christian practical reasoning must begin from an accepted christological standard. Christians ought to expect that there will be diverse ways of accounting for God's activity in Christ. Indeed, the acceptance of four canonical gospels rather than any one of them or a single harmony of them testifies to this. Further, the very nature of trinitarian relations suggests that the Spirit will always be re-expressing the Logos. As John Milbank has noted, "Somehow, because the divine *actus* is *infinite*, and therefore 'interminably terminated' it comprises a non-temporal dynamic or mutual 'play' between infinite 'conclusion' of expression in the Son, and an endless 're-opening' of that conclusion by the desire of the Spirit which re-inspires the paternal *arche*." On the same page Milbank develops this point further when he claims, "The need for mediation then becomes more purely the interpretive exigency which belongs together with the reality of historical 'absence' – an absence which, as indeterminacy of meaning, was already an aspect even of Christ's presence on earth. A 'trinitarianism without reserve' will project this exigency back into God himself. This is only possible if the Son is considered also as *Logos*, meaning an infinite aesthetic plenitude of expression, which yet does not predetermine, in 'totalizing' fashion, a freedom of interpretation."[43] Further, as I already noted in chapter 2, cultural and temporal change will indicate that simply repeating prior formulations word for word will not guarantee that one continues to say the same thing. Nevertheless, within this trinitarian "freedom of interpretation," subsequent alternative formulations would have to demonstrate that they

---

[43] Milbank, "The Second Difference," in *The Word Made Strange* (Oxford: Blackwell, 1997), p. 187. See also the chapter entitled, "A Christological Poetics."

maintain continuity with prior christological standards. How can this be argued for? A basic minimum measure of continuity would have to be reflected in the judgment that any new formulations, taken together with prior ones, still render a single unsubstitutable subject.[44] Further, in regard to the formation and evaluation of new Christ-focused formulations, many of the points I have argued for in regard to Christian interpretation of scripture apply here as well. For example, issues about how to discern the work of the Spirit, matters of word-care, practices of interpretive charity as well as forgiveness, repentance, and reconciliation would all come into play here. Moreover, these considerations also point to the issues of ecclesial authority which I wish to take up in a moment.

In addition to being Christ-focused, Christian practical reasoning also relies on human exemplars. Paul points to himself, Timothy, and Epaphroditus as examples of those who have properly and analogically extended the story of Christ in their own lives. As Phil. 3:12–16 makes very clear, Paul is not claiming any sort of perfection or completion for himself. Even so, he immediately follows this disclaimer with a call to "join in imitating me" (4:17). One of the ways in which Christians can draw appropriate analogies from their christological standard to their own situation is by finding apposite exemplars and imitating them. Indeed, the best way to learn the habits of the practically wise is to find appropriate exemplars to imitate.

At least two things need to be said about this. First, as I indicated above, this imitation is not an attempt to replicate isomorphically the exemplar. Practical reasoning is the activity of noting similarities and differences between a model and the particular context in which one tries to live in a manner appropriate to that model. What one strives for is non-identical repetition.

Even in Philippians, Paul offers his own reflections about his choice of life over death as an example of putting the needs of others before one's own desires in 1:19–26. He also, however, presents Timothy's and Epaphroditus' actions as similar examples of this disposition distinct from Paul's own example. One might even note the brief comments directed to Euodia and Syntyche as an example by means of antithesis of the dispositions and actions Paul desires for the Philippians. There is both analogical continuity between these characters, and individual and communal differentiation. Rather than a sameness that obliterates difference, Paul's language of imitation is designed to produce an ordered, harmonious diversity.[45]

---

[44] I take this formulation from Hans Frei's *The Identity of Jesus Christ* (Philadelphia: Fortress Press, 1975).

[45] This is against the claims of Elizabeth Castelli, who treats all pauline language of imitation as valorizing a difference obliterating sameness. See *Imitating Paul*, especially pp. 15–21.

Secondly, as I have already briefly noted, the primary ways in which one is formed to be practically wise in general, and a practically wise reader of scripture in particular, is by attending to the habits and practices of those who are already more advanced in this process.[46] This includes both those who are alive and quite close at hand and those who are temporally, culturally, and/or geographically distant. In regard to the interpretation of scripture, Christians will need to mark, remember, and attend to those who preceded them in the faith and who were accomplished interpreters of scripture. The more and better that contemporary Christians attend to such exemplars, the more they will tend to interpret like them. Moreover, the interpretive views and conclusions of these past and present masters of scriptural interpretation will become part of the conventional ways in which Christians come to read particular texts. This is not to say that contemporary Christians will always accede to and replicate those views and conclusions. There may be good reasons for countering the conventions in certain cases. Nevertheless, as Christians are formed to be practically wise readers, the judgments of those wise readers cannot help but become crucial elements in current debates and discussions.

In the various chapters of this book I have attempted to engage a variety of pre-modern interpreters in making my various arguments. No doubt someone whose professional training was in historical theology could have made better use of this vast body of material. Nevertheless, as I indicated in the introduction, Christians need to rediscover and re-appropriate the pre-modern history of biblical interpretation. If Christians are to be formed as scriptural interpreters in ways that combat the modern tendency to fragment theological activity into an array of discrete disciplines, then they will find a host of exemplars among pre-modern interpreters. In addition, exemplars will be found in the African-American Christian tradition and other contexts that have resisted or avoided the professionalizing of theology. Again, Christians should not assume that simply by replicating the words of Augustine, Aquinas, Martin Luther King Jr, or Julian of Norwich they will become practically wise readers of scripture. Repetition may be a place to begin formation, but it is not, ultimately, the mark of the practically wise. The aim of forming Christians to

---

[45] In his fourth homily on Jeremiah (para. 5) Origen succinctly puts forth a similar view when he enjoins his audience to: "Read the Scriptures; look to those who were justified and those who were not; Imitate the just and guard against walking in the ways of the unjust." See *PG* 13.293.

be practically wise readers of scripture is so that they can interpret in ways that would be recognizable to these (and other) exemplars. In theory, one could imagine a practically wise interpreter in the present carrying on debates, discussions, and arguments with these exemplars in ways that both parties could recognize and engage with – despite the temporal, cultural, and geographical distance between them. This aspect of Christian practical reasoning raises issues of ecclesial authority. These questions arise as soon as one begins to struggle with questions about who counts as an exemplar, and why? How does one properly engage exemplars? How are disputes finally adjudicated? Who teaches whom? I will say more about these issues in a moment.

Having indicated the importance of practical reasoning for Christian interpretation of scripture, in this particular section I have discussed the characteristics of Christian practical reasoning. I also want to discuss briefly how this formation might better take place. Here I can only hope to offer some very general considerations.[47] While practical wisdom is an essential virtue for Christian interpretation of scripture, it is by no means only applicable to scriptural interpretation. I have focused on the formation of practically wise readers of scripture. In fact, however, Christians seek to form their members into practically wise people – people who can deploy the skills, virtues, and dispositions needed to live holy lives, growing in deeper communion with God and others. In this light, the formation of practically wise interpreters cannot be separated from issues involved in the process of Christian formation more generally. Such formation takes place in a variety of ways and contexts, and Christians and Christian communities must attend to them all.

The most obvious practices of formation for my particular purposes are those related to baptism and catechesis. Whether catechesis follows or precedes baptism, the crucial point is to note its connection to baptism. That is, if baptism initiates one into the covenant people of God and thereby joins an individual to that people formed by the death and resurrection of Jesus and journeying under the Spirit's guidance towards the kingdom of God, then catechesis helps those individuals to complete that journey successfully. This is done by introducing and beginning to provide the conceptual, moral and spiritual resources Christians will need to complete their journey. As I already noted, this must involve the development of scriptural knowledge. It is clear that Christians can no longer presume (if they ever really could) that regular

[47] For what follows I am deeply indebted to L. G. Jones' as yet unpublished essay, "A Dramatic Journey Into God's Dazzling Light."

church attendance and general cultural awareness would provide Christians with a basic grasp of biblical content. Moreover, catechesis must also provide an initial context within which scripture can be interpreted in the light of the ends towards which Christians live their lives. At present, very few churches attend to catechesis with anything like the diligence it requires. There are, however, some hopeful signs of a revival in this respect.[48]

These aside, however, contemporary Christians have two significant obstacles to overcome in any attempt to re-invigorate their catechetical practices. First, they must fight against a general cultural disposition that religious belief is a private, individual matter, immune to communal formation and discipline. This disposition serves to underwrite the conviction that individuals can make up their theology, prayer, and worship as they go along, picking and choosing what suits them best.[49] Secondly, Christians must recognize that Christian education takes time.[50] It cannot be accomplished in small weekly doses. In cannot be limited to the young either. This is particularly the case when Christian education for children becomes a form of child care that separates children from the worship of the community.

In addition to formal catechesis, the liturgy of the church has a great power to form the lives of its participants. If baptism brings Christians into a people on a dramatic journey towards God, then the eucharist represents that drama, inviting believers to participate in it, and, as they are formed by their participation, empowering them to go forth from the eucharist in the power of the Spirit to continue that dramatic activity in the wider world. More particularly, through the ministry of the word, Christians can be formed to read scripture as a crucial aspect of their struggles to carry on their journey towards God in the specific contexts in which they find themselves. If this is so, then it is safe to assume that such formation will be aided by attention to the detail, atmosphere, and performance of a community's liturgical life.

These activities can be furthered by corporate Bible studies. Such gatherings cannot, however, work on their own apart from common patterns of formation and prayer. In the absence of these patterns there is a tendency for Bible studies to become opportunities for individuals to express and confirm

---

[48] The best examples I know of are the Roman Catholic Rite of Christian Initiation for Adults and the "Catechesis of the Good Shepherd" based on the work of Sofia Cavalletti.
[49] For a trenchant analysis of these cultural phenomena as they work themselves out in contemporary "spiritualities" see the January 1997 volume of *Modern Theology*.
[50] For a stunning account of how global culture industries, particularly mediated through television, render us unable to learn appropriately Christian patterns of thought, action, and feeling, see Michael Budde, *The (Magic) Kingdom of God* (Boulder: Westview Press, 1997).

their individual prejudices.[51] Without question, there is much more to be said about issues of Christian formation. My concern has been to make some general comments about various ways in which the task of forming people to be practically wise interpreters of scripture can be fitted within a more general pattern of Christian formation. At this point, and by way of conclusion, I need address issues of ecclesial authority which have been standing in the background of many of the chapters in this book and which I explicitly noted in this chapter.

Ecclesial Authority

In this chapter I have already noted that questions about the ways in which the Christ-focused narratives which constitute the standard from which Christian practical reasoning moves directly invoke questions of ecclesial authority. That is, while I have indicated the importance of forming such Christ-focused accounts and how these accounts might be formed, I have not specified who forms and authorizes these Christ-focused accounts. While I have discussed the role of exemplars in Christian practical reasoning, I have not determined who decides questions about which figures count as exemplars and which should be ignored or avoided.

Moreover, while I have already discussed the importance of word-care for the debates and discussions constitutive of a lively tradition, I have only alluded to the questions about those occasions when attempts to extend a tradition into the present actually break the tradition. Further, while I have indicated some of the factors which should play a role in making such determinations, I have not spoken about who makes those determinations and how they are made.

I have spoken about how the church in Acts came to reach a crucial theological decision based on testimony about the work of the Spirit. Yet Galatians, the focus of the next chapter, indicates how difficult it was to institute that judgment. Further, if in a manner analogous to the patterns of Acts 10–15 some Christians were to come (as some clearly have already come)

---

[51] See Robert Wuthnow's study of small groups in America, *Sharing the Journey* (New York: Free Press, 1994). Wuthnow found that over half of the small groups he surveyed were organized around Bible study. This, however, did not actually significantly help people learn more about the Bible or its interpretation. In fact, people tended to leave a Bible study as soon as their interpretation was challenged by another. Some small Bible studies counter this habit by forbidding anyone to criticize the interpretations of another.

to the view that, based on the well-attested presence of the Spirit in their lives, homosexual Christians (as homosexuals) should not be barred from any aspect of Christian life and ministry, how might such a view become normative for Christians generally?

I have addressed the importance of the character of the interpreter in helping to adjudicate various interpretive disputes in the light of Paul's reading of the Abraham story in Galatians. I have not, however, specified what, if any, relationships there are between character and ecclesial office and authority.

Throughout this book I have both argued implicitly, and often tacitly assumed, that the authority of scripture is not a property of the biblical texts any more than a meaning or an ideology is property of those texts. That is, authority is not something that has been inserted into the Bible which can then later be found, abstracted, analyzed, and either followed or ignored. Rather, scriptural authority must be spoken of in connection with the ecclesial communities who struggle to interpret scripture and embody their interpretations in the specific contexts in which they find themselves. I have said much about the habits, practices, and convictions essential to those communities who would read scripture as authoritative. I have spoken about aspects of the common life of these communities which will enhance their struggles to interpret and embody scripture. Although all of these issues are tied up in greater or lesser degrees with judgments about the authority of these communities, I have left it until now to address them specifically. There are several reasons for this. First, the issues and discussions of ecclesial authority are both historically diverse and theologically complex enough to require independent volumes ranging well beyond the scope of this book and my own expertise. Secondly, and more importantly, while the arguments in this book imply and invest authority in Christian communities' interpretation of scripture, I do not think that the arguments depend on a single account of ecclesial authority in order to work.[52]

Having said that, there are at least two theological considerations that would have to be part of any account of ecclesial authority that would also be compatible with my account of Christian scriptural interpretation. First, my account demands a notion of ecclesial authority that recognizes that the Spirit has been and still is at work in the lives of Christians and Christian communities. Secondly, my arguments about scriptural interpretation presuppose and underwrite a view of the church as the body of Christ, and as such

[52] In this book I have been concerned with, in the language of William Christian, "primary doctrines;" and matters of ecclesial authority are best characterized as dealing with "governing doctrines." See *The Doctrines of Religious Communities,* chs 1 and 2.

its practices must manifest a christological character appropriate to this identity. One of the crucial reasons for this is seen in my discussion of character and interpretation in chapter 5. It is not simply Paul's account of his own life that provides him with the interpretive authority he exercises in Galatians. Rather, it is the christological density of that account which underwrites Paul's authority – "I have been crucified with Christ; it is no longer I who live, but Christ who lives in me" (Gal. 2:20). Without this, Paul's exercise of interpretive authority would be dependent upon his goodness, his rhetorical power, or his institutional might. Hence, ecclesial authority must always retain such a christological focus and cruciform shape. While this may rule out some notions of ecclesial authority, I do not expect it to rule out very many.

Further, I think there are some notions of ecclesial authority which are distinctly at odds with the arguments of this book. On the one hand, my arguments would be incompatible with any notion of ecclesial authority which renders decisions based on managerial and marketing considerations.[53] While this may seem obvious, it is also important to recognize the popularity of such views among vast numbers of American Christians.[54] Further, even within episcopal polities, which might seem well insulated from such strategies, the image of bishop as CEO of a diocese is often implicitly if not explicitly operative. Within such a model, ecclesial authority will ultimately become subject to consumer choice. This would effectively frustrate the communal practices and habits and disciplines essential to interpreting scripture with the aim of faithfully worshipping and living before the triune God.

At the same time, Christians interpret and embody scripture as a constitutive part of their participation in a particular tradition, Christianity. In this light, Christians should expect that scriptural interpretation will always be marked by a level of debate, discussion, and argument. Without some level or argument the tradition would come to an end. Hence, any account of ecclesial authority must work to enable shape and sustain interpretive discussion, argument, and debate.[55]

[53] For an excellent theological discussion and evaluation of such views see Philip D. Kenneson, "Selling[out] The Church in the Marketplace of Desire," *Modern Theology* 9 (1993), pp. 319–48.

[54] As Kenneson notes in regard to George Barna's *Marketing the Church* (Colorado Springs: Nav Press, 1988), which is one of the standard works arguing for a marketing and managerial approach to the church, as of its eighth printing in 1992 the book had sold 44,000 copies.

[55] While the market-driven account and an authoritarian account are different extreme positions, they are not incompatible with each other.

Having ruled out these extreme accounts of ecclesial authority, there are some other considerations which it would be important for me to incorporate into any future account of ecclesial authority. Many of the arguments I have made may seem particularly well suited to the lives of individual congregations. I do not want to dispute that. In fact, it is as a part of particular congregations that the vast majority of Christians interpret and embody scripture. Most commonly, their arguments, debates, and discussions are with people they are relatively close to. I do not, however, think that a purely congregational account of ecclesial authority would be adequate to my arguments. Christians, and local congregations in particular, cannot interpret and embody scripture as if they were the first and only Christians ever to do so. Christians are part of the one, holy catholic and apostolic Church. While these notions can be, and have been, variously interpreted, at the very least they testify to the fact that Christians are incorporated into a temporally and geographically extended and culturally diverse body that, at the same time, claims to be one. Any account of ecclesial authority would need to consider how, within the context of God's grace, the Church's catholicity and its ultimate communion is established and maintained.[56] This consideration would seem to start to circumscribe more tightly the number of viable accounts of ecclesial authority. At the same time, any serious theological account of ecclesial authority could not ignore the serious conflicts which have divided Christians in the past and the persistence of those divisions today. At this point is should be clear that these considerations push one into both well-trodden and exceedingly complex paths that I am not yet able to address with anything like the adequacy they deserve.

I began this book as an attempt to create some openings in which to discuss and reflect upon Christian interpretation of scripture in ways that took seriously both the centrality of scripture to Christian life and worship and the importance of particular Christian convictions and practices. This has led me to traverse ground both old and new. To the extent that this is old ground, this book is a call to Christians to rediscover, re-invigorate, and re-appropriate important elements of their past practices and convictions which may have fallen into disrepair. To the extent that I am doing anything new, I am offering

---

[56] In this regard see J. A. DiNoia's comment regarding the teaching office of the Roman Catholic church, ". . . all of the activities of the Catholic community – including its teaching activities – can be understood only when seen as directed toward fostering ultimate communion. It is in this context that a properly theological account of the role of the magisterium can be advanced." See "Communion and Magisterium: Teaching Authority and the Culture of Grace," *Modern Theology* 9 (1993), p. 407.

a call to Christians, and Christian biblical scholars in particular, to begin to reflect differently on the contexts in which biblical interpretation takes place and on the particular interests that should be constitutive of Christian scriptural interpretation. Most importantly, however, I have tried to show the integral connections between Christian scriptural interpretation, Christian doctrine and practices, and Christians' abilities to form and sustain a certain type of common life. Recognizing, extending, and maintaining these connections intact will become one of the most important tasks for Christians as they engage scripture in the various contexts in which they find themselves.

BIBLIOGRAPHY

Adam, A. K. M. "Docetism, Käsemann and Christology: Why Historical Criticism Can't Protect Christological Orthodoxy," *Scottish Journal of Theology* 49 (1996), pp. 391–410.

—— *Making Sense of New Testament Theology*, Macon: Mercer University Press, 1995.

—— Review of *New Horizons in Hermeneutics,* in *Modern Theology* 10 (1994), pp. 433–4.

—— *What is Postmodern Biblical Criticism?*, Minneapolis: Fortress Press, 1995.

Alexander, L. "Hellenistic Letter Forms and the Structure of Philippians," *Journal for the Study of the New Testament* 37 (1989) pp. 87–101.

Barclay, J. "Mirror Reading a Polemical Letter: Galatians as a Test Case," *Journal for the Study of the New Testament* 31 (1987) pp. 73–93.

Barrett, C. K. "The Allegory of Abraham, Sarah and Hagar in the Argument of Galatians," in *Essays on Paul*, Philadelphia: Westminster Press, 1982, pp. 154–69.

—— *The Gospel According to St. John*, 2nd edn, London: SPCK, 1975.

Barth, M. *Ephesians,* 2 vols, Garden City: Doubleday, 1974.

Barton, J. "Reading the Bible as Literature: Two Questions for Biblical Critics," *Literature and Theology* 1 (1987), pp. 135-63.

—— *Reading the Old Testament*, Philadelphia: Westminster, 1984

Bauckham, R. "James and the Jerusalem Church," in R. Bauckham (ed.), *The Book of Acts in its Palestinian Setting*, Grand Rapids: Eerdmans, 1995, pp. 415–80.

Benhabib, S. *Situating the Self*, Cambridge: Polity Press, 1992.

Betz, H. D. *Galatians*, Philadelphia: Fortress Press, 1979.

Bible and Culture Collective *The Postmodern Bible*, New Haven: Yale University Press, 1995.

Bledstein, B. *The Culture of Professionalism*, New York: W. W. Norton, 1976.

Blowers, P. "The *Regula Fidei* and the Narrative Character of Early Christian Faith," *Pro Ecclesia* 6 (1997), pp. 199–228.

Bonhoeffer, D. *No Rusty Swords*, trans. C. H. Robertson, London: Collins, 1970.

Borgen, P. "Catalogues of Vices, The Apostolic Decree, and the Jerusalem Meeting" in *Early Christianity and Hellenistic Judaism*, Edinburgh: T. & T. Clark, 1996, pp. 233–51.

Brett, M. G. *Biblical Criticism in Crisis?*, Cambridge: Cambridge University Press, 1991.

—— "Four or Five Things to do with Texts," in D. J. A. Clines, S. E. Fowl, and S. E. Porter (eds), *The Bible in Three Dimensions*, Sheffield: Sheffield Academic Press, 1990, pp. 357–77.

—— "Motives and Intentions in Gen. 1," *Journal of Theological Studies* 42 (1991), pp. 1–16.

Bruce, F. F. *The Acts of the Apostles*, 3rd edn, Grand Rapids: Eerdmans, 1990.

Budde, M. *The (Magic) Kingdom of God,* Boulder: Westview Press, 1997.

Caird, G. B. *New Testament Theology*, completed and ed. by L.D. Hurst, Oxford: Clarendon Press, 1994.

Calvin, J. *Sermons on Ephesians*, rev. of 1557 translation of A. Golding, London: Banner of Truth Trust, 1973.

Capper, B. "The Palestinian Cultural Context of the Earliest Christian Community of Goods," in R. Bauckham (ed.), *The Book of Acts in its Palestinian Setting*, Grand Rapids: Eerdmans, 1995, pp. 323–56.

Carroll, R. *The Bible as a Problem for Christianity,* Philadelphia: Trinity Press International, 1991.

Cartwright, M. G. "Ideology and the Interpretation of the Bible in the African-American Christian Tradition," *Modern Theology* 9 (1993), pp. 141–58.

Castelli, E. *Imitating Paul: A Discourse of Power*, Louisville: Westminster/John Knox Press, 1991.

Childs, B. *Biblical Theology of the Old and New Testaments*, Minneapolis: Fortress Press, 1993.

—— "The Sensus Literalis of Scripture: An Ancient and Modern Problem," in H. Donner et al. (eds), *Beiträge zur alttestamentliche Theologie: Festschrift für Walter Zimmerli*, Göttingen: Vandenhoeck and Ruprecht, 1977, pp. 80–94.

—— "Toward Recovering Theological Exegesis," *Pro Ecclesia* 6 (1997), pp. 16–26.

Christian, W. Sr *The Doctrines of Religious Communities*, New Haven: Yale University Press, 1987.

Clines, D. J. A. *The Esther Scroll*, Sheffield: Sheffield Academic Press, 1984.

Cosgrove, C. "The Law Has Given Sarah No Children," *Novum Testamentum* 29 (1987), pp. 219–35.

Critchley, S. *The Ethics of Deconstruction*, Oxford: Blackwell, 1992.

Dannenburg, L. and Müller, H. -H. "On Justifying The Choice of Interpretive Theories," *Journal of Aesthetics and Art Criticism* 43 (1984), pp. 7–16.

Davidson, D. "A Coherence Theory of Truth and Knowledge," in E. LePore (ed.) *Truth and Interpretation,* Oxford: Blackwells, 1986, pp. 307–19.

—— "On the Very Idea of a Conceptual Scheme," in *Inquiries into Truth and Interpretation,* Oxford: Oxford University Press, 1984, pp. 183–99.

Davies, P. R. *Whose Bible Is It Anyway?,* Sheffield: Sheffield Academic Press, 1995.

Dawson, D. *Allegorical Readers and Cultural Revision in Ancient Alexandria*, Berkeley: University of California Press, 1992.

Derrida, J. *Limited Inc.* Evanston: Northwestern University Press, 1988 [Fr. 1972].

—— *Of Grammatology*, trans. G. Spivak, Baltimore: Johns Hopkins University Press, 1976 [Fr. 1967].

—— "Plato's Pharmacy," in *Dissemination*, trans. Barbara Johnson, Chicago: University of Chicago Press, 1981 [Fr. 1977], pp. 66–172.

DiNoia, J. A. "Communion and Magesterium: Teaching Authority and the Culture of Grace," *Modern Theology* 9 (1993), pp. 403–18.

Droge, A. "Mori Lucrum: Paul and Ancient Theories of Suicide," *Novum Testamentum* 30 (1988), pp. 263–86.

Droge, A. and Tabor, J. D. *A Noble Death: Suicide and Martyrdom among Christians and Jews In Antiquity*, San Francisco: Harper and Row, 1992.

Dunn, J. D. G. *Jesus, Paul and the Law Studies in Mark and Galatians*, Louisville: Westminster/John Knox Press, 1990.

—— *Jesus and the Spirit* London: SCM, 1975.

—— *Unity and Diversity in the New Testament*, London: SCM, 1977.

Dunne, J. *Back to the Rough Ground*, Notre Dame: University of Notre Dame Press, 1993.

Ebeling, G. "The Meaning of 'Biblical Theology'," in *Word and Faith*, trans. J. Leitch, Philadelphia: Fortress Press, 1960, pp. 79–97.

Elliott, N. *Liberating Paul*, Maryknoll: Orbis, 1994.

Evans, C. F. "Is 'Holy Scripture' Christian?," in *Is "Holy Scripture" Christian and Other Questions*, London: SCM, 1971.

Firestone, R. "Abraham's Son as the Intended Sacrifice: Issues in Qu'ranic Exegesis," *Journal of Semitic Studies* 34 (1989), pp. 95–131.

Fish, S. *Is There a Text in This Class?*, Cambridge, MA: Harvard University Press, 1980.

Fowl, S. E. "Christology and Ethics in Phil. 2:5–11," in B. Dodd and R. P. Martin (eds), *Where Christology Began*, Louisville: Westminster/John Knox Press, 1998, pp. 140–53.

—— "Could Horace Talk with the Hebrews? Translatability and Moral Disagreement in MacIntyre and Stout," *Journal of Religious Ethics* 19 (1991), pp. 1–20.

—— "The Ethics of Interpretation, or What's Left Over After the Elimination of Meaning," in D. J. A. Clines, S. E. Fowl and S. E. Porter (eds), *The Bible in Three Dimensions*, Sheffield: Sheffield Academic Press, 1990, pp. 379–98.

—— "How to Read the Spirit and How the Spirit Reads," in J. Rogerson et al. (eds), *The Bible and Ethics*, Sheffield: Sheffield Academic Press, 1995, pp. 348–65.

—— "Learning to Narrate Our Lives in Christ," in C. R. Seitz and K. Greene-McCreight (eds), *Theological Exegesis: Experiments in Canonical Criticism*, Grand Rapids: Eerdmans, 1998.

—— "Making Stealing Possible: Criminal Reflections on Building an Ecclesial Common Life," *Perspectives* (September 1993), pp. 14–17.

—— "Receiving the Kingdom as a Child: Children and Riches in Luke 18:15ff.," *New Testament Studies* 39 (1993) pp. 153–8.

—— *The Story of Christ in the Ethics of Paul*, Sheffield: Sheffield Academic Press, 1991.

—— "Texts Don't Have Ideologies," *Biblical Interpretation* 3:1 (1995), 1–34.

—— "Who can Read Abraham's Story?," *Journal for the Study of the New Testament* 55 (1994), pp. 77–95.

Fowl, S. E. and Jones, L. G. *Reading in Communion: Scripture and Ethics in Christian Life,* Grand Rapids: Eerdmans, 1991.

Frei, H. *The Identity of Jesus Christ,* Philadelphia: Fortress Press, 1975.

—— "The 'Literal Reading' of Biblical Narrative in the Christian Tradition: Does it Stretch or Will it Break?," in F. McConnell (ed.), *The Bible and the Narrative Tradition,* New York: Oxford University Press, 1986 pp. 36–77.

Frend, W. H. C. *The Donatist Church,* 2nd edn, Oxford; Clarendon Press, 1985.

Gadamer, H.-G. *Truth and Method,* New York: Seabury, 1975.

Garrett, S. " 'Lest the Light in You Be Darkness': Luke 11:33–36 and the Question of Commitment," *Journal of Biblical Literature* 110:1 (1991), pp. 93–105.

Gaventa, B. R. *From Darkness to Light: Aspects of Conversion in the New Testament,* Philadelphia: Fortress Press, 1986.

—— "Galatians 1 and 2: Autobiography as Paradigm," *Novum Testamentum* 28 (1986), pp. 309–26.

—— "The Singularity of the Gospel," in J. Bassler (ed.), *Pauline Theology,* Minneapolis: Augsburg Fortress, 1991, vol. 1, pp. 147–59.

Giddens, A. "Four Theses on Ideology," *Canadian Journal of Political and Social Theory / Revue canadienne de théorie politique et sociale* 7 (1983) pp. 8–21.

Gottwald, N. K. *The Hebrew Bible: A Socio-Literary Introduction,* Philadelphia: Fortress Press, 1985.

—— *The Tribes of Yahweh,* New York: Orbis, 1979.

Haenchen, E. *The Acts of the Apostles,* trans. B. Nobel and G. Shinn, Philadelphia: Westminster Press, 1971.

Hahn, F. "Die Worte vom Licht, Lk 11, 33–36," in P. Hoffman et al. (eds), *Orientierung an Jesus: Zur Theologie der Synoptiker,* Freiburg: Herder and Herder, 1973, pp. 107–38.

Hamm, D. "Luke 19:18 Once Again: Does Zacchaeus Defend or Resolve?," *Journal of Biblical Literature* 107 (1988), pp. 431–7.

Hansen, G. W. *Abraham in Galatians,* Sheffield: Sheffield Academic Press, 1989.

Hauerwas S. *After Christendom,* Nashville: Abindon, 1991.

—— "Gay Friendship: A Thought Experiment in Catholic Moral Theology," *Irish Theological Quarterly* (forthcoming).

—— "A Story Formed Community," in *A Community of Character,* Notre Dame: University of Notre Dame Press, 1981, pp. 9–35.

Hays, R. B. "Awaiting the Redemption of Our Bodies," *Sojourners* 20 (July 1991), pp. 17–21.

—— "The Corrected Jesus," *First Things* (May 1994) pp. 43–8.

—— *Echoes of Scripture in the Letters of Paul,* New Haven: Yale University Press, 1989.

—— *The Faith of Jesus Christ,* Chico, CA: Scholars Press, 1983.

—— *The Moral Vision of the New Testament,* San Francisco: Harper San Francisco, 1996.

—— "On the Rebound: A Response to Critiques of *Echoes of Scripture in the Letters of Paul,"* in J. Sanders and C. Evans (eds), *Paul and the Scriptures of Israel*, Sheffield: Sheffield Academic Press, 1993, pp. 70–96.

Hirsch, E. D. "Meaning and Significance Reinterpreted," *Critical Inquiry* 11 (1984), pp. 202–25.

—— *Validity in Interpretation*, New Haven: Yale University Press, 1967.

Holmberg, B. *Paul and Power*, Philadelphia: Fortress Press, 1978.

Hoover, R. W. "The Harpagmos Enigma: A Philological Solution," *Harvard Theological Review* 64 (1971) pp. 95–119.

Hübner, H. *Das Gesetz bei Paulus*, Göttingen: Vandenhoeck and Ruprecht, 1978.

Jameson, F. "The Ideology of the Text," *Salamagundi* 31–2 (1975), pp. 204–46.

Jeanrond, W. "After Hermeneutics: The Relationship Between Theology and Biblical Studies," in F. Watson (ed.), *The Open Text*, London: SCM, 1993, pp. 95–101.

—— "Criteria for New Biblical Theologies," *Journal of Religion* 76 (1996), pp. 233–49.

—— *Text und Interpretation als Katagorien theologischen Denkens*, Tübingen: Mohr, 1986.

Johnson, L. T. *The Acts of the Apostles*, Collegeville: Michael Glazier, 1992.

—— *The Gospel of Luke*, Collegeville: Michael Glazier, 1991.

—— *The Real Jesus*, San Francisco: Harper San Francisco, 1995.

—— *Scripture and Discernment*, Nashville: Abingdon, 1996.

Jones, L. G. "A Dramatic Journey into God's Dazzling Light," forthcoming.

—— *Embodying Forgiveness*, Grand Rapids: Eerdmans, 1995.

—— "Taking Time for the Spirit," *The Christian Century* (April 29, 1992), p. 451.

Jowett, B. "On the Interpretation of Scripture," *Essays and Reviews*, 7th edn, London: Longman and Green, 1861.

Käsemann, E. "Vom theologischen Recht historisch-kritischer Exegese," *Zeitschrift für Theologie und Kirche* 64 (1967), pp. 253–81.

Kennedy, G. A. *The New Testament through Rhetorical Criticism*, Chapel Hill: University of North Carolina Press, 1984.

Kenneson, P. "Selling[out] the Church in the Marketplace of Desire," *Modern Theology* 9 (1993), pp. 319–48.

Kugel, J. and Greer, R. *Early Biblical Interpretation*, Philadelphia: Westminster Press, 1986.

Lash, N. "Ministry of the Word or Comedy and Philology," *New Blackfriars* 6 (1987), pp. 472–83.

—— "What Authority has Our Past?" in *Theology on the Way to Emmaus*, London: SCM, 1986, pp. 47–61.

Levenson, J. *The Hebrew Bible, The Old Testament and Historical Criticism*, Louisville: Westminster/John Knox Press, 1993.

Levinas, E. *Totality and Infinity*, trans. A. Lingis, Pittsburgh: Duquesne University Press, 1969.

Lincoln, A. T. *Ephesians*, Waco: Word, 1990.

—— *Paradise Now and Not Yet*, Cambridge: Cambridge University Press, 1981.

Lindbeck, G. Review of *Biblical Hermeneutics in Historical Perspective: Studies in Honor of Karlfried Frochlich*, in *Modern Theology* 10 (1994), pp. 101–6.

—— "The Story Shaped Church: Critical Exegesis and Theological Interpretation," in S. E. Fowl (ed.), *The Theological Interpretation of Scripture: Classic and Contemporary Readings*, Oxford: Blackwell, 1997, pp. 39–52.

Longenecker, R. *Biblical Exegesis in the Apostolic Period*, Grand Rapids: Eerdmans, 1975.

Lull, D. *The Spirit in Galatia*, Atlanta: Scholars Press, 1980.

Luther, M. "Treatise on Good Works," trans. J. Atkinson, in vol. 44 of *Luther's Works*, Philadelphia: Fortress Press, 1968.

Lyons, J. *Semantics*, vol. 1, Cambridge: Cambridge University Press, 1977.

MacIntyre, A. *After Virtue*, 2nd edn, Notre Dame: University of Notre Dame Press, 1984.

—— "Epistemological Crises, Dramatic Narrative and the Philosophy of Science," *The Monist* 60 (1977), pp. 453–72.

—— *Three Rivals Versions of Moral Inquiry*, Notre Dame: University of Notre Dame Press, 1990.

—— *Whose Justice? Which Rationality?*, Notre Dame: University of Notre Dame Press, 1988.

Marks, H. "Pauline Typology and Revisionary Criticism," *Journal of the American Academy of Religion* 52 (1984), pp. 71–92.

Marshall, B. "Aquinas as Post-Liberal Theologian," *The Thomist* 53:3 (1989), pp. 353–406.

Martyn, J. L. "Events in Galatia: Modified Covenantal Nomism versus God's Invasion of the Cosmos in the Singular Gospel: A Response to J. D. G. Dunn and B. R. Gaventa," in J. Bassler (ed.), *Pauline Theology*, vol. 1, Minneapolis: Augsburg Fortress, 1991, pp. 160–79.

Meeks, W. A. "A Hermeneutics of Social Embodiment," Harvard Theological Review 76 (1989), pp. 176–86.

—— "The Man From Heaven in Paul's Letter to the Philippians," in *The Future of Early Christianity: Essays in Honor of Helmut Koester*, Minneapolis: Augsburg Fortress, 1991, pp. 329–36.

Mesters, C. *Defenseless Flower*, trans. F. McDonagh, Maryknoll: Orbis, 1989.

Milbank, J. "Can a Gift be Given? Prolegomena to a Future Trinitarian Metaphysic," in L. G. Jones and S. E. Fowl (eds), *Rethinking Metaphysics*, Oxford: Blackwell, 1995, pp. 119–61.

—— *Theology and Social Theory*, Oxford: Blackwell, 1990.

—— *The Word Made Strange*, Oxford: Blackwell, 1997.

Mink, L. "History and Fiction as Modes of Comprehension," *New Literary History* 1 (1970) pp. 541–58.

Mitchell, A. C. "Zacchaeus Revisited: Luke 19:18 as Defense," *Biblica* 71 (1990), pp. 153–76.

Moore, S. *Literary Criticism and the Gospels: The Theoretical Challenge*, New Haven: Yale University Press, 1989.

—— *Mark and Luke in Poststructuralist Perspective*, New Haven: Yale University Press, 1992.

—— *Poststructuaralism and the New Testament*, Minneapolis: Fortress Press, 1994.

Morgan, R. "Can Critical Study of Scripture Provide a Doctrinal Norm?," *Journal of Religion* 76 (1996), pp. 206–32.

—— *The Nature of New Testament Theology*, London: SCM, 1973.

Mosala, I. G. *Biblical Hermeneutics and Black Theology in South Africa*, Grand Rapids: Eerdmans, 1989.

Neale, D. *None But the Sinners,* Sheffield: Sheffield Academic Press, 1991.

Ochs, P., *The Return to Scripture in Judaism and Christianity*, ed. and introduced by P. Ochs, New York: Paulist, 1993.

Ollenburger, B. "Biblical Theology: Situating the Discipline," in J. T. Butler, E. Conrad, and B. Ollenburger (eds), *Understanding the Word*, Sheffield: Sheffield Academic Press, 1985, pp. 37–62.

—— "What Krister Stendahl 'Meant' – A Normative Critique of Descriptive Biblical Theology," *Horizons in Biblical Theology* 8 (1986), pp. 61–98.

Phillips, G. "The Ethics of Reading Deconstructively, or Speaking Face to Face: The Samaritan Woman meets Derrida at the Well," in E. Malbon and E. McKnight (eds), ¡*The New Literary Criticism and the New Testament*, Sheffield: Sheffield Academic Press, 1994, pp. 283-325.

—— " 'You are Either Here, Here, Here, or Here': Deconstruction's Troubling Interplay," *Semeia* 71 (1995), pp. 193–213.

Pickstock, C. *After Writing: On the Liturgical Consummation of Philosophy*, Oxford: Blackwell, 1998.

Pontifical Biblical Commission "Interpretation of the Bible in the Church," 1993 [Eng. 1994].

Quine, W. V. O. *Word and Object,* Cambridge, MA: Harvard University Press, 1960.

Räisänen, H. *Beyond New Testament Theology*, London: SCM, 1990.

—— *Paul and the Law*, Philadelphia: Fortress Press, 1983.

Rogers, E. F. Jr "How The Virtues of the Interpreter Presuppose and Perfect Hermeneutics: The Case of Thomas Aquinas," *Journal of Religion* 76:1 (1996), pp. 64–81.

Rorty, R. "Texts and Lumps," *New Literary History* 17 (1985), pp. 1–16.

Rose, G. *Judaism and Modernity*, Oxford: Blackwell, 1993.

Rosen, S. "Antiplatonism," in *The Ancients and Moderns: Rethinking Modernity*, New Haven: Yale University Press, 1989, pp. 37–84.

Rowland, C. "An Open Letter to Francis Watson on *Text, Church and World*," *Scottish Journal of Theology* 48 (1995), pp. 507–17.

Sanders, E. P. *Paul, The Law and the Jewish People*, Philadelphia: Fortress Press, 1983.

Schlier, H. *Der Brief an die Epheser*, Düsseldorf: Patmos Verlag, 1962.

Schneiders, S. *The Revelatory Text*, San Francisco: Harper Collins, 1991.

Schuchard, B. G. *Scripture within Scripture*, Atlanta: Scholars Press, 1992.

Schüssler-Fiorenza, E. *In Memory of Her*, New York: Crossroad, 1983.

Schütz, J. H. *Paul and the Anatomy of Apostolic Authority*, Cambridge: Cambridge University Press, 1975.

Schwehn, M. *Exiles from Eden*, New York: Oxford University Press, 1993.

Segal, A. *Paul the Convert*, New Haven: Yale University Press,1990.

Seitz, C. "Human Sexuality Viewed from the Bible's Understanding of the Human Condition," *Theology Today* 52 (July 1995), pp. 236–46.

Siker, J. *Disinheriting the Jews: Abraham in Early Christian Controversy*, Louisville: Westminster/John Knox Press, 1991.

—— "Homosexuals, The Bible and Gentile Inclusion," *Theology Today* 51 (July 1994), pp. 219–34. Reprinted in J. Siker (ed.), *Homosexuality in the Church: Both Sides of the Debate*, Louisville: Westminster/John Knox Press, 1994, pp. 178–94.

Söding, T. "Inmitten der Theologie des neuen Testaments," *New Testament Studies* 42 (1996), pp. 161–84.

Steinmetz, D. "The Superiority of Pre-Critical Exegesis," in S. E. Fowl (ed.), *The Theological Interpretation of Scripture: Classic and Contemporary Readings*, Oxford: Blackwell, 1997, pp. 26–38.

Stendahl, K. "Biblical Theology, Contemporary," in G. Buttrick (ed.), *The Interpreter's Dictionary of the Bible*, Nashville: Abingdon, 1962, vol. 1, pp. 418–32.

Stout, J. *The Flight from Authority*, Notre Dame: University of Notre Dame Press, 1984.

—— "What is the Meaning of a Text?," *New Literary History* 14 (1982), pp. 1–12.

Surin, K. *The Turnings of Darkness and Light*, Cambridge: Cambridge University Press, 1989.

Tannehill, R. *The Narrative Unity of Luke–Acts*, 2 vols, Minneapolis: Fortress Press, 1990.

Tanner, K. "Theology and the Plain Sense," in G. Green (ed.), *Scriptural Authority and Narrative Interpretation*, Philadelphia: Fortress Press, 1987, pp. 59-78.

Thielman, F. *From Plight to Solution*, Leiden: Brill, 1989.

Thiselton, A. C. *New Horizons in Hermeneutics*, Grand Rapids: Zondervan, 1992.

Wadell, P. *Friendship and the Moral Life,* Notre Dame: University of Notre Dame Press, 1989.

Wansink, C. *Chained in Christ*, Sheffield: Sheffield Academic Press, 1996.

Watson, F. "A Response to Professor Rowland," *Scottish Journal of Theology* 48 (1995), pp. 518–20.

—— *Text, Church and World*, Grand Rapids: Eerdmans, 1994.

—— *Text and Truth*, Edinburgh: T. & T. Clark, 1997.

Weber, M. "Science as Vocation," in *From Max Weber: Essays in Sociology*, trans. and ed. H. H. Gerth and C. Wright Mills, New York: Oxford University Press, 1977, pp. 129–56.

West, G. *Biblical Hermeneutics of Liberation*, Pietermaritzburg: Cluster Publications, 1991.

—— "Some Parameters of the Hermeneutic Debate in the South African Context," *Journal of Theology for Southern Africa* 80 (1992), pp. 3–13.

Wheeler, S. *Wealth as Peril and Obligation*, Grand Rapids: Eerdmans, 1995.

Williams, R. "Interiority and Epiphany: A Reading of New Testament Ethics," *Modern Theology* 13 (1997), pp. 29-51.

—— "The Suspicion of Suspicion: Wittgenstein and Bonhoeffer," in R. Bell (ed.), *The Grammar of the Heart*, San Francisco: Harper and Row, 1988, pp. 36–53.

Witherington, B. *Conflict and Community in Corinth*, Grand Rapids: Eerdmans, 1995.

Wrede, W. "The Tasks and Methods of 'New Testament Theology'," in R. Morgan *The Nature of New Testament Theology*, London: SCM, 1973, pp. 68–116.

Wright, N. T. *The Climax of the Covenant: Christ and the Law in Pauline Theology*, Minneapolis: Fortress Press, 1992.

Wuthnow, R. *Sharing the Journey*, New York: Free Press, 1994.

Wyschogrod, M. "The 'Shema Israel' in Judaism and the New Testament," in H. G. Link (ed.), *The Roots of Our Common Faith*, Geneva: WCC Faith and Order Paper, 119, 1983.

Yeago, D. "The New Testament and Nicene Dogma," in S. E. Fowl (ed.), *The Theological Interpretation of Scripture: Classic and Contemporary Readings*, Oxford: Blackwell, 1997, pp. 87–101.

INDEX